T0319994

International Knowledge and Innovation Networks

NEW HORIZONS IN REGIONAL SCIENCE

Series Editor: Philip McCann, *Professor of Economics, University of Waikato, New Zealand and Professor of Urban and Regional Economics, University of Reading, UK*

Regional science analyses important issues surrounding the growth and development of urban and regional systems and is emerging as a major social science discipline. This series provides an invaluable forum for the publication of high-quality scholarly work on urban and regional studies, industrial location economics, transport systems, economic geography and networks.

New Horizons in Regional Science aims to publish the best work by economists, geographers, urban and regional planners and other researchers from throughout the world. It is intended to serve a wide readership including academics, students and policy makers.

Titles in the series include:

International Knowledge and Innovation Networks

Knowledge Creation and Innovation in Medium-technology Clusters

Riccardo Cappellin

University of Rome Tor Vergata, Italy

Rüdiger Wink

Leipzig University of Applied Sciences, Germany

NEW HORIZONS IN REGIONAL SCIENCE

Edward Elgar

Cheltenham, UK • Northampton, MA, USA

Published by
Edward Elgar Publishing Limited
The Lypiatts
15 Lansdown Road
Cheltenham
Glos GL50 2JA
UK

Edward Elgar Publishing, Inc.
William Pratt House
9 Dewey Court
Northampton
Massachusetts 01060
USA

A catalogue record for this book
is available from the British Library

Library of Congress Control Number: 2009925928

Mixed Sources
Product group from well-managed forests and other controlled sources
www.fsc.org Cert no. SA-COC-1565
© 1996 Forest Stewardship Council
FSC

ISBN 978 1 84844 441 6

Printed and bound by MPG Books Group, UK

Contents

About the authors

Riccardo Cappellin is Full Professor of Economics at the University of Rome Tor Vergata and teaches courses in Economics of Innovation and in Regional Economics. His publications cover fields such as: economics of technological change, regional economics and policy, European integration, federalism, industrial economics, labour economics, transport economics and urban economics. His recent research focuses on the network concept in the process of knowledge creation and innovation in a spatial perspective. He has coordinated several research projects on innovation policies and regional policies for various institutions.

Rüdiger Wink is Professor for International Economics at Leipzig University for Applied Sciences (HTWK) and Senior Research Fellow at Ruhr Research Institute for Regional and Innovation Policy (RUFIS) in Bochum, Germany. Before that, he was inter alia Senior Research Fellow at the European Research Institute at the University of Birmingham, UK, and research assistant at the German Council for the Federal Government on Global Change. His main research fields cover innovation, technology environmental and labour market policies based on economic theories of institutional evolution.

1. Introduction

Riccardo Cappellin and Rüdiger Wink

This book aims to increase the understanding of the process of knowledge creation and innovation in medium-technology sectors in the EU and to identify the characteristics of knowledge and innovation networks within regional clusters and the barriers to their enlargement at the European level. It investigates strategies that SMEs in medium-technology industries apply to adjust their knowledge creation processes to global structural challenges.

The topic discussed in this book is absolutely crucial for the future of the European economy, as medium-technology industries are not only the dominant sectors for European exports into the global markets, but also still the fastest-growing sectors in international trade. The focus on high-technology sectors and knowledge-intensive business services found in many studies of international organizations, expert groups and scientists misses the point that these new activities are not independent from the traditionally strong manufacturing sectors in Europe, such as medium-technology industries. For example, bio-pharmaceutical inventions will only find their markets when they are linked with more traditional tools from medicine technology (medium-technology engineering plus electronics); modern materials are reducing the weight and increasing the flexibility and functionality of cars; aeroplanes and big machines are developed in cooperation with medium-technology machinery; high-technology electronics and chemical sectors, and new laser technologies have to be linked with optical and machinery industries to develop new products. Thus, integrative technologies are capable of developing connections between medium-technology industries and high-technology segments. Many economic studies forecast relocations of low-technology industries towards the fast-growing emerging markets, like China and India, and extend these forecasts also to the whole medium-technology segment. This general perspective, however, neglects the importance of technological interdependence between the incumbent medium-technology capabilities and new high-technology knowledge streams. Our investigation particularly looks at the implications these linkages have on the medium-technology industry SMEs in Europe.

Due to the underestimation of the role medium-technology sectors will play in the future, the actual scientific insights on how knowledge in these industries is generated, examined and commercialized is limited. Most studies simply transfer the observations from high-technology sectors with their strong role of formal R&D, capital equipment and patents as typical output, to medium-technology sectors, thus neglecting the specificities of these industries. These specificities in innovation processes particularly refer to the concepts of 'synthetic knowledge' and integrative technologies, which mean that firms in the medium-technology sectors are able to connect general insights on modern technologies to concrete and very specific engineering problem solutions. Hence, medium-technology industries follow their own rationale in knowledge creation.

Within this book, we first analyse in Chapter 2 the role of medium-technology sectors in the European economy and some major characteristics of these sectors on the basis of the available indicators of export, value-added, employment, human capital and R&D. The aim of this introductory empirical analysis is to demonstrate the importance of medium-tech sectors and to underline the need to design an approach to European innovation policy that considers the specific factors and processes determining knowledge creation and innovation in the medium-technology sectors.

Then, we investigate three main groups of questions addressed to three different target groups. First, in Chapter 3:

- How do medium-technology industry SMEs cope with the structural changes in internationalized markets? Which role do national and international networks play in this adjustment process? Which best practices can be observed at the firm level?

Chapter 3 takes up the strategic management perspective of medium-technology SMEs. Most international management studies on new markets and strategies deal with processes in big multinational firms. In addition, new high-technology start-up firms acting as 'born global' are another attractive case study. However, medium-technology SMEs are often seen as outdated due to their lack of management resources and formal R&D as well as their poor international experience and linkages. Within this chapter, we look at strategies that medium-technology SMEs in different European regions can develop to overcome their structural weaknesses and to adjust their knowledge production process.

Traditionally, networks play an important role for medium-technology SMEs, as network linkages help them to share responsibilities within value chains and knowledge on specific machines and products. This traditional function of networks, however, has changed in a remarkable direction towards knowledge networks and it is one of the major results of our study to show how these new knowledge network structures are used to exploit the traditional strengths of capabilities in medium-technology SMEs in generating tacit knowledge by combining general insights on technological processes with very specific and concrete problem solutions. Hence, innovation performance in medium-technology industries has to be measured in a different way than using the same – more formal and analytical – knowledge indicators such as those in high-technology industries, where patents, licences or R&D contracts play a major role. Instead, a more differentiated view on knowledge creation and commercialization in the European regions is needed to understand the interplay between medium-technology SMEs, large multinational firms, high-technology specialist services and public research units. These network structures need to be very specific, as they combine the traditional networks of medium-technology SMEs, driven by personal and social linkages, with advanced knowledge-intensive organizations, where cognitive proximity and R&D activities play a major role. Thus, the traditional pattern of very innovative high-technology firms and research institutes on one side and on the other, outdated medium-technology SMEs without any competitiveness in future global markets and earmarked to be replaced in the near future, can no longer hold and has to be replaced by a differentiated view on the very specific strengths of European medium-technology companies and the sources of their competitiveness based on capabilities to bridge the gap between different types of knowledge. Case studies from empirical research serve as illustrations to explain the practical experiences with this new pattern of integrative knowledge generation.

Next, in Chapter 4, we ask:

● Which theoretical concepts are able to explain the observed changes in medium-technology industries? Which theoretical recommendations can be made to enhance the internationalization of knowledge flows in medium-technology industries between different European regions?

Chapter 4 investigates the theoretical dimension of the topic. Concepts of innovation theory are mainly focused on high-technology knowledge generation and hardly consider the relational and evolutionary aspects of innovation processes. Knowledge generation in medium-technology industries follows a different rationale, as the network linkages between the firms integrate personal and cognitive issues and the knowledge created is highly specific and tacit. Therefore, this part of the book provides an original theoretical framework, which particularly adds and links three different elements to the existing understanding of innovation.

First, knowledge generation and production is connected with cognitive sciences to understand the linkage between the individual knowledge processing within the individual brain and the exchange of knowledge content within interactions based on joint codes of communication. This perspective has immanent impact on the understanding of innovation processes, as it helps to identify the preconditions for actual and successful cooperation in knowledge creation and the necessary investments that cooperation partners have to take to build up knowledge network structures.

Second, an evolutionary and spatial perspective is introduced by replacing the understanding of innovation as a concrete result of formalized knowledge production processes with an understanding of innovation as an expression of capabilities gained within interactions with other actors and through the informal processing of one's own experiences. This understanding fits much better with the situation of medium-technology SMEs, which usually improve their products and processes continuously by enhancing the capabilities of their employees embedded within internal processes and interactions. Instead of a more linear interpretation of innovation processes, where formal R&D investments and formal collaborations between highly qualified individuals lead to new knowledge, our theoretical concept considers a more systemic approach based on the complex interaction between individuals, the reciprocal sharing of their knowledge and the generation of new ideas in the framework of frequent communication and of application aimed at solving concrete problems.

In particular, this book aims to highlight the regional/spatial character of the cognitive process of interactive learning and of knowledge creation. Innovation processes within firms are related to the external links between the various firms in the local and the international economy and these spatial links are crucial in a long-term perspective. Regional knowledge networks are analysed based on the approach of cognitive economics rather than of economic geography. In fact, this more modern systemic model of the process of innovation, based on concepts derived from cognitive sciences and focused on networks, interactive learning process and the development of creative capabilities, is different from the traditional linear model, which focuses on R&D and technology transfers. The theoretical perspective on cognitive economics and its linkages with regional social and innovation networks offers new insights to existing cluster policy discussions.

Third, an institutional and territorial dimension is integrated by linking the insights of innovation processes in medium-technology SMEs with the emergence, adjustment and extension of network structures. Again, existing theoretical concepts on innovation are hardly able to explain the complex structure of networks, the specific role of geographical and other forms of proximity and the microeconomic decisions behind participation in networks. By explaining the preconditions for knowledge creation and exploitation in medium-technology SMEs, we are able to identify the driving forces that lead to different and specific network structures in different types of regions and sectors. The book illustrates that governance is a distinct model of regulation of economic relationships different from the traditional orthodox free market model and it is more appropriate for the management of knowledge relations especially in medium-technology sectors. It highlights the role of intermediate institutions in explaining the concentration of these sectors in coordinated market economies rather than in liberal market economies. The concept of 'territorial knowledge management' (TKM), which investigates the preconditions that knowledge networks have to meet for successful knowledge generation processes, highlights criteria to measure the existing capabilities and needs within knowledge networks, and offers recommendations for firms and policy-makers in the improvement and steering of their networks. In particular, it shows the necessary extensions and adjustments in networks, when interregional and international network structures are required. Here, the traditional means of medium-technology SMEs within networks cannot work and instruments of regional policies often fail to build up new structures for these extended networks. Based on our theoretical framework, we are able to explain necessary adjustments and reforms in existing networks.

Finally, in Chapter 5, we ask:

● Which political recommendations can be drawn from the empirical observation and theoretical explanation? What could be a suitable European policy to strengthen integrative knowledge capabilities in medium-technology industries and to enhance the access of SMEs to international knowledge networks in these fields?

In Chapter 5, the focus is directed at political rationales and instruments and aims to reach some conclusions for regional, national and supranational policy-makers in Europe. The empirical case studies examined in the research have been investigated in order to identify recipes for success on a regional level and the implications of these recipes for national and supranational strategies. The best practices in policy clearly show that policy instruments in the medium-technology sectors need to connect strategic, knowledge and institutional aspects within their rationale. In particular, Austrian and French experiences with strategic programmes like 'competence centres' and 'poles of competitiveness' help to overcome typical scarcities within SMEs and to contribute to building sustainable long-term infrastructures for knowledge networks. Additionally, examples from Germany, France and the United Kingdom stress the importance of institutional support for international linkages, for example by harmonization of qualification standards and joint safety and environmental regulation.

The book focuses on the issue of the European enlargement of regional networks and the various obstacles hindering the SMEs in medium-technology sectors. In particular, innovation policies increasingly require a European dimension. In fact, not only high-technology sectors, but also medium-technology sectors need to be integrated in a European knowledge economy, as they represent a major component of European international competitiveness. Moreover, regional innovation systems specialized in medium-technology sectors require that the effects of market mechanism are integrated by European policy and institutions, in order to ensure a continuous growth and a long-term sustainability, by managing the economic, political, social and environmental imbalances related to economic and technological change.

The first insights of the research were used in discussion with practitioners on the regional, national and European level. Within a Policy Forum on 'Regional Competence Centres and European Knowledge and Innovation Networks' in Rome,[1] concrete experiences were presented and discussed. As a result of this discourse, general statements were developed to explain what the role of policy could be within these new regional knowledge networks and the process towards internationalization of network interactions. This step resulted in some concrete policy recommendations. By adopting a governance approach to cooperation between policy and firms, we explain the specific role each actor has to play to support the emergence of knowledge networks for medium-technology industries and how the funding responsibilities have to be allocated. The analysis focuses on the concept of competence centres as a new tool of innovation policy on a regional and European level. The most important implications of this approach are the inclusion of strategic long-term initiatives transferred to projects, the support by independent knowledge providers, the strategic support by regulation and international fairs and the diversified concept of technology platforms instead of exclusive sectorial instruments. Finally, we discuss the opportunities and preconditions for using this approach for an intensification of knowledge network interactions between the regions in the incumbent and new EU member states.

Having shared our views with many practitioners and experts on the innovative capabilities of medium-technology sectors as a specific source of strength for European economies, we believe that the reading of this book will be interesting for students and researchers in postgraduate management and innovation studies as well as for managers of SMEs and multinational industrial firms and for experts in innovation policies at the regional and European level.

ACKNOWLEDGEMENTS

The results presented in this book are based on the autonomous research of the authors and on the results of an empirical study executed in the European project 'IKINET – International Knowledge and Innovation Networks for European Integration Cohesion and Enlargement' between 2004 and 2008, funded within the 6th European Framework on Research, Technology and Development (CIT2-CT-2004-506242). Eight units contributed to the results of this study:

- University of Rome Tor Vergata, Italy, led by the coordinator of the overall project, Riccardo Cappellin;
- Polish Academy of Science, Warsaw, Poland, led by Staszek Walukiewicz;
- Ruhr Research Institute for Regional and Innovation Policy (RUFIS), Bochum, Germany, led by Rüdiger Wink;
- Centre for Advanced Studies at Cardiff University, United Kingdom, led by Phil Cooke;
- Joanneum Research, Graz, Austria, led by Michael Steiner;
- Autonomous University of Madrid, Spain, led by Javier Alfonso-Gil and Antonio Vazquez-Baquero;
- National Institute for Agricultural Research (INRA), Paris, France, led by Andre Torre;
- Applica SpI, Brussels, Belgium, led by Terry Ward.

The authors wish to thank all research partners in the IKINET project for their contribution to the empirical research and to the discussions on the theoretical concepts and on the political experiences and recommendations.

They wish to especially thank Staszek Walukiewicz for his friendly and effective participation in the Steering Committee and for his contribution to the discussions on the policy implications.

The authors also acknowledge partial support from the FP6 European Integrated Project EURODITE: 'Regional Trajectories to the Knowledge Economy: A Dynamic Model', Project no. 006187.

In order to give the readers a more complete perspective of the complex tightly linked issues to be considered, the authors have integrated the specific contributions emerging from the IKINET project with results drawn from other projects, studies and discussions and they are therefore solely responsible for the opinions presented here.

The authors wish to thank Luigi Orsenigo for continuous, friendly and fruitful discussions while elaborating this research; Giuseppe Vullo for the assistance in the statistical elaborations and in the organization of the research activities; and Suzanne Mursell and the editing service by Edward Elgar for the precise and well-thought revision and editing leading to very useful improvements in the text.

NOTE

1. The contributions to this forum can be downloaded at http://www.ikinet.uniroma2/contributions.htm.

2. The role and characteristics of medium-tech sectors

Riccardo Cappellin

While innovation policies mainly focus on the development of high technologies and R&D investments, European industry is still characterized by a strong specialization in medium-technology sectors, such as machinery, transport equipment and chemical products.[1] (See Box 2.1 for definitions of industry technology categories.)

2.1 THE ROLE OF MEDIUM-TECHNOLOGY SECTORS IN INTERNATIONAL TRADE

Medium-technology manufacturing sectors represent the largest component in the trade of OECD countries (56.3%) and their share in the period 2000–05 has continuously increased, while the shares of both low-technology and high-technology products have decreased (Table 2.1).

The most recent data for the exports of European countries indicate the same importance and the same trend of the medium-technology sectors. In particular, the share of medium-technology sectors in total manufacturing exports is greater than or close to 50% in almost all European countries and it increased during the 2000–03 period in the following countries: Germany, Italy, United Kingdom, Austria, Denmark, Finland, France, Netherlands, Portugal and Sweden. An opposite trend is only indicated in the following countries: Belgium, Greece, Ireland and Spain. In fact, the share of the exports by the high-technology sectors has decreased in all countries indicated above with the exception of Belgium, Greece, Ireland, Portugal and Spain, where the increase of the share of high-tech sectors is mainly determined by the sharp decrease of the share in low-technology sectors (as in Belgium, Ireland and Portugal) and in medium low-technology sectors (as in Greece and Spain) (Table 2.2).

These trends are explained both by the crisis of the ICT sectors after the 2000 speculative bubble and by the large and continuous increase of

---

BOX 2.1   MANUFACTURING INDUSTRY
TECHNOLOGY CATEGORIES

Definition: The four manufacturing industry technology categories
are defined as follows (NACE codes are given in brackets):

1. High-tech: office machinery and computers (30), radio, televi-
sion and communication equipment and apparatus (32), medical,
precision and optical instruments, watches and clocks (33),
aircraft and spacecraft (35.3), pharmaceuticals, medicinal chemicals and botanical products (24.4).

2. Medium-high-tech: machinery and equipment (29), electri-
cal machinery and apparatus (31), motor vehicles, trailers and
semi-trailers (34), other transport equipment (35), chemicals and
chemical products excluding pharmaceuticals, medicinal chemicals and botanical products (24 excluding 24.4).

3. Medium-low-tech: coke, refined petroleum products and
nuclear fuel (23), rubber and plastic products (25), non-metallic
mineral products (26), basic metals (27), fabricated metal products except machinery and equipment (28), building and repairing
of ships and boats (35.1).

4. Low-tech: food products and beverages (15), tobacco products (16), textiles (17), wearing apparel; dressing and dyeing of
fur (18), tanning and dressing of leather; manufacture of luggage,
handbags, saddlery and harness (19), wood and products of
wood and cork, except furniture (20), pulp, paper and paper
products (21), publishing, printing and reproduction of recorded
media (22), furniture and other manufacturing (36), recycling
(37).

Sources: European Commission, 2005; European Union, 2000; Felix, 2006.

---

the importance in international trade of the so-called emerging economies, such as Brazil, Russia, India and China (BRIC countries). In fact,
the imports and exports of these countries from and to European countries mainly concentrate in products characterized by a medium or low
technology.

Table 2.1   Structure of OECD^a manufacturing trade^b by technology intensity

	Share in Total Manufacturing Trade (%)					
	2000	2001	2002	2003	2004	2005
High technology (HT)	26.7	25.8	25.2	24.5	24.4	24.1
Medium-high technology (MHT)	37.6	38.0	38.8	39.3	39.0	38.7
Medium-low technology (MLT)	15.1	15.0	14.9	15.5	16.5	17.6
Low technology (LT)	20.1	20.7	20.9	20.7	19.6	19.0

Notes:
a.   Excludes Luxembourg and Slovak Republic.
b.   Average value of total OECD exports and imports of goods.

Source: OECD, STAN Indicators database, March 2005, www.oecd.org/sti/stan/indicators/.

2.2   THE COMPETITIVENESS OF THE EUROPEAN UNION IN MACHINERY AND TRANSPORT EQUIPMENT

Within the medium-technology manufacturing sectors, the machinery and transport equipment sector (with the exclusion of office and telecom equipment) is the most important component. Exports of this sector of the European Union are 1.6 times the exports of United States and 2.7 times the exports of China. Moreover, the trade balance of the European Union in this sector is highly positive and it is 6.8 times higher than that of China, and even higher than that of Japan (Table 2.3).

These data confirm that the competitiveness of the European Union exports in the medium-technology sectors is of key importance in the European foreign trade balance and highlight the increasing importance of innovation and knowledge as the key competitiveness factors in these sectors. In fact, the fast growth of emerging countries represents an opportunity for the European exports of medium-technology manufacturing sectors, as these countries mainly need specialized products from the medium-technology investment good sector. This opportunity, however, can only be exploited if firms in the European medium-tech sectors are able to continuously innovate in order to avoid the delocation of these productions away from European regions and countries. Thus, medium-tech industrial sectors in Europe should increasingly base their international competitiveness on innovation and the capability to create new knowledge.

Table 2.2 Composition of manufacturing exports of goods by technology intensity (2003 shares and absolute change in shares in the 2000–03 period) (%)

		HT	MHT	MLT	LT				HT	MHT	MLT	LT
Germany	2003	19.11	52.5	14.6	13.79	Greece		2003	12.49	16.48	29.21	41.81
	00/03	-1.04	1.44	-0.16	-0.23			00/03	2.76	2.06	-6.51	1.68
Italy	2003	11.04	39.84	18.96	30.17	Ireland		2003	53.62	30.28	2.59	13.51
	00/03	-0.58	1.06	0.27	-0.74			00/03	3.47	-0.68	-0.37	-2.43
United Kingdom	2003	32.9	37.7	13.12	15.82	Netherlands		2003	31.06	29.48	16.07	23.39
	00/03	-3.59	2.19	0.37	1.21			00/03	-1.53	2.17	-1.26	0.62
Austria	2003	14.89	40.67	18.27	26.17	Portugal		2003	11.81	30.85	15.55	41.78
	00/03	-0.82	0.39	-0.53	0.96			00/03	1.52	-0.59	1.41	-2.35
Belgium	2003	19.41	42.1	16.94	21.55	Spain		2003	10.82	47.0	18.95	23.22
	00/03	5.45	0.67	-2.73	-3.4			00/03	0.66	0.08	-1.57	0.82
Denmark	2003	21.54	29.07	13.07	36.32	Sweden		2003	21.95	38.36	17.32	22.36
	00/03	0.88	1.2	-0.89	-1.18			00/03	-6.86	4.62	0.8	1.42
Finland	2003	23.97	24.53	21.07	30.42							
	00/03	-3.36	0.78	3.64	-1.06							
France	2003	22.47	42.05	15.25	20.23							
	00/03	-3.16	2.61	0.09	0.47							

Source: OECD, STAN Indicators database.

Table 2.3   The competitiveness of the European economy in medium-technology sectors (in millions, US dollars, at current prices)

		European Union (27) external			United States			Japan			China		
		Exports	Imports	Net exports	Exports	Imports	Net exports	Exports	Imports	Net exports	Exports	Imports	Net exports
Manufactures	2000	666.608	608.538	58.070	648.907	968.207	−319.300	449.686	212.666	237.020	219.859	169.883	49.976
	2007	1406.496	1187.164	219.332	909.393	1409.631	−500.239	640.881	314.428	326.453	1134.805	677.633	457.172
Office and Telecom Equipment (OTE)	2000	83.962	145.289	−61.327	153.399	215.544	−62.145	108.179	60.866	47.313	43.498	44.427	−929
	2007	117.920	238.606	−120.686	134.934	262.074	−127.140	103.124	69.680	33.444	347.113	226.279	120.834
Machinery and Transport Equipment except OTE	2000	278.629	189.413	89.216	258.801	348.408	−89.607	221.482	45.202	176.279	39.102	47.504	−8.402
	2007	625.079	327.546	297.533	401.475	491.377	−89.902	348.757	80.920	267.837	229.932	186.181	43.751
Machinery and Transport Equipment	2000	362.591	334.702	27.889	412.200	563.952	−151.752	329.661	106.068	223.593	82.600	91.931	−9.331
	2007	742.999	566.152	176.847	536.409	753.451	−217.042	451.881	150.599	301.282	577.045	412.460	164.585

Source: World Trade Organization (2008).

2.3   A COMPARISON BETWEEN EU-15 AND US FOREIGN TRADE

Medium-technology sectors show a similar share in total exports both in the EU-15 (59.06%) and in the United States (61.36%). Their share is also almost three times higher than the export shares of the high-tech sectors both in the EU and in the United States (Table 2.4a).

The performance of medium-technology sectors should be interpreted in the framework of the almost opposite evolution of the trade flows in the two areas. In particular, total European exports in the period 2000–05 have increased much more (74.64%) than US exports (13.13%) and European imports have increased (58.70%) less than European exports. Moreover, US imports have increased (28.22%) more than US exports. That has led to a large increase of the US trade deficit (58.27%), while the trade surplus of the EU has greatly increased (208.75%) (Table 2.4b). The trade balance of the European Union is positive and it represents 23.11% of the imports, while the trade balance of the US is negative and exports are 41.26% lower than the imports (Table 2.4a). These trends indicate the increasing competitiveness of European manufacturing exports, as these have been able to increase despite an appreciation of the euro by 14.3% with respect to the US$ in the 2000–05 period. On the other hand, the devaluation of the US dollar has not helped a worsening of the US trade balance.

The European exports in the medium-tech sectors are much higher (78.40%) than those of the United States. The trade balance of the European Union in medium-technology sectors is positive and it is compensating for the trade deficit in the high-tech and low-tech sectors. In particular, the exports in these sectors are 65.36% higher than imports in the European Union, while they are 18.57% lower than imports in the United States. In fact, medium-technology sectors represent a negative component in the negative trade balance of the United States, although the size of the US trade deficit for medium-tech sectors is lower than the US trade deficits in the high-tech and low-tech sectors.

The medium-tech sectors assume a positive role in the structure and in the evolution of the trade balance both for the EU and for the US economy. In fact, a point of similarity between the European Union and the United States is the fact that the evolution of the trade balance of medium-tech sectors in the period 2000–05 has been more positive than that of the high-tech and low-tech sectors. In the EU, the positive balance in the medium-tech sectors has increased 144%, while the deficit of the high-tech sectors has slightly decreased and the deficit of the low-tech sectors has increased by 73%. In the United States, the negative balance

Table 2.4   A comparison between EU-15 and US foreign trade

(a)	Export Ratio	Export Share (%)		Trade Balance/ Import (%)	
	EU/US	EU	US	EU	US
	2005	2005	2005	2005	2005
High tech	166.56	17.09	19.02	–8.43	−48.64
Medium tech	178.40	59.06	61.36	65.36	−18.57
Low tech	225.25	23.84	19.62	−11.17	−66.09
TOTAL	185.34	100.00	100.00	23.11	−41.26

(b)	Export Change (%)		Import Change (%)		Trade Balance Change (%)	
	EU	US	EU	US	EU	US
	2000– 2005	2000– 2005	2000– 2005	2000– 2005	2000– 2005	2000– 2005
High tech	89.38	4.27	73.24	36.08	−10.05	*100.72*
Medium tech	78.57	14.64	51.91	18.74	144.12	*40.80*
Low tech	57.28	17.99	58.89	37.43	*72.97*	*50.12*
TOTAL	74.64	13.13	58.70	28.22	208.75	*58.27*

Source: Our elaborations on OECD International Trade by Commodities Statistics: United States – SITC Rev. 3, Vol. 2007; European Union – 15 Extra EU – SITC Rev. 3, Vol. 2006.

in the medium-tech sectors has increased by 41% or less than the deficit of the high-tech sectors (100%) and the deficit of the low-tech sectors (50%) (Table 2.4).

2.4   EMPLOYMENT IN SMALL AND MEDIUM-SIZED FIRMS

The share of small firms (1–49 employees) on total manufacturing employment is particularly large in the following countries: Cyprus, Portugal, Italy, Spain, Greece, Netherlands, Norway, Latvia and Estonia. When the medium-sized firms are also considered (50–249 employees), the share of SMEs in manufacturing employment is greater than 50% in almost all European countries (Table 2.5).

Table 2.5   Employment in manufacturing by firm size (%)

	Total	Small	Medium	Large
		(1–49 emp.)	(50–249 emp.)	(≥250 emp.)
Belgium	100.00	26.83	25.19	47.98
Bulgaria	100.00	28.72	35.15	36.13
Denmark	100.00	26.18	27.34	46.48
Germany	100.00	21.75	24.27	53.98
Estonia	100.00	32.35	37.68	29.97
Ireland	100.00	21.90	30.91	47.19
Greece	100.00	46.20	23.98	29.82
Spain	100.00	48.35	24.50	27.15
France	100.00	29.70	22.61	47.69
Italy	100.00	48.70	24.99	26.31
Cyprus	100.00	63.19	22.14	14.68
Latvia	100.00	33.15	35.96	30.89
Lithuania	100.00	27.76	35.20	37.04
Luxembourg	100.00	16.48	21.73	61.79
Hungary	100.00	27.95	25.86	46.18
Netherlands	100.00	34.33	29.85	35.82
Austria	100.00	26.21	27.23	46.56
Poland	100.00	24.96	32.09	42.95
Portugal	100.00	51.30	29.47	19.24
Romania	100.00	21.66	28.04	50.30
Slovenia	100.00	23.18	28.08	48.73
Slovakia	100.00	15.40	27.41	57.19
Finland	100.00	23.14	23.73	53.13
Sweden	100.00	24.57	23.29	52.14
UK	100.00	27.97	26.22	45.82
Norway	100.00	33.87	28.18	37.95

Note: Annual enterprise statistics on manufacturing subsections DF-DN (incl. coke, chemicals, plastics, minerals, metals, machinery and transport equipment) and total manufacturing (NACE D) 2005.

Source: Our elaborations on the Eurostat database on Science and Technology.

2.5   EMPLOYMENT OF MEDIUM-TECH SECTORS IN THE ECONOMY AND IN MANUFACTURING INDUSTRY

Manufacturing industry represents less than a fifth (18.21%) of the total employment in the European Union in 2006. In particular, the

Table 2.6   EU-27 – employment in technology and knowledge-intensive sectors (% shares of total employment)

	2000	2004	2005	2006
High-technology manufacturing sector	1.27	1.11	1.07	1.08
Medium-high-technology manufacturing sector	6.13	5.66	5.51	5.52
Medium-low-technology manufacturing sector	4.66	4.44	4.34	4.36
Low-technology manufacturing sector	8.23	7.75	7.55	7.25
Total manufacturing sector	20.3	18.96	18.46	18.21
Total knowledge-intensive services: NACE Rev. 1.1 codes 61, 62, 64 to 67, 70 to 74, 80, 85 and 92	30.34	32.18	32.36	32.78
Total less-knowledge-intensive services: NACE Rev. 1.1 codes 50, 51, 52, 55, 60, 63, 75, 90, 91, 93, 95 and 99	33.12	33.32	33.71	33.67
Other sectors	16.24	15.54	15.47	15.34
TOTAL	100	100	100	100

Source: Eurostat database in Science and Technology.

manufacturing high-technology sectors, on which innovation policies mostly concentrate, represent only 1.08% of total employment, while manufacturing medium-technology sectors have a much greater importance since they represent 9.88%. Knowledge-intensive services figures indicate a large and increasing importance (Table 2.6).

Employment in manufacturing in the European Union in 2006 is especially concentrated in medium-tech sectors (21.098 million). These sectors are more important than low-tech sectors (15.473 million) and much more important than high-tech sectors (2.295 million). Medium-tech manufacturing represents, in 2006, 54.3% of total manufacturing employment, while high-tech manufacturing represents only 5.9% and low-tech manufacturing 39.8%. The share of medium-technology sectors in manufacturing industry employment is particularly important in the largest and most industrialized countries in the European Union, such as: Luxembourg, Germany, Czech Republic, Sweden, Austria, Belgium, France, United Kingdom, Italy, Slovakia, Slovenia, Spain and Denmark. Conversely, the high-tech industry seems to be dispersed in a rather different typology of countries. In fact, the share of high-tech manufacturing in total manufacturing is especially important in: Ireland, Malta, Finland, Hungary, United Kingdom, Germany, France, Austria, Slovakia, Italy, Sweden and the Czech Republic. As expected, the low-technology sectors are mostly concentrated in the countries that indicate a lower level of economic development. In fact, the share of low-tech manufacturing in total manufacturing is especially important in: Latvia, Lithuania, Cyprus, Bulgaria, Estonia, Portugal, Greece, Romania, Netherlands, Poland, Malta, Spain, Hungary, Denmark, Slovenia and Ireland.

The growth rate in the period 2000–06 of employment in medium-high-tech manufacturing (3.1%) and in medium-low-tech manufacturing (6.9%) has been greater than that in low-tech manufacturing (0.6%), while employment in high-tech manufacturing has decreased (–3.4%). With the exception of only a few countries, the share of medium-tech manufacturing industry on total manufacturing has increased in all EU countries during the period 2000–06. The countries where the growth rate of medium-high-tech manufacturing has been the highest are: Latvia, Slovakia, Austria, Greece, Czech Republic, Spain, Estonia, Italy, Hungary and Slovenia. The countries where the growth rates of medium-low-tech manufacturing have been the highest are: Latvia, Estonia, Lithuania, Slovenia, Spain, Cyprus, Slovakia, Czech Republic and Italy (Table 2.7).

2.6 HUMAN RESOURCES IN SCIENCE AND TECHNOLOGY IN MANUFACTURING AND SERVICE SECTORS

Skilled workers are unevenly distributed between the various manufacturing sectors. In fact, their share of total employment in 2006 is much higher in the case of high-tech manufacturing (49.2%) than for low-tech manufacturing. Medium-high-technology manufacturing (34.9%) and medium-low-technology manufacturing (21.0%) have intermediate values. Moreover, this share is constantly increasing in the period 2004–06 both in manufacturing and in the overall economy. These data indicate the importance of human capital in determining the technology level of the industrial sectors. The corresponding shares in the knowledge-intensive service (59.0%) and also in the less knowledge intensive services (27.3%) are higher than the average value in the manufacturing industry (26.4%). Thus, manufacturing industry is less intensive in human capital than service activities (see Box 2.2 and Table 2.8).

Table 2.7 Annual data on employment by technology intensive sectors at the national level (2000–2006 percentage change and 2006 share)

	High Tech Change	Medium High Change	Medium Low Change	Low Change	Total Manuf. Change	High Tech Share	Medium High Share	Medium Low Share	Low Share	Total Manuf. Share
EU-27	-3.37	3.10	6.86	0.65	2.56	5.90	30.35	23.94	39.81	100.0
Austria	-30.76	27.66	3.10	-15.33	-2.02	7.21	29.60	29.22	33.96	100.0
Belgium	-18.85	-5.45	-9.54	-6.31	-7.42	3.96	33.70	25.00	37.34	100.0
Bulgaria	-0.29	-6.09	-1.32	21.54	10.74	2.21	18.22	16.84	62.74	100.0
Croatia	–	–	–	–	–	2.60	21.96	22.30	53.13	100.0
Cyprus	98.46	-0.85	14.70	-6.23	-0.69	1.38	8.43	24.07	66.12	100.0
Czech Republic	39.90	16.30	10.56	-8.10	6.42	5.94	30.88	30.36	32.83	100.0
Denmark	-20.63	-0.60	-20.92	-15.38	-12.48	5.17	34.11	20.27	40.46	100.0
Estonia	-13.01	6.79	48.47	-3.64	4.50	5.00	12.77	20.19	62.05	100.0
Finland	9.44	-6.37	-6.78	-12.86	-7.63	11.53	26.22	23.00	39.25	100.0
France	-16.07	-10.52	-5.92	-17.79	-12.55	7.30	31.67	25.90	35.12	100.0
Germany	-5.11	-0.97	-9.03	-7.27	-5.03	7.76	41.02	22.07	29.15	100.0
Greece	7.37	16.82	5.88	-8.32	-1.73	1.89	16.07	22.17	59.87	100.0
Hungary	19.14	4.23	3.86	-19.43	-5.83	11.24	27.05	20.81	40.91	100.0
Ireland	-5.92	2.86	-18.69	-10.95	-8.68	19.97	22.78	17.17	40.08	100.0
Italy	39.03	4.78	9.58	-12.46	0.07	6.09	30.03	26.46	37.42	100.0
Latvia	22.05	264.67	160.86	-27.74	-7.83	0.96	10.75	17.41	70.88	100.0
Lithuania	1.16	-23.36	42.79	0.88	2.40	3.53	10.48	16.31	69.68	100.0
Luxembourg	-8.13	-37.26	-28.01	-3.83	-23.64	2.91	12.50	57.00	27.59	100.0
Malta	-18.66	-19.48	-21.15	-17.13	-18.53	17.96	19.61	15.77	46.67	100.0
Netherlands	-28.49	-26.37	4.87	6.16	-4.63	4.90	19.63	22.08	53.39	100.0

Table 2.7 (continued)

	High Tech Change	Medium High Change	Medium Low Change	Low Change	Total Manuf. Change	High Tech Share	Medium High Share	Medium Low Share	Low Share	Total Manuf. Share
Poland	–	–	–	–	–	2.84	22.27	24.61	50.28	100.0
Portugal	–7.77	–6.28	1.19	–13.73	–9.58	2.22	15.06	22.00	60.71	100.0
Romania	–9.26	–6.60	–23.32	8.87	–2.53	1.45	24.16	17.64	56.76	100.0
Slovakia	84.72	48.13	11.41	–9.18	13.16	6.74	29.41	26.73	37.12	100.0
Slovenia	33.85	4.17	30.50	–18.35	–0.26	3.92	27.02	28.77	40.30	100.0
Spain	–7.16	8.48	27.17	–0.91	8.21	2.80	25.44	29.06	42.70	100.0
Sweden	–34.96	–9.21	–3.46	–12.41	–11.17	6.03	36.42	23.75	33.80	100.0
Turkey	–	–	–	–	–	1.39	17.90	19.33	61.39	100.0
UK	–31.28	–18.18	–17.17	–21.08	–20.19	7.86	34.74	22.22	35.19	100.0

Source: Our elaborations on the Eurostat database on Science and Technology.

BOX 2.2   HUMAN RESOURCES IN SCIENCE AND TECHNOLOGY

Human resources in science and technology (HRST) indicate individuals who fulfil at least one of the following conditions: having successfully completed education at the third (tertiary) level (ISCED '97 version levels 5a, 5b or 6) in an ST (science and technology) field of study and/or working in an ST occupation where the above formal qualification is normally required (ISCO '88 COM codes 2 or 3). In particular, according the Canberra Manual (on human resources, 1995), the seven broad fields of study in ST are: natural sciences, engineering and technology, medical sciences, agricultural sciences, social sciences, humanities and other fields.

2.7   THE CHARACTERISTICS OF THE MEDIUM-TECH SECTORS AND OF HIGH- AND LOW-TECH SECTORS

Medium-technology industry represents 57.9% of manufacturing exports, 53.3% of manufacturing employment and 47.8% of manufacturing value-added, while the share of high-tech industry is only 17.1% in European manufacturing exports, 19.5% in manufacturing value-added and 5.8% in manufacturing employment (Figure 2.1).

The comparison of the shares of the medium-technology sectors in the EU-27 exports, value-added, employment, employees with tertiary education and R&D allows us to identify various characteristics of these sectors in relation to high-technology and low-technology sectors (Table 2.9a). In particular, as indicated by Figure 2.1, medium-technology sectors not only have a much greater relevance than high-tech sectors, but also have a different 'technology profile' from that of the high-tech sectors. In fact, medium-tech sectors indicate a very high share of total exports, total employment of qualified workers and total employment, while the high-tech sectors indicate a relatively large value of the shares of total value-added and especially of R&D.

The share of medium-tech manufacturing sectors of total EU-27 exports to the rest of the world in 2005 (57.9%) is almost three times that of high-technology sectors (17.1%). The share of total EU value-added of medium-tech manufacturing sectors (47.8%) is more than double that of high-technology sectors (19.5%). The ratio between the share

Table 2.8   EU-27 – share of HRST in total employment

		HRST			Employment			Share (%)		
		2004	2005	2006	2004	2005	2006	2004	2005	2006
Total	All NACE[a] branches – total	70636	73175	76096	205687	209353	213482	34.3	35.0	35.6
Manufacturing	Manufacturing sector	9894	9957	10263	39002	38657	38866	25.4	25.8	26.4
	High-technology manufacturing sector	1051	1062	1128	2271	2226	2295	46.3	47.7	49.2
	Medium-high-technology manufacturing sector	3971	3976	4116	11644	11526	11795	34.1	34.5	34.9
	Medium-low-technology manufacturing sector	1889	1870	1954	9137	9093	9304	20.7	20.6	21.0
	Low-technology manufacturing sector	2983	3049	3064	15951	15812	15473	18.7	19.3	19.8
Market services	Services: NACE Rev. 1.1 sections G to Q = 50 to 99	56287	58500	60884	134733	138311	141848	41.8	42.3	42.9
Knowledge intensive	Total knowledge-intensive services: NACE Rev. 1.1 codes 61, 62, 64 to 67, 70 to 74, 80, 85 and 92	38429	39615	41279	66194	67737	69975	58.1	58.5	59.0
	Knowledge-intensive high-technology services: NACE Rev. 1.1 codes 64, 72, 73	3677	3898	4096	6628	6839	7077	55.5	57.0	57.9
	Knowledge-intensive market services (excluding financial intermediation and high-tech services): NACE Rev. 1.1 codes 61, 62, 70, 71, 74	7867	8150	8742	15811	16255	17039	49.8	50.1	51.3

Knowledge intensive	Knowledge-intensive financial services: NACE Rev. 1.1 codes 65, 66, 67	3 384	3 545	3 700	5 944	6 109	6 285	56.9	58.0	58.9
	Other knowledge-intensive services: NACE Rev. 1.1 codes 80, 85, 92	23 501	24 022	24 741	37 811	38 534	39 575	62.2	62.3	62.5
Less knowledge intensive	Total less-knowledge-intensive services: NACE Rev. 1.1 codes 50, 51, 52, 55, 60, 63, 75, 90, 91, 93, 95 and 99	17 858	18 885	19 605	68 539	70 574	71 873	26.1	26.8	27.3
	Less-knowledge-intensive market services: NACE Rev. 1.1 codes 50, 51, 52, 55, 60, 63	8 950	9 476	9 855	46 222	47 148	48 197	19.4	20.1	20.4
	Other less-knowledge-intensive services: NACE Rev. 1.1 codes 75, 90, 91, 93, 95, 99	8 909	9 409	9 750	22 317	23 426	23 675	39.9	40.2	41.2
Other sectors		4 455	4 718	4 949	31 952	32 385	32 768	13.9	14.6	15.1

Note: ᵃNACE – Nomenclature Générase des Activités Économiques dans les Communautés Européennes.

Source: Our elaboration on Eurostat database.

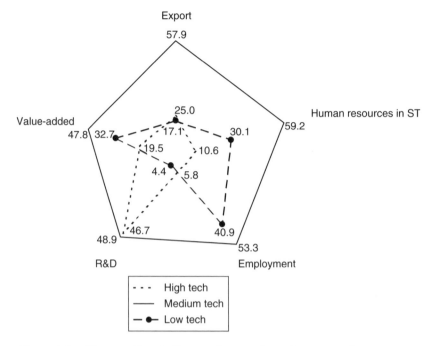

Figure 2.1   Shares of key indicators in manufacturing sectors by technology intensity (%)

of medium-technology sectors in export and in value-added (121.1%) indicates that these sectors have a higher propensity to exports than the manufacturing average and that this propensity is greater than that of high-tech sectors (87.6%). This propensity is almost double that of the low-tech sectors (76.5%). The share of total EU employment of medium-tech manufacturing sectors is almost ten times greater (53.3%) than that of high-technology sectors (5.8%) (Table 2.9b and Figure 2.2).

On the other hand, as expected, the productivity, measured by the ratio between the value-added share and the employment share is higher for high-technology sectors (336.2%) than for medium-tech manufacturing sectors (89.7%). Similarly, the propensity to invest in R&D (ratio R&D share/value-added share) and also the content of qualified human resources (ratio HRST share/employment share) are all higher in high-technology sectors (239.5%; 182.4%) than in medium-tech manufacturing sectors (102.3%; 111.2%). The difference between the two sectors is clearly indicated by the different relevance of qualified human resources (that is, a proxy of 'human capital') and of R&D (that is, a proxy of 'codified knowledge') in these sectors. In fact, the content of qualified

Table 2.9 *(a) Shares of key indicators and (b) relative intensity of indicators.*

(a) Shares of key indicators in manufacturing sectors by technology intensity in the EU (%).

	Manufacturing	High Tech	Medium Tech	Low Tech
Export*	100.0	17.1	57.9	25.0
Value-added**	100.0	19.5	47.8	32.7
Employment***	100.0	5.8	53.3	40.9
Human resources in ST***	100.0	10.6	59.2	30.1
R&D****	100.0	46.7	48.9	4.4

(b) Relative intensity of selected indicators with respect to total manufacturing of the various sectors (%) (*ratios between shares*)

	Manufacturing	High Tech	Medium Tech	Low Tech
Export/Value-added	100	87.6	121.1	76.5
Value-added/ Employment	100	336.2	89.7	80.0
HRST/Employment	100	182.4	111.2	73.7
HRST/Value-added	100	54.5	123.9	92.2
R&D/Value-added	100	239.5	102.3	13.5
HRST/R&D	100	22.7	121.1	685.2

Sources: *2005; OECD STAN Indicators, 2007; **2003; Key Figures 2007; ***2004; Eurostat database, Science and Technology; ****2004; Key Figures 2007.

labour per unit of value-added for medium-tech manufacturing sectors (123.9%) is more than double that of high-technology sectors (54.5%), as can be measured by the ratio between the share of HRST (human resources in science and technology) and the share of value-added of the manufacturing total. On the other hand, the high-technology sectors have a R&D share/value-added share ratio (239.5%) that is double that (102.3%) of the medium-tech manufacturing sectors. In fact, the HRST share/R&D share ratio indicates that medium-tech manufacturing sectors (121.1%) and even more low-technology sectors (685.2%) combine a much higher level of human resources with a unit of R&D than high-technology sectors (22.7%). Thus, knowledge that is embedded in people or 'tacit knowledge' is much more important for medium-tech manufacturing sectors than for high-technology sectors (Table 2.9a and Figure 2.2).

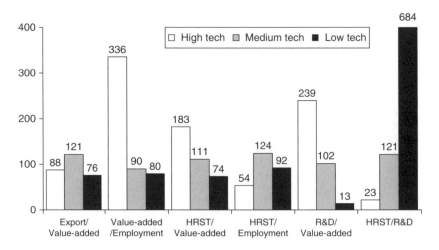

Figure 2.2   Relative intensity of selected indicators with respect to total
manufacturing of the various sectors

2.8   THE RELATIVE INTENSITY OF HUMAN CAPITAL IN THE EU AND US

The share of medium-technology sectors in total manufacturing exports is rather similar in both the European Union (57.9%) and in the United States (61.4%). Also, the share of medium-technology sectors in total manufacturing value-added is rather similar in both the European Union (47.8%) and in the United States (44.6%). On the other hand, the share of medium-technology sectors in total manufacturing employment is much higher in the European Union (53.3%) than in the United States (44.7%). This difference is mainly explained by the much lower share of the high-tech sectors in total employment in the European Union (5.8%) and in the US (12.6%) (cf. Table 2.9a and Table 2.10).

A comparison of the share of HRST employees in total employment in manufacturing and in services indicates that the gap in the use of qualified human resources between manufacturing and services is much larger in the United States than in most of the European countries (Table 2.11). In fact, the share of HRST in total employment in services (41.7%) is higher in the United States than in various European countries, such as Italy (39.0%), France (35.3%), Spain (30.6%) and the United Kingdom (29.1%) and slightly lower than in Germany (43.9%), Sweden (44.4%) and Switzerland (45.0%). On the other hand, the corresponding HRST share in total employment in manufacturing industry

Table 2.10   Shares of key indicators in manufacturing sectors by technology intensity in the United States (%)

	Manufacturing	HT	MT	LT
Export (2005)*	100.0	19.0	61.4	19.6
Value-added (2003)**	100.0	18.6	44.6	36.8
Employment in tot. manuf. (2003)***	100.0	12.6	44.7	42.7

Sources: * Our elaborations on OECD ITCS International Trade by Commodities Statistics – United States – SITC Rev. 3 Vol. 2007; ** our elaborations on OECD STAN Indicators database; *** our elaborations on OECD STAN Indicators database.

is much lower in the United States (14.1%) than in the European countries, such as Sweden (26.1%), France (26.0%), Switzerland (24.6%), Germany (24.2%), the United Kingdom (19.0%), Italy (17.8%) and Spain (16.4%). Thus, the ratio between the shares of HRST in manufacturing and those in services is much lower in the United States (33.8%) than in the European countries, where this ratio has values between 73.5% in France and 45.6% in Italy. This indicates a greater capability of the EU manufacturing industry to use qualified human resources than the US manufacturing industry. In fact, both the absolute values of the share of HRST employees in total employment in the manufacturing industry and the ratio of this latter with respect to the corresponding share in services are higher in most European countries than in the United States. These data and the high trade deficit of the United States in industrial products indicate the importance of human capital in determining the higher international competitiveness of European industry in relation to US manufacturing.

2.9   CONCLUSIONS

While innovation policies mainly focus on the development of high technologies and R&D investments, European industry is still characterized by a strong specialization in medium-technology sectors, such as machinery, transport equipment and chemical products. Medium-technology sectors have achieved high success in industrial restructuring in recent years and play a key role in European competitiveness. The analysis of key statistical indicators for the manufacturing sectors classified by technology intensity indicates that medium-technology sectors have very different characteristics from the manufacturing high-technology sectors on which innovation policies mostly

Table 2.11   Share of HRST employees by industry, 2004 (%)

	Manufacturing	Services	Ratio of Manufacturing: Services
France	26.0	35.3	73.5
Austria	26.0	37.2	70.0
Finland	27.2	39.1	69.5
United Kingdom	19.0	29.1	65.1
Ireland	19.2	29.8	64.4
Denmark	24.9	42.1	59.1
Sweden	26.1	44.4	58.9
Belgium	21.2	36.1	58.8
Germany	24.2	43.9	55.2
Switzerland	24.6	45.0	54.6
Spain	16.4	30.6	53.5
Netherlands	22.5	44.1	50.9
Norway	21.1	41.8	50.5
Czech Republic	19.9	40.2	49.5
Luxembourg	20.7	45.2	45.8
Italy	17.8	39.0	45.6
Australia	15.8	37.1	42.6
Slovak Republic	16.0	38.8	41.1
Poland	15.4	39.2	39.3
Greece	11.8	31.3	37.7
Hungary	13.3	36.3	36.7
Canada	13.0	36.0	36.1
Iceland	13.4	38.8	34.5
United States	14.1	41.7	33.8
Japan	7.1	21.0	33.8
Portugal	8.2	25.8	31.7

Source: OECD Science, Technology and Industry: Scoreboard 2007, ANSKILL database.

concentrate. In particular, the following empirical results seem to highlight the need for specific innovation policies for the medium-technology sectors:

- Medium-technology manufacturing sectors represent the largest component in the trade of OECD countries (56.3%) and their share in the period 2000–05 has continuously increased, while the shares of both low-technology and high-technology products have decreased.
- The share of medium-technology sectors in total manufacturing exports is greater than or close to 50% in almost all European

countries and it has increased during the 2000–03 period. The trade balance of the European Union in medium-technology sectors is positive and it is compensating the trade deficit in the high-tech and low-tech sectors.

- High-technology sectors represent only 1.08% of total European employment, while manufacturing medium-technology sectors have a much greater importance since they represent 11.61%.
- The share of medium-technology sectors in manufacturing industry employment is particularly important in the largest and most industrialized countries in the European Union. Moreover, with the exception of only a few countries, the share of medium-tech manufacturing industry on total manufacturing has increased in all EU countries during the period 2000–06.
- Medium-technology industry represents 57.9% of European manufacturing exports, 53.3% of manufacturing employment and 47.8% of manufacturing value-added, while the share of high-tech industry is only 17.1% in European manufacturing exports, 19.5% in manufacturing value-added and 5.8% in manufacturing employment.
- Medium-technology sectors do not only have a much greater relevance than high-tech sectors, but also have a different 'technology profile' from that of the high-tech sectors. In fact, medium-tech sectors indicate a very high share of total exports, total employment of qualified workers and total employment, while the high-tech sectors indicate a relatively large value of the shares of total value-added and especially of R&D. Therefore, conventional innovation policies focusing on R&D incentives might fail the need for innovation in medium-tech sectors.
- The intensity of human capital is closely related to the technology level of the industrial sectors. Medium-technology manufacturing sectors have intermediate values of highly qualified workers in total employment and this share is constantly increasing.
- The difference between the medium-tech and high-tech sectors is clearly indicated by the different relevance of qualified human resources (that is, a proxy of 'human capital') and of R&D (that is, a proxy of 'codified knowledge') in these sectors. In fact, medium-tech manufacturing sectors and even more low-technology sectors combine a much higher level of human resources with a unit of R&D than high-technology sectors. Thus, knowledge that is embedded in people or 'tacit knowledge' is much more important for medium-tech manufacturing sectors than for high-technology sectors.
- The share of medium-technology sectors of total manufacturing exports is rather similar in both the European Union (59.4%) and

in the United States (61.4%). Also, the share of medium-technology sectors in total manufacturing value-added is rather similar in both the European Union (47.8%) and in the United States (44.6%). A point of similarity between the European Union and the United States is the fact that the evolution of the trade balance of medium-tech sectors in the period 2000–05 has been more positive than that of the high-tech and of the low-tech sectors.

- A comparison of the share of HRST employees in total employment in manufacturing and in services indicates that the gap in the use of qualified human resources between manufacturing and services is much larger in the United States than in most of the European countries. This indicates a greater capability of the EU manufacturing industry to use qualified human resources than the US manufacturing industry.
- These statistics indicate the importance of medium-tech sectors and underline the need to design an approach to European innovation policy that considers the specific factors and processes determining knowledge creation and innovation in these sectors.

NOTE

1. We thank Giuseppe Vullo for having provided assistance in the preparation of the statistics presented in this chapter.

3. Innovation patterns and best practices in medium-technology networks

Rüdiger Wink

3.1 INTRODUCTION

The last chapter showed the increasing importance of medium-tech sectors and the specificities of innovation in these sectors from a macro perspective. Within this chapter, the focus will turn to the role of small and medium-sized enterprises (SMEs) in the medium-tech sectors and their contributions to the successful restructuring of EU medium-tech industries. The major backbone of this chapter is an empirical study on innovation processes in medium-technology SMEs in different European regions. Original qualitative and quantitative data was collected to get a better understanding of the organization of the innovation processes, the role of organizational learning, networks and international linkages for SMEs in the medium-technology manufacturing sector. The medium-technology manufacturing sector was chosen as most of the European firms are engaged in this sector and many new high technologies need close connections to the knowledge base of the established technologies in the medium-technology sector to achieve market breakthroughs and diffusions. In particular for lagging regions, medium-technology manufacturing segments are the only innovation areas possible when considering the existing resources. As already explained in Chapter 2, data on the market share of European exporters in global trade show that medium-technology market shares are dominated by European firms, while for low- and high-technology products the European market shares are remarkably smaller. Thus, medium technologies should be in the strategic focus of European industrial policy despite the fact that most empirical studies on innovation processes have so far concentrated on high-technology segments.

Seven regions were selected to cover the variety of starting conditions and challenges of the European regions within the global competition and a specific cluster specialized in a medium-technology sector has also been selected:

- Ile de France as one of the most advanced metropolitan areas with a large R&D infrastructure and many big industrial companies: optics cluster;
- Hamburg as one of the most advanced metropolitan areas with a high share of business-related services and a smaller industrial basis: aeronautic cluster;
- Madrid as a metropolitan area of the Southern European member states with a huge growth in recent years: aeronautic cluster;
- Styria as an old-industrial area with huge success in the restructuring process towards a knowledge-intensive industrial area: automotive cluster;
- Wales as an old-industrial area with high growth rates due to foreign investments, but less R&D investments than Styria: aeronautic cluster;
- Campania as a lagging region in the incumbent member states with growth rates in R&D and qualification levels: aeronautic cluster;
- Silesia as a lagging region in the new member countries with a long industrial history but huge structural challenges: mining machinery cluster.

For every region, a typical sub-sector of the medium-technology sector was chosen. For Hamburg, Madrid, Wales and Campania the sector of investigation was aeronautics due to the regional relevance of the industry in terms of employment and innovation. Aeronautics covers a wide range of different technologies and serves as a typical example of many integrative technologies, where new high-technology research, for example on new 'intelligent' materials (adaptronics) and electronic technologies, has to be connected with more traditional engineering knowledge on mechanical and hydraulic processes. These integrative technologies are seen as a major challenge to innovation processes, as insights from different disciplines and technological sectors have to be connected (Akbar, 2003; Benzler and Wink, 2005).

Furthermore, the aeronautics sector is in all investigated regions a sector of strategic relevance for future growth within global competition and, due to the cooperation within the EADS/Airbus consortium and within the Boeing supply chain, a perfect example of interregional knowledge transfers (Wink, 2009a, on the relationship between supply chains and transregional learning).

The investigated sector in Paris was the optical sector, where technological developments also required close connections between very advanced and specialized high-technology firms with long experience in established medium-technology markets (Benzler and Wink, 2005). Furthermore, the optical sector seemed to be a perfect example, with lots of interregional firm cooperation between specialized regions in the EU.

In Styria, the mechanical sector played a major role in the restructuring process with many linkages to the automotive and new material markets. Again, relatively strong linkages to other European regions could be expected (Steiner and Hartmann, 2006).

Finally, in Silesia the mining sector was investigated, as this sector has dominated the region for more than a century, many R&D institutes are located in the region and new international investments stress the importance of this sector for the region against the background of increasing energy prices all over Europe. Interregional linkages could particularly be expected due to the international investors (see Cantwell and Piscitello, 2005; Piscitello and Rabbiosi, 2006, on the linkages between investments by multinational firms and international knowledge transfers).

The empirical studies were based on a case study approach. Instead of collecting a small amount of quantitative data from a large number of firms and organizations, several in-depth interviews with different key persons in the firms were carried out to receive more detailed information about actual processes within single firms. By using this in-depth analysis and integrating qualitative information, a more differentiated picture on the innovation networks in Europe and prerequisites for interregional knowledge interactions could be achieved (Box 3.1).

In the following, an overview will be presented of the most important results of this empirical analysis.

3.2   CHARACTERISTICS OF THE FIRMS AND CLUSTERS OF INVESTIGATION

Within this section, some quantitative data are shown to illustrate the framing conditions for innovation processes within the firms and clusters.

First of all, regional data are shown to underline the differences between the investigated regions. The data were collected and elaborated by the Applica team within the IKINET consortium based on Eurostat data. Figure 3.1 shows differences in GDP. Based on GDP per capita, Hamburg is the wealthiest region in the whole EU (see also European Commission, 2007). On the other hand, the GDP per capita in Silesia is below 30% of the average of the EU-25.

BOX 3.1   METHODOLOGY: DESIGN OF THE
          EMPIRICAL ANALYSIS

The empirical analysis consists of four single steps. First, a more general statistical overview was collected to describe the general economic background for the seven clusters investigated. Here, the indicators described the general economic performance of the regions, inter alia considering the GDP per capita in purchasing power standards (PPS), the sectoral structure of the regional economy, inter alia by looking at the distribution of employment along different sectors, the availability of human capital and other demographic factors, described inter alia by the level of education for different age groups in the region, and formal innovation input and output, expressed inter alia by R&D investments, innovative products and patent data.

Second, industrial firms and other organizations were identified for the case study approach. The core of the case studies was in every region a set of 15 industrial firms of the investigated sector. These firms were selected on the basis of a 'snowball effect' to guarantee that direct linkages between the firms could be observed. First interviews in firms were used to ask which other firms in the region were the most important partners in the context of innovation, and these firms were then taken into the set of interviews and also asked which were the most important partners in the regions for them. Besides the industrial firms, other groups of potential actors within a regional knowledge network were selected on the basis of the snowball effect: R&D service organizations; engineering and business-related service organizations; private or semi-public consultancy and support organizations (for example, chambers, industrial associations); public regional and federal organizations; financial service organizations.

All in all, 35 case studies were elaborated in all investigated regions. Furthermore, the information gathered from the snowball effect – the mutual assessment of importance by the firms and organizations in the region – could be integrated into a formal social network analysis based on the NetMiner II software. The network structures showed the importance of linkages between single firms and organizations in the clusters referring to material linkages as well as different kinds of knowledge linkages (pre-competitive R&D collaboration, joint R&D and sales of R&D results).

By investigating these linkages, it was possible to analyse the importance of single organizations and firms as nodes in the network and the factors determining the relative importance of nodes in the networks (for further details on this methodology and further hints on the methodology see Steiner and Ploder, 2008).

Third, a set of questions for qualitative analysis of innovation processes in the firms and organizations was used. This questionnaire dealt with five main topics: (1) the innovation history of the case and the recognition of general structural changes in the market environment; (2) the organization of internal innovation processes, including the role of formal knowledge as well as tacit knowledge in different forms, and the relevance of tools of innovation management; (3) the organization of human resource management, including recruitment criteria, the share of foreign and highly skilled as well as female personnel and the age structure and loyalty in the firms; (4) the relevance and structure of local networking, including driving forces for networking, the role of personal linkages and other forms of proximity and possible hindrances in regional networking; (5) the relevance and experiences with interregional networking, factors in selecting possible partners, differences in regional networking experiences, hindrances and preconditions for successful interregional networks. This qualitative information was used for a report on every case study by the research units.

Fourth, questionnaires with quantitative indicators were used to identify firm-specific criteria to explain the observations in the case studies and differences between the regions. The quantitative part was structured along the dimensions of territorial knowledge management (TKM), which will be explained later on in Chapter 4. Thus, the groups of indicators cover: the overall performance and characteristics of the firms and organizations; the accessibility of knowledge in the single cases; the receptivity of the firms and organizations; the creativity in the firms and organizations; the regional identity expressed by the single cases; the governance of network structures on regional or interregional level. This information was used to explain differences in the importance of every single organization for the regional networks – being in the centre as a node or at the periphery with poor linkages – as well as the differences between the networks, referring to the density of interactions, complexity of cooperation and openness to interregional linkages.

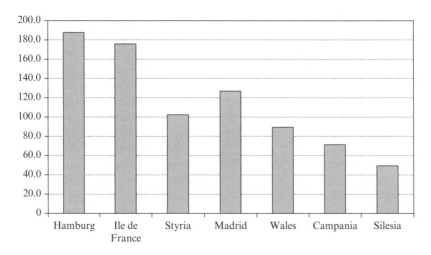

Source: Eurostat.

Figure 3.1   GDP per head in PPS, EU = 100, 2005

Figure 3.2 illustrates differences between the regional labour markets. The high per capita income in Hamburg mainly originates from the high share of business-related services. High-technology services and industrial employment does not play a major role in the region. In general, the metropolitan regions show the expected high share in the service sector, while Styria and Wales have relatively high shares of employment in the manufacturing sector. The two lagging regions have, overall, relatively low shares in manufacturing and services.

Figure 3.3 offers a comparison of the R&D expenditure structure within the regions. Here, Styria and Ile de France are the highest performers. Within the lagging region of Campania and Silesia (Poland) as well as in Wales the share of public R&D expenditures is higher than private business R&D expenditures, which illustrates the structural weaknesses in these areas. These differences between the regions correspond to the results for patent performance, where again Ile de France is the leading investigated region and only Hamburg as the second-ranked investigated region shows a remarkably better relative result than for the comparison of R&D input. Sterlacchini (2008), however, shows that the relevance of R&D inputs and qualification for economic growth processes differs across the European regions, with mainly North European countries benefiting from the intensity of R&D and higher education.

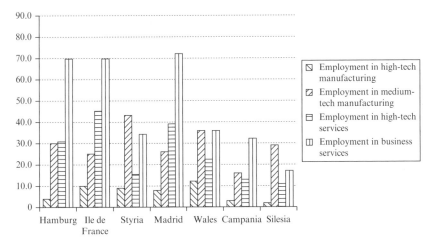

Source: Eurostat.

Figure 3.2   Employment in sectors as % of total working population, 2004

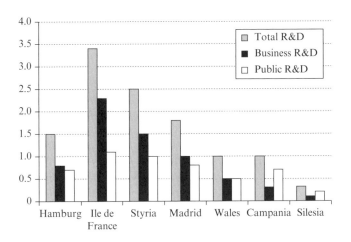

Source: Eurostat.

Figure 3.3   R&D expenditures as % of GDP, 2004

This general overview of the regions served as a starting point for the interregional comparison and followed the expected pattern of differences according to the types of regions selected (metropolitan, old-industrial, lagging, and so on). The interviews with the firms and organizations provided further quantitative data to illustrate the differences between the investigated regions. The quantitative data collected consisted of seven parts and covered those fields that reveal information on the capabilities of firms and organizations to participate in knowledge interaction (see the explanation of the seven perspectives of territorial knowledge management (TKM) in Chapter 4 and Figure 4.18):

- size and growth of the firms and organizations;
- the capability of the firms and organizations to access new knowledge based on R&D cooperation and expenditures;
- the capabilities of firms and organizations to access knowledge outside the region;
- the internal human resources and organizational capabilities of the firms and organizations;
- the capabilities to enhance the local or regional identity of the firms and organizations;
- the internal potentials to improve creativity;
- the capabilities of the firms and organizations in the context of customer orientation.

In contrast to many other studies on innovation based on quantitative indicators (see, for example, the Scoreboard approaches by the European Commission, 2005 and the OECD, 2007), this structure followed a theoretical concept integrating the complexity of innovation processes and considering the linkages between internal capabilities of the firms and organizations and the external relationships to cooperation partners inside and outside the regions. This also allowed the identification of crucial indicators that explain different structures and performances in different types of networks. We will come to the implications of these correlations in the next section when we discuss the results of the qualitative part of the interviews.

The quantitative data provided by the interviewed firms and organizations followed the expected patterns within the regions. Thus, the original objective of the project – to get an overview of innovation processes in SMEs from the medium-technology manufacturing sectors in different types of regions – could be achieved. For examples of these differences, the structure of firms within the regions can be observed. The firms in Hamburg, the metropolitan region with relatively weak concentration on R&D but strengths in private business services, are relatively small and concentrated on their region. Wales as an old-industrial region with structural weaknesses in R&D has firms with a relatively strong international market orientation, in particular due to the high relevance of international investors attracted by public funding. Styria has a diversified set of firms with differences in size, international orientation and R&D, similar to Ile de France and Madrid. Campania as an incumbent lagging region has a relatively high number of small firms with R&D more concentrated on public institutes, while Silesia has at least some firms with higher shares of R&D and international orientation due to long experience in the sector.

The number of firms with experience of R&D cooperation with foreign firms is highest for Styria, the successfully restructured old-industrial region, and lowest for Hamburg, the metropolitan region with relatively low concentration on private R&D. Correspondingly, a relatively high number of firms in Styria have experience with EU-funded projects. The Campania cluster also has a remarkably high number of firms with experience in public funding, in particular due to the high relevance of public funding in lagging regions.

The experiences in the quantitative part of the interviews demonstrated that the method of structuring the quantitative indicators along different functions within a territorial knowledge management approach actually improved the understanding of structural differences between the regions. The correlations in the next section will reveal more on this explanatory potential. Future research with larger firm sets and access to more data will be helpful in reaching a deeper understanding of SME innovations than provided by the existing CIS and Innovation Scoreboard comparisons based only on quantitative innovation input and output data that neglect the specificities of innovation in medium-technology SMEs.

3.3   INNOVATION PROCESSES IN EUROPEAN MEDIUM-TECHNOLOGY SMES

3.3.1   The Organization of Innovation Processes

The traditional view of medium-technology SMEs is based on the recognition of firms with severe scarcities of resources (Bougrain and Haudeville, 2002; Frormann, 2006). While in the traditional industrial model, survival of these firms was still possible despite strategic weaknesses due to scarce resources, structural changes to new market environments for European industries raise doubts on the future competitiveness of medium-technology SMEs. These structural challenges are formulated from customers, financial intermediaries, human capital markets, product markets as well as international markets.

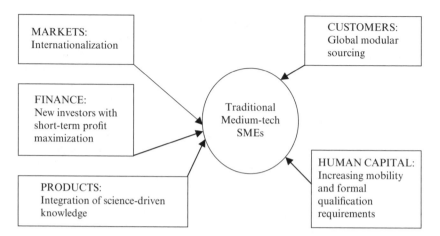

Figure 3.4   Threats to the traditional medium technology SME approach

Figure 3.4 illustrates the new pressures on the traditional model forcing traditional SMEs to adjust their innovation processes.

The typical criticisms of traditional medium-technology SMEs include the following:

1. The firms are too embedded in their local environment with too little experience and too few contacts at international level.

Traditional value chains in local production systems with a strong emphasis on geographical proximity and close social contacts have been adjusted to more differentiated value systems with production in many different international regions and more responsibilities and risks for the small members. Brenner and Mühlig (2007) describe driving forces for the emergence and evolution of clusters, and Carbonara, Giannoccaro and Pontrandolfo (2002) provide a theoretical framework for evolutionary changes of cooperation in production systems. In both lines of argument, the initial formation is driven by attractive local production factors and the realization of mutual gains by cooperation. With time, however, the requirements for partners within the cooperative systems become more and more differentiated with a strong position of multinational actors and specialized system suppliers. Accordingly, SMEs in medium-technology sectors are forced to develop strategies for relocation of standardized production processes to cope with increasing cost competition. The suppliers do not only have to follow their most important customers all over the world, but also increasingly often have to take the risks of developing new markets, including foreign exchange rate risks and sales risks. Thus, SMEs need a deeper knowledge of the cultural, legal and economic specificities of foreign markets, and have a lack of management capacity with foreign experience and foreign contacts (see Dunning, 1988; Johanson and Vahlne, 1990, on traditional concepts for internationalization processes). As a result, many conventional SMEs lose their status in industrial value chains, which switch from local production systems to formal international agreements.

2. The firms do not have the necessary resources to develop system competencies within modern international value chain management.

In the last two decades, multinational films have drastically reduced their level of integration and their absolute number of suppliers (Brandes, Lilliecreutz and Brege, 1997; Quinn, 2000). Instead of making a high number of single contracts with suppliers of single components, they outsource complete modules of their products to system suppliers, who have the responsibility to find partners with sufficient capabilities to keep a specified formal level of quality. Engineering service firms have specialized in expertise to modularize production process and to govern international outsourcing processes (Coviello and Martin, 1999; Jack, As-Saber and Edwards, 2006; Ilyas et al., 2008). For many traditional SMEs used to personal contacts with their major customers and to a high level of specialization for certain components, the step towards the emergence of competencies assumed for system suppliers is too far. They do not have the necessary diversity of technological experience, management experience to guarantee specific formal qualities of whole supply chains and financial strengths to take the risk of responsibility for whole modules.

In many papers on management theories in the 1990s, the emergence of 'virtual enterprises' was seen as a possible solution for firms not willing or able to integrate too many single functions of a production process into one single firm, as cooperation was only based on actual needs (Warnecke, 1993; Womack and Jones, 1994). Other models called for strategic alliances to overcome deficits in single firms (Bleeke and Ernst, 1995; Bougain and Haudeville, 2002). For all these organizational models, however, the participating firms and their management had to offer specific capabilities, technological equipment, experience in and access to different markets and the resources to govern these loose cooperation processes. For most of the traditional SMEs in medium-technology sectors, these prerequisites were not a given. Consequently, virtual corporations were kept to a small segment (mostly in high-technology segments), and strategic alliances were mainly driven by big multinational firms. The traditional SMEs, however, are under constant pressure to be downgraded to a position as fourth- or fifth-tier suppliers within a value chain, eliminated from modular value chains, or to become formal parts of firm groups merged for the purpose of forming new system suppliers.

3. The firms are too small and too restricted to encourage private investors to take larger risks within innovative markets.

The traditional model of finance for European SMEs focused on medium-technology industries was based on a strong dependence on the private equity of the entrepreneur, his/her family and friends and on a close relationship to one single local bank (Frormann, 2006; El Hajj Chehade and Vigneron, 2007). Short-term rates of return were less important in such a model, and most of the credits provided by the banks were backed up by mutual trust and experience with the business model of the firm (Karl and Wink, 2006). These conditions are no longer a given. Banks came under increasing pressure to consider quantitative risk management indicators, requiring larger rates of private equity as back-up for credits and to focus on short-term performance of credit demanders. Thus, firms have to look for private investors to improve their risk position. Private equity funds became important actors in the capital markets, and many of them concentrate on SMEs with hidden strengths to unveil short-term profit potentials, causing severe changes in the strategic management processes of the firms. These changes also affect the role of the firm founder or members of the firm-founding families, who lose their often-dominant position in formulating corporate principles and defining strategic technological developments. Additionally, venture capitalists can influence growth processes of SMEs not only by offering capital for new investments but also by spreading information on potential regional partners and regional market strategies (Zook, 2004). As a consequence, SMEs either have to adjust their strategies towards short-term profit interests, including decreasing relevance of long-term loyalty to employees and firm-specific routines within innovation processes, or become increasingly restricted in their growth and investment potential, as the necessary financial resources and contacts to adjust to new requirements in value chain systems and internationalized markets are not available. In the long term, the independence of the SMEs can in these cases no longer be obtained.

4. The firms can no longer rely on long-term loyalty of human capital and internal emergence of specific competencies but have to be competitive in recruiting high potentials.

Similar to the context of finance, customer management or spatial dimensions of markets, the conditions for SMEs to develop their own human resource management has changed drastically in recent years (Heneman, Ledford and Gresham, 2000). Traditionally, SMEs are not as focused on formal qualifications in their recruitment as bigger firms, and rely on long-term development of firm-specific qualifications to create and enhance their own firm-specific tacit knowledge base. Employees stay for a long time within the companies and have few incentives to move to bigger firms, as they may only have irreversible firm-specific competencies that would not be demanded (and paid for) by the bigger firms in the same way. The departing employees would lose their sovereignty of position due to the higher level of hierarchies and formalized decision-making processes in bigger firms.

With the changing knowledge requirements of employees, who also have to understand the more theoretical content of new technologies to link this with engineering insights on specific machines (Duhovnik et al., 2003), SMEs become increasingly reliant on specific experts, who need to have high formal qualifications and experience of specific applications (Florida, Mellander and Stollarick, 2007). Thus, they have to compete with bigger firms, which use larger salaries and modern human resource management styles as inducements in recruitment. As a consequence, firms need to adjust their human resource strategies and organization (Nonaka and Konno, 1998; McCracken and Wallace, 2000; Swanson, 2001). On the one hand, they need to enhance the exchange and formalization of former tacit knowledge to become less dependent on the knowledge of single employees (see Nonaka, 1994; Stein and Zwass, 1995; Steels, 2000; Tiwana, 2001, on single approaches for technological solutions to the formalization and storage of knowledge within the firms). On the other hand, they need to offer attractive working conditions and career prospects to their key employees to compensate for restrictions on salaries compared with the bigger firms. Examples in this context include the role of skill-based payments or the reorganization of the work environment towards projects (Thompson and LeHew, 2000; Zingheim and Schuster, 2002; Bredin and Söderlund, 2006). Instruments like stock options, however, can only rarely be used by SMEs despite their attractiveness for managers because those firms, in most cases, are not listed at the stock exchange (Mehran, 1995; Poutsma, de Nijs and Poole, 2003). Thus remains the question of how medium-technology SMEs can overcome their difficulties in attracting highly qualified experts.

5.   The firms need to integrate new knowledge elements into traditional engineering solutions.

This final point refers to differences in the knowledge content needed. Traditionally, medium-technology industries need specific knowledge on production processes, equipment and products, which was primarily based on engineering knowledge (Vincenti, 1990; De Vries, 2003). This knowledge was usually developed along single applications and problem solutions with only a few general theoretical basics (König, 1993). The change towards integrative technologies connecting traditional medium-technology industries with modern science-driven technologies requires analytical skills to apply general theoretical concepts from nature sciences to specific problem solutions (Liyanage, Nordberg and Wink, 2007; Quintana-Garcia and Benavides-Velasco, 2008). Big companies mainly use two approaches to overcome this challenge: either to build up communities-of-practice within their firm consisting of engineers with combinative knowledge skills and more theory-driven researchers with analytical skills (Brown and Duguid, 1991; Handly et al., 2006; Amin and Roberts, 2008; Duguid, 2008) or to outsource specific knowledge requirements to specialized spin-offs within the value chain (Quinn, 2000; Harada, 2003; Mol, 2005). For SMEs, these options are only rarely available, as they are restricted in their attraction of specified experts and pooling of diversified skills within their firm (Hoffman et al., 1998; Wickramasinghe and Sharma, 2005) and they need to offer attractive knowledge to gain and obtain access to knowledge-intensive value chains (Miotti and Sachwald, 2003; Karlsson and Andersson, 2007). Our study also served to investigate whether and under which circumstances joint development between medium-technology SMEs within knowledge networks can really be a solution to overcoming these restrictions to development (see Danilovic and Winroth, 2006, on observations of these changes towards self-organizing systems of SME cooperation within value chains).

* * *

In the following, we present best practice strategies within our regions of investigation to show how European medium-technology industry SMEs are able to stay at the top of international competitiveness despite these specific structural challenges. As shown by the diversity of influences on the innovation processes in medium-technology SMEs, adjustments in the organization of innovation processes affect the whole corporate organization itself: (1) internally: strategic development of new products and processes, human resource development, facilitation of cooperation between engineers and other experts on production with employees in marketing, finance and other functional divisions and so on; (2) externally: positioning within the market based on redefinition of customized products, diversification of markets or inclusion of knowledge-intensive services into the product portfolio, new forms of cooperation within value chains, modes of entry into foreign markets amongst others.

All these changes cannot be realized without a complete restructuring of the organization, its culture, shape and processes. Many scientific and management papers deal with the problem of adjusting an organization, when the adoption of a new technology – for example, information technology tools – requires new organizational processes. Utterback (1996) and Christensen (1997) provide examples of firms that have been successful innovators at an initial stage of technological development but failed to adjust their organization at later stages. For medium-technology SMEs, these challenges are even stronger, as they have to include technological paradigms from other disciplines to extend and diversify their knowledge base. Thus, they have to develop openness and flexibility within their organizational structure to adjust to changing market conditions as well as cognitive openness to knowledge from different disciplines. Theories of revolutionary changes argue that disruptive changes in the influencing environment are necessary to overcome organizational inertia, while simultaneously the reactions within the organization have to be accepted and attainable (Reger et al., 1994; Gustafson and Reger, 1995).

Another possible factor influencing changes could be charismatic managers convincing the members of the organizations that their original beliefs are no longer suitable (Reger et al., 1994). Power (2006), however, provides in this context insights on the differences in the willingness to adopt B2B technologies within Australian SMEs in fast-growing consumer goods segments, with senior managers being more negative in their perception of technological tools than managers in functional areas.

In the following, we will look at the direction, range and driving forces of strategies within our regions of investigation. We distinguish four typical strategic options (see also Table 3.1) that relate pure strategies of strategic management (quality, cost differentiation, niche), which, for example, Michael Porter already defined years ago (Porter, 1990), to knowledge management:

3.3.1.1 Complete strategic turn towards spin-offs with science-driven knowledge

This option is typical for SMEs that started their business during or after the structural changes and do not have the usual problems of lock-in structures and mentalities within their organizations. These industrial SMEs are based on entrepreneurial decisions by former employees in bigger firms or by former researchers from universities and research institutes (Callan, 2001; European Commission, 2002; Parhankangas and Arenius,

2003). Although most of the literature deals with high-technology spin-offs and start-ups (Caryannis et al., 1998; Klepper, 2001; OECD, 2001), these firms also play a major role in knowledge transfers within medium-technology sectors (Lockett, Wright and Franklin, 2003; Siegel, Westhead and Wright, 2003; Agarwal et al., 2004). The entrepreneurs have a specified knowledge that is relevant for medium-technology sectors, but due to their recent experiences with formal R&D processes also have capabilities to cooperate and exchange knowledge with representatives from big firms and basic research institutes (Kechidi et al., 2007). This science-driven knowledge usually integrates a larger share of analytical knowledge and requires a basic abstract understanding, which can only be attainable by people with continuous contacts in academic environments. Thus, these types of firms are perfect candidates for a complete transition towards supply of more analytical knowledge and more science-driven markets, which connect medium-technology products with high-technology services (see Ekeledo and Sivakumar, 1998; Gronroos, 1998, for examples of marketing services, and UNCTAD, 2005, for examples from R&D services).

According to the focus in many scientific papers on high-technology spin-offs, most authors stress the positive role of spin-offs for the knowledge economy in knowledge-intensive agglomerations, as in these regions critical masses of research institutes, universities and R&D departments of big firms can be found (Karlsson, 1997; Egeln et al., 2004; Cantner and Graf, 2006; Andersson and Hellerstedt, 2008; Broström, 2008). Within our sample of investigation, the agglomerative areas of Ile de France, Styria or Madrid showed a relatively high share of young firms that were founded as spin-offs from bigger firms and use an original element on a specific part of the value chain in the bigger firm to formulate a new business model and to focus on the requirements of international value chain systems. For the original parent companies, these spin-offs leave more options to focus their core competencies on, while still strategically exploiting former knowledge investments (see López Iturriaga and Martin Cruz, 2008, for similar results in a sample of 3462 Spanish firms).

Another model is spin-offs from public R&D institutes, as several companies in the German case of the aeronautical cluster in Hamburg demonstrated. Even in the Middle and Eastern European countries, former specialized public research facilities, for example in the Silesian mining industry, can form the nucleus for new businesses. These firms are able to provide formalized knowledge via highly qualified staff, technological equipment and advanced knowledge management practices. They prefer to stay as specialized spin-offs instead of using internal or external growth to maintain their independence and to be sufficiently flexible in their market strategies. Within modern modular value chain systems, they are integrated as specialized providers who are able to cooperate directly with the original equipment manufacturers (OEMs) or leading system suppliers (Jack et al., 2006). A typical example of this is the 'concurrent engineering' approach by Airbus in the aeronautical sector, where Airbus engineers work simultaneously online on specific technological problem solutions with selected engineers from major system suppliers and specialized small firms (Hayward, 2005; Alfonso-Gil and Talbot, 2007; Alfonso-Gil and Vazquez-Baquero, 2009; Jalabert et al., 2008). This approach can be seen as part of a strategy towards a more collaborative supply chain management to reduce uncertainties and coordination costs within the value chain (Kilger and Reuter, 2002), while still trying to keep elements of central planning to ensure overall efficiency of the production process (see Pibernik and Sucky, 2006, on an approach to systemizing alternatives of more centralized or decentralized supply chain planning).

For the majority of established conventional SMEs, this strategic turn cannot be a realistic option, as they lack the necessary qualifications of their staff, technical equipment and management expertise (Wickramasinghe and Sharma, 2005). Additionally, the break in the organizational culture would be too severe if they tried to overcome these deficiencies by explicit strategies only to focus on staff with academic backgrounds, to invest in R&D facilities and technologies to cope with OEM standards or to replace the management. For the future of European SMEs, however, this is an important growth model in regions with highly qualified staff and private or public R&D facilities. To connect medium-technology sectors with integrative innovations, it will be crucial to combine these locational advantages with specific qualifications in engineering and related disciplines (see Hall, 1974, for investigations on the relationship between engineering research and scientific progress). Examples of cross-disciplinary qualification and research from the two aeronautics clusters in France and Germany show the opportunities of this approach.

3.3.1.2 Increase the diversification of sales markets to improve the exploitation of the knowledge

Traditionally, many SMEs work closely with a few customers, based on personal linkages mostly within the same region (see Carbonara et al., 2002; Carabelli, Hirsh and Rabellotti, 2006 on the traditional perspectives on industrial districts and their transition towards new patterns of production). These personal linkages play a major role in overcoming barriers to cooperation driven by lack of trust in potential partners and lack of confidence in the existence of mutual benefits of cooperation by complementary knowledge (see Chetty and Agndal, 2008 for a case study). The product development within this traditional model was highly specialized according to the requirements of the few customers, and the market strategy of the conventional SMEs was restricted to the industrial segment they were used to. These 'relational' or 'social' proximities (see Rallet and Torre, 1998; Boschma, 2005; Davenport, 2005; Torre and Rallet, 2005 on concepts for different forms of proximities) between suppliers and major customers lose their relevance in a market environment where multinational firms adjust their sourcing strategies to international and modularized markets. The multinational firms care less for social or relational linkages than for superior knowledge and complementary effects of the knowledge base secured by cognitive or organizational proximities (see Wink, 2009b, on these changes and the terminology of proximity dynamics). In a later section, we will explain in more theoretical detail the relationships between different types of proximities and knowledge interactions in medium-technology sectors.

Many successful SMEs reacted to this change by increasing their independence from major customers. Diversification of sales markets is a feasible strategy in those industries, where a specific technology or know-how in production processes is not restricted to one single product group or industry but to several industries with similar needs and possible applications (Wink, 2007; Quintana-Garcia and Benavides-Velasco, 2008). For a long time, the range of diversification in medium-technology industries was restricted, as the combinative knowledge of the engineers only made it possible to connect requirements from specific customers to tailor-made problem solutions at specialized machines (Vincenti, 1990). The switch towards integrative technologies, where the incumbent industrial knowledge is combined with the more analytical knowledge of science-driven research, increases the range of diversification due to the more general knowledge base of technological functionality (Benzler and Wink, 2005). Consequently, cluster strategies make use of these options for diversification by inviting customers from different sectors without direct rivalry to work with suppliers from the more advanced science-driven technologies as well as with those suppliers from medium-technology segments who are able to apply their problem solutions to different requirements (Bathelt, Malmberg and Maskell, 2004; Brenner, 2004; Capello and Faggian, 2005; Christensen and Drejer, 2005).

As an example, the cluster Carbon Fibre Competence Network (CFK) in Stade – close to the centre of our investigated area Hamburg – consists of non-competing members along the whole value chain of composite materials within different markets, from R&D service suppliers, specialized medium-technology SMEs, advanced spin-offs, specialists in logistics and waste management to public administration, financial services providers and big OEMs. Due to the diversity of the OEMs included (aeronautical, automotive, chemical companies as examples), SMEs can explore new sales markets they did not think of in their past as exclusive suppliers for specific market segments. Similarly, the Styrian industry is no longer characterized by one or two dominant sectors, as in the 1980s, but changed towards a diversified technology-based economy, where techno-logical solutions might be created in cooperation with one specific sector, often the automotive industry, but transferred to other industrial markets (see Steiner and Hartmann, 2006, for more details on these changes). This active approach, instead of passively waiting for hints from the dominant OEM or other major customers, leaves the SMEs much more strategic potential within global competition. Therefore, successful SMEs normally do not concentrate more than one-third of their business on one specific sales market, and even within this market look for different customers.

3.3.1.3   Focus on niche strategies with innovative products

Another group of successful SMEs based its strategies on a consequent exploitation of original strengths of traditional medium-technology indus-try SMEs lying in the specific value of tacit knowledge embedded exclu-sively in the firms' human capital and market experiences (Meyer, 2006). Here, the firms focus on a relatively small market, but aim to be the 'best' in these niches. This model for firms, often cited as 'hidden champions' (Simon, 1996), could be observed in our sample, for example when looking at Austrian machinery firms specializing in supplying specific parts for Formula 1 racing cars or suppliers in the aeronautical value chain concen-trated on designing and producing specific parts of the cabin interior (for example, child protection seats or specially designed kitchens). The crucial premises for the success of this strategy are the continuous superiority of the firms' knowledge in the market, primarily strengthened by ongoing learning curve effects in product development, and the exclusiveness of this knowledge protected by strict rules on secrecy (Liyanage et al., 2007; Venohr and Meyer, 2007).

Furthermore, the attractiveness of market niches crucially depends on their long-term development potential, which means technological options for the future, affected purchase power, but also the flexibility in the market towards innovative products. The civil aeronautics market can be seen as an example of these restrictions on flexibility, as new items developed by the suppliers first have to be integrated into the regulatory environment for the civil aircraft production, which means that the OEMs have to finance the registration and examination procedures of the regulatory authorities, and this is only realistic if the OEMs expect additional sales in the airline market with these new items. Thus, security and environmental innovations in these niche markets could face problems of implementation if the necessary additional market pressure is not brought to bear. Growth for these niche markets is in most cases only possible with further internationalization to achieve proximity to the most important and growing sales markets. Hence, firms choosing this strategy look for modes to enter foreign markets without losing the specificities of their skills and organizational culture (Venohr and Meyer, 2007). For many Italian industrial districts with their high level of specialization, these strategic processes not only affect single SMEs but also whole cooperative structures of SMEs, which started on a regional level and internationalize jointly (Cappellin, 2004a; Federico, 2005; Mariotti, Muhnelli and Piscitello, 2008). We will look later in this chapter at the specific challenges that internationalization of cluster structures and networking pose to medium-technology SMEs.

3.3.1.4   Intensified formal cooperation to build up critical masses
As explained at the beginning of this chapter, some general structural changes in global markets directly affect the competitiveness of business models based on small production units. System suppliers need a critical size to build up necessary competencies over the whole module they are responsible for and to take the additional financial and management risks the OEMs require (see Qi, Bard and Yu, 2004; Iakovou, Vlachos and Xanthopoulos, 2007, on a taxonomy of risks within a supply chain). Financial service providers require a minimum size of firm to offer specific market instruments, for example in mezzanine segments (Karl and Wink, 2006). OEMs require a critical size of potential cooperation partners in R&D to guarantee that the partners are able to finance their R&D equipment and staff (see Mazaud and Lagasse, 2007, on the example of Airbus). In particular, in sectors like aeronautics with huge demand disruptions along long product cycles, uncertainties due to foreign exchange rate risks and rising complexity of value chains after long periods of vertical integration, OEMs look for suitable partners to share risks.

Hence, SMEs in medium-tech sectors come under pressure to adjust their visible size. Contrasting this tendency towards greater size, small units are still quite efficient in strengthening the incentives of the individual employee to improve his or her knowledge base, as they have less hierarchies and formal structure (see Lindkvist, 2004, on approaches to overcoming disincentives by hierarchies). Traditionally, informal cooperation between firms helped to exploit the best of both sides – economies of scope by total size of all cooperating firms and decentralized structures by small structures. Typical examples of this were local production systems and industrial districts (Piore and Sabel, 1984; Pycke, Becattini and Sengenberger, 1990; Paniccia, 2002). This informal way of increasing organizational size, however, might lead to restricted results in the changed market environment, as they are not necessarily included in calculations for bank credits or orders by sourcing OEMs.

More intensified ways of cooperation with a higher degree of formalism could be a solution to adjust to these changed needs. These formal approaches could range from consortium contracts to joint holdings. Consortium contracts are encouraged by large countries in those cases where the consolidation within the supply chain was thus far not possible due to a lack of system suppliers, political influences on sourcing or too great a diversity of the knowledge base, for example in the aeronautics sector (Wink, 2007). The most ambitious attempt to form a holding of SMEs within our sample could be observed in Hamburg, where the local association of aeronautical SMEs supported the formation of a holding acting as one single supplier, who should be able to offer one or several systems. The experiences of this case, however, also showed the difficulties of this strategy, as the founders did not succeed in attracting sufficient important suppliers for the holding and were therefore not able to meet the standards expected by Airbus.

Summing up, the four observed strategies show possible responses by medium-technology SMEs to the general strategic challenge explained at the beginning. Challenges, however, remain for every SME to identify its best strategic response in its own specific case. Thus, Table 3.1 shows the strengths and the limits of the described strategies.

This overview stresses that there is not only one single strategic challenge that the SMEs have to meet. They also have to develop their strengths in knowledge creation and networking to keep necessary premises for the realization of the alternative strategic options. Within the next sections we therefore look at these aspects.

3.3.2 Knowledge Creation

Most scientific papers on knowledge creation deal with the creation of new, often radical, knowledge in high-technology sectors (see Abernathy and Clarke, 1985; Capello, 1999; Liyanage et al., 2007, for an overview of the literature). Here, typically capital-intensive investments in huge R&D laboratories and excellent staff lead to new scientific insights that can be transformed into new products and processes (see Junold and Wink, 2006, and Roper, Du and Love, 2008 on the knowledge value chain in the stem cell business). This requires analytical knowledge, as the core of the innovation is based on the theoretical cognition process leading to new explicit knowledge, which can be laid down in written texts for publications, manuals or patent applications (see Karlsson, 1997; Cantner and

Table 3.1   Strategic opportunities for medium-technology industry SMEs

Strategy	Possible Benefits	Restrictions
Spin-offs with more formalized knowledge base	Better adjustment to modern supply chains, specialization in high-value niches, protection of strategic independence	Necessary formal knowledge base; high formal qualifications of the workforce, high R&D investments needed; restricted to spin-offs from big firms or research institutes
Diversification of sales markets	Independence from single customers, broader range of cooperation for knowledge interaction, reduction of market risks	Applicability of knowledge to different industrial sales markets, access to technological clusters, flexibility of marketing strategies
Focus on niche markets with innovative products	Less competitive pressure from big companies, fewer needs for diversified recruitment and product development strategies	Exclusiveness of knowledge, sales potential within the niche market, technological and market development potential of the niche
Intensification of formal cooperation	Protection of independence and compliance with requirements from OEMs and financial markets, exploitation of scale economies	Compatibility of partners, design of cooperation, sustainability of cooperation structures, dependence on personal contacts

Graf, 2006 on social network investigations based on patent information). In medium-technology industries, most of the knowledge is still synthetic, combining general theoretical thoughts with the specificities of single production processes and equipment. Consequently, a lot of specified and embedded knowledge is needed to develop new products and services.

These traditional strengths, however, are threatened by the changed market environments already mentioned in a more general overview at the beginning of the chapter and directly affecting knowledge production processes. Figure 3.5 visualizes these threats to knowledge creation.

1.   The firms are increasingly forced to formalize their knowledge base.

As already explained above, medium-technology SMEs are used to developing primarily tacit knowledge focused on very specific unique problem solutions within production processes and are often dependent on the capabilities of single employees. Knowledge management models

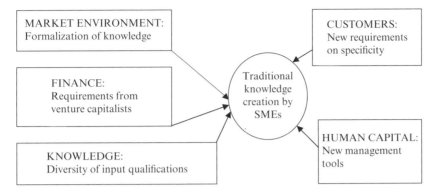

Figure 3.5   Threats to the traditional knowledge creation processes of medium-technology SMEs

and tools deal with processes to formalize the embedded knowledge of employees and to make it accessible to other members in the organizations (Szulanski, 1996; Davenport and Pruzak, 1998; Van der Bent, Paauwe and Williams, 1999). These models and tools, however, are typically restricted to big firms, while SMEs – particularly in medium-technology sectors – face specific impediments within the processes of developing and implementing their knowledge management systems. Tan and Hung (2006) present a taxonomy of these impediments using the example of ISO 9000-based systems. They refer to impediments at the level of top management, as lack of vision due to missing experiences with knowledge management systems and their use, lack of suitable corporate rules and values, as well as lack of management resources (Gore and Gore, 1999). Other levels include information technology that might not be suitable to the needs and potentialities of SMEs (see Grant, 1996, on the functions of information technology), lack of education and training of employees (Grieves, McMillan and Wilding, 2006) and organizational structures on the firm or supply chain level that are not sufficiently open to creating incentives for the employees and managers to exchange their knowledge (O'Dell and Grayson, 1998; Gold, Malhotra and Segars, 2001).

Despite these problems in adjusting, OEMs require in modern supply chain systems the proof of certain qualifications and procedures according to formalized industry or firm norms, for example by the big multinational automotive or aeronautics producers (see Kohtamaki and Kautonen, 2008; Ruiz-Torres and Mahmoodi, 2008, on general considerations for OEMs to structure their supply chain). This formalization is particularly important in a market environment, where supply chains not only serve the function of efficient physical delivery along the production process, which mainly poses challenges for logistical systems, but also a market mediating function to develop fast responses to new needs of demand and innovative product and process changes (see Fisher, 1997; Fisher et al., 1997, for a distinction between these two functions). The latter function mainly requires flexibility and speed, making it necessary that every member within the supply chain is able to create new problem solutions and adjust its processes to new requirements (see Selldin, 2004; Olhager, Selldin and Wikner, 2006, on the impact for downstream processes in the value chain). Collaborative improvements between supply chain members can only be achieved if the necessary information on the interfaces is accessible, thus requiring a formalization of the embedded knowledge (Tether, 2002; Gutierrez and Serrano, 2008; Wink, 2009b). Furthermore, this formalization helps the OEMs to identify the specific value and potential of future improvements of each member within the chain (see Martinez and Bititci, 2006, on the challenges for this identification).

For the incumbent SMEs, the need for formalization of knowledge often means huge additional investments in new staff, participation with programmes of consultancy service companies and equipment. Furthermore, the shifting of R&D risks from OEM to the supplier also implies increasing expectations in formal R&D investments by the SMEs, which often lack necessary financial means, organizational routines and qualified human capital (Frormann, 2006). As a consequence, SMEs have to look at adjusting their traditional way of knowledge creation towards the new expectations without losing their competitive advantage of specificity.

2.   The firms need to adjust to structural market changes towards customization.

Traditionally, the SMEs of our investigation are used to providing specific solutions, thus to working closely with their customers. Within the traditional value chain of medium-technology industries, however, this often means only cooperating with one big firm, which acts as a mass producer within international markets. During the last decades, most of these markets have been affected by changes towards customization, which means that the variety of final products becomes bigger, the speed to find flexible specification increases and the industrial products have to be connected with an increasing share of services (see D'Aveni, 1994, Danov, Brock Smith and Mitchell, 2003; Santalainen, 2006, on 'hypercompetition' as the new challenge for strategic management). These changes cause new requirements for supplying SMEs, as they have to cooperate more closely with the OEM on the necessary services, have to be prepared for new specifications and service demands and need to accelerate their adjustment processes (see Tether and Tajar, 2008, on experiences with organizational innovations in supply chains driven by specialized service firms). This again requires additional capabilities of the human capital and the management, which is hard to acquire by SMEs due to the competition in this labour market segment with big firms. Studies in the Hamburg aeronautics cluster, for example, show that the firms do not have knowledge of their actual potentials in technology marketing, including opportunities and premises to expand into related markets, to internationalize their products, integrate other production technologies or use other marketing strategies within their original markets (Teichert and Harder-Nowka, 2007). Without this knowledge, however, strategic development of knowledge creation and commercialization processes is hardly possible. Thus, the successful turn towards customized products and increasing flexibility of knowledge created crucially depends on the sustainability of business models by medium-technology industry SMEs.

3. The firms need to cope with formal and often standardized requirements by venture capital markets.

We have already referred to the general challenges for medium-technology SMEs caused by capital markets. The change from the traditional close and personal relationships with one local bank to more formal and standardized transactions with several actors in the capital market increases the importance of formal financial criteria, which SMEs are often unable to meet (Karl et al., 2004). In the context of knowledge creation, an additional uncertainty affects the relationship, as the actual market success of a knowledge production process is difficult to anticipate and actors in the venture capital markets usually look for formal securities to reduce the risk of an adverse selection or a hold-up problem, when knowledge asymmetries between investor and firm could lead to inefficient investment decisions and huge losses (Blum and Müller, 2004). For high-technology firms, these formal securities usually consist of patents, market research studies by third parties or first contracts with customers (Wink, 2004a). These options are less available for medium-technology SMEs, because patents are in these cases less common than secrecy and protection of tacit knowledge (see Alfonso-Gil and Talbot, 2007, on the hermetic culture of the SMEs in the aeronautical sector), and the risk-shifting policies by OEMs lead to concentration of more financial risk on the side of suppliers, thereby causing additional risks for investors. Furthermore, as the high profit rates of completely new markets are less realistic in the more mature markets of medium-technology industries, venture capitalists would therefore be less interested in these markets (Jeng and Wells, 2000; Schertler,

2003). The discussion on the influence of private equity funds on SMEs in many EU countries, with several complaints of short-term pressure on the management to raise profit rates for investors by cutting costs and increasing dividends for investors, illustrates the fears that are accompanied by the increasing importance of capital markets for investment finance in the SME segment (see UNCTAD, 2007, on the supportive impact of private equity funds on developed economies). Therefore, medium-technology SMEs need to look for adjustments towards the expectations of the capital markets and alternative instruments to cover their gap in the financial resources necessary for more R&D investments and adjustments of knowledge creation processes.

4. The firms need more diverse knowledge to build up skills for integrative technologies.

Integrative technologies are characterized by close linkages between modern high technology and science-driven technologies and applications from incumbent medium-technology industries, as, for example, in the case of composites as new materials for cars or aeroplanes connected with modern sensor or other electronic features (see Asheim, 2002; Benzler and Wink, 2005, for further examples and implications; Garcia-Vega, 2006, on the importance of technological diversification for innovations). For SMEs in the medium-technology industries, this implies cooperation with partners whose cognitive codes – style of communication, technical terms, heuristics to find problem solutions or methodologies – are completely different from their experiences, which are restricted to communication within their specific supply chain and concentrated on very specific applications (see Bhatt, 2000; Hassink, 2005, on the challenges caused by path-dependencies within organizational learning processes; Grabher and Ibert, 2006, on the risks for firms, if the management restricts knowledge interactions to a few personal contacts). Thus, they need time and new experiences to find new codes with new partners, for example from universities or public research institutes or research-intensive spin-offs, and possibly new staff to manage these new knowledge linkages.

These linkages pose challenges not only for the cognitive patterns of potential partners, but also for organizational and cultural structures and processes, as strategies for better mutual understanding have to be implemented and accepted by all members in the affected organizations. Orlikowski (2002) provides strategies for diversified organizations to improve knowledge interactions between different parts of the organizations. These strategies range from measures to find a common identity and opportunities for frequent F2F contacts, to the arrangement of individual opportunities for knowledge exchange along single problems and activities to lower the access barriers for new participants to existing knowledge interactions (see Wink, 2007, for an application to the framework of different forms of proximity between organizations). Such activities, however, are only sufficiently attractive if the connection between the different knowledge bases offers clearly visible profits in the short term. Here, entrepreneurial visions by the top managers in the SMEs are essential to convince their employees to overcome the barriers to cooperation (see Witt, 2000, on the cognitive influence of visionary entrepreneurs). In the fifth chapter, we will take a look at political strategies to overcome barriers between the medium-technology SMEs and potential partners from science-driven segments, which should add to the best practice experiences we collect in this chapter.

5. The firms need new organizational procedures and human resource management tools to cope with the expectations of highly qualified human capital.

Human resource and knowledge management within traditional SMEs was mainly driven by a dominant role of highly specified capabilities developed in long-term routines and a strong hierarchy between top management and the other levels. Many family-owned SMEs are based on paternalistic approaches with a caring style by the firm owners on many different even private levels of the employees, which is accompanied by a high dominance of the norms, principles and values of the family (Frormann, 2006; Venohr and Meyer, 2007). The employees hired often did not have high formal qualifications, but increased their knowledge base continuously by being integrated into production routines and development processes. The long-term loyalty of the employees and low share of fluctuation was not questioned, as the employees' qualifications were often too specific to be transferred to other – bigger and better-paying – firms (see Boisot, 1998; Drejer, 2000; Keogh and Steward, 2001, on the changing requirements for employees in knowledge economies).

The aeronautical sector is a special example of these observations of high firm loyalty, as the close linkage towards the defence sector further restricts the access for foreigners to the labour markets and the share of foreign employees within the firms in the SMEs is still far below 5% on average. So far, most of the investigations on barriers to learning within organizations refer to experiences in big firms. Here, cognitive barriers on the individual level are caused by defence routines and missing incentives for active improvements of the personal knowledge base, structural barriers due to weak communication systems and competition between different departments, and social barriers due to problems within the relationships between employees and an organizational culture, which discourage open interactions (Argyris, 1993; Schein, 1996; Grieves et al., 2006). Within SMEs in the medium-technology sector, however, the risks that barriers restrict changes towards learning processes are also prominent, as long experience within given structures restricts the recognition of benefits by changing organizational structures and routines (see Chiarvesio, di Maria and Micelli, 2004, for experiences from Italy).

With the increasing pressure to adjust to the requirements for more formalized knowledge and cooperation with more science-driven firms, the SMEs also have to look for formally better qualified work staff and new tools to motivate these employees with different expectations than less qualified employees and to reduce the dependence of the firms' knowledge base on single individuals, as the mobility of highly qualified staff is higher than for lower qualified employees. Richard Florida (2002) discussed this changing importance of the 'creative class' by looking at those factors attracting a highly qualified and creative workforce to a location or organization. On the level of human development tools, different options seem suitable for attracting highly qualified work staff to medium-technology SMEs:

- increasing the level of independence and self-responsibility of the highly qualified employees by corporate entrepreneurship programmes (Hayton, 2005; Amo, 2006);
- contracting based on co-entrepreneurship, for example with self-employed knowledge experts (Lubatkin, Florin and Lane, 2001; Pavlovich and Corner, 2006);
- creating incentives by offering skill-based payments to enhance the commitment to the organization and strengthen the role of highly qualified workforce (Al-Waqfi and Agarwal, 2006);
- redefining the SME organization on a project-based structure with more responsibilities and monetary incentives for highly qualified or specifically qualified and loyal employees (see Gann and Salter, 2000; Grabher, 2004; Hung et al., 2007, on extending the perspective to interorganizational project-based interactions);
- integration into the ownership of the firm in the case of outstanding values of an expert or manager (Poutsma et al., 2003).

On the level of organizational structures, management has to strengthen participation of employees within strategic decisions, look for additional incentives to intensify the identification of the employees with the firm and to improve the formalization of individual tacit knowledge, for example by using more documentations of knowledge creation processes, building communities-of-practice in the firm or implementing intranet tools with clear and transparent organization rules to quickly find concrete hints on problem solutions and incentives to enable the employees to support each other with reported solutions or other experiences (see Brown and Duguid, 1991; Argyris and Schön, 1996, on these general approaches within learning organizations). Again, it will be a question of how the conventional European SME model in the medium-technology industries can be adjusted to these requirements without losing its traditional strengths.

* * *

In the following, we summarize best practice examples of our investigated cases to show how these adjustments can succeed. We differentiate three strategic priorities in the context of knowledge creation (see also Table 3.2):

3.3.2.1 Further education and other human capital strategies
Traditionally, SMEs show weaker performances in R&D and patent indicators, as they often lack necessary resources to follow such strategic directions in knowledge creation processes. In contrast, the development of personal skills has always been a major strategic aspect, as the availability of specific skills builds a competitive advantage in particular over bigger firms. For a long time, skill development was integrated into daily production practices to build up routines and firm-specific embedded knowledge (Bougrain and Haudeville, 2002). The new structural requirements mentioned at the beginning of this section, however, refer to skills that help to create linkages between the SMEs and suitable partners or between incumbent markets and new strategic sales market options. Consequently, the importance of further education not only inside firm routines but also within external modules increases. Our investigation shows that those SMEs that are able to change their strategies towards new and diversified markets or intensify their strengths in niche markets, are also characterized by higher rates of external further education than other SMEs. Thus, strategic human capital development can be seen as a way to cope with traditional weaknesses of SMEs in the availability of formalized qualifications and knowledge (McCracken and Wallace, 2000; Swanson, 2001).

Additionally, the more advanced and innovative SMEs show more interest in new knowledge management tools like communities-of-practice or strategic problem-solving circles (Drejer, 2000; Duhovnik et al., 2003). These adjustments towards management practices within bigger firms, however, reach their limits where SMEs fear too much administrative effort to introduce organizational changes or where they cannot see direct connections to concrete problem solutions. Here again, the importance of external pressures and visible effects to overcome defence routines and general fears of too much change must be stressed.

3.3.2.2   Cooperation strategies

Cooperation has always been a 'must' for SMEs to overcome scarcities of resources within one single firm (Steiner, 1998; Torre and Gallaud, 2004). Within the changing environment for knowledge creation, however, these cooperation strategies become increasingly affected by deliberations of strategic knowledge development and adjustment of knowledge creation potentials (Lublinski, 2003; Bathelt et al., 2004). Thus, cooperation strategies within our best practice cases can include different options and partners. In most cases, cooperation with local universities or technology intermediaries is a central element (Wink, 2004b; Markman et al., 2005; Sparrow, Mooney and Lancaster, 2006). This way of cooperation can help to compensate for two different scarcities in medium-technology SMEs: the lack of R&D investments, causing limitations to necessary equipment for exploration and examination of new technological ideas, and the lack of national and international partners from science-driven sectors with their specific cognitive codes and norms of cooperation (see Feller, Ailes and Roessner, 2002; MacPherson, 2002, for case studies). The local partners can then act as gatekeepers for the SMEs and can facilitate the structural change within the firm, as at least the communication can be developed by frequent face-to-face contacts and social control in geographical proximity (Wink, 2004b). Other partners for cooperation can be collaborators within the supply chain, for example to develop joint qualification or further education schemes or to finance joint R&D equipment, or specialized knowledge-intensive service providers, which are particularly present in metropolitan regions (Muller and Zenker, 2001; Fawcett and McCarter, 2008). In some cases, chambers and business associations support the strategic changes particularly by offering further education schemes or organizing joint social events (see Wink, 2007, on the case of Hamburg). One important difference between these cooperation strategies in medium-technology SMEs and cooperation in big firms or high-technology SMEs is the dominance in the former of personal and social linkages as well as common identities to build up necessary trust and acceptance of mutual dependence, which otherwise would be only seen as too fierce restrictions to sovereignty of the firm (Dupuy and Torre, 2006; Chetty and Agndal, 2008). Cognitive and formal linkages, which are more usual for high-technology cooperation or cooperation in big firms, are ties that are still seen as too weak to form, in particular, the necessary trust in the reliability of the partners (Nooteboom, 2002).

3.3.2.3   New financial instruments

The traditional method of finance between a local bank and the medium-technology SMEs was based on mutual trust and personal linkage (El Hajj Chehade and Vigneron, 2007). Due to long-term relationships, the bank management was able to understand the business model of the SME and its market chances and risks, and the SME management accepted the informal influence by the bank based on recommendations for credit offered. With the environment changing towards more formal criteria and the increasing influence of capital markets, SMEs fear losing the control mechanisms based on personal linkages and their original sovereignty. Therefore, they hesitate to use modern capital market instruments to overcome their capital scarcities and still look for credit, which becomes relatively more expensive for them, as they are rarely able to comply with formal risk standards. Suitable options to prevent these additional costs or scarcities without being completely dependent on foreign investors are mezzanine instruments, which can also be used for the funding of single projects or investments (Karl et al., 2004). Within the aeronautical market as well as the automotive industry, OEMs normally call for tenders in the case of introducing a new model and suppliers have to apply for orders, which cause relatively high initial investments, but should lead to continuous inflows for several years. These initial investments are often too high for small companies, in particular if the future inflows are connected with participation in sales market risks of the OEM (Wink, 2007). If the OEM accepts the sales market risk and offers long-term credit, then it is possible for the SME to outsource the project risk and the credit funding to a project firm with limited liability. The prerequisite for this, however, is the availability of securities by the OEM. If this is not given, then mezzanine instruments like silent partnerships or the provision of participation certificates could be used to increase the share of private equity without losing any sovereignty in the management. For many incumbent SMEs with long traditions of being kept out of the capital market, these instruments are still too unknown and uncertain to be accepted (see Karl et al., 2004, for further links to empirical sources). Our investigation, however, shows that with generational changes in the SME management, the variety of instruments for risk funding becomes wider to facilitate the finance necessary for the strategic adjustment of knowledge creation processes.

As in the case of the organization of innovation processes, Table 3.2 sums up the major opportunities and risks of the strategic options we found in our best practice investigation. Despite an adjustment towards

Table 3.2   Opportunities and risks of knowledge creation strategies by medium-technology SMEs

Strategies	Opportunities	Risks
Further education and human capital development	Extension of formal qualifications, diversification of skills available, building up linkages to other sectors	Restriction to firm-specific requirements, increasing risks to lose highly qualified staff, remaining need for formal R&D
Cooperation strategies	Selection of partners to compensate for existing deficits in knowledge creation, use of existing personal and social linkages	Restrictions to personal and social linkages might limit cooperation with high-technology partners, dependence on gatekeepers, reduced sovereignty
New financial instruments	Increasing flexibility to cope with financial requirements in supply chain systems, options to protect sovereignty	Limits to acceptance and information in traditional SMEs, need to adjust legal entities, dependence on support by OEMs in single cases

the general challenges of knowledge creation in industrial markets, the strategies of SMEs are still specific, as they crucially focus on internal human capital development and personal linkages within their cooperation strategies. In the following section, we will discuss the implications of these findings for local networking by medium-technology SMEs.

3.3.3   Local Networking

Local networking has already been a typical strategy for medium-technology SMEs to cope with requirements in supply chains (Cappellin, 2003a). Due to structural changes within the industrial markets, however, the conditions for local networking also changed. Consequently, there is not one specific network model for all European regions, but networks can be based on different objectives, entry requirements and modes of cooperation (see, for concepts to systemize existing network and cluster structures, Gordon and McCann, 2000; Bottazzi, Dosi and Fayiolo 2002; Iammarino and McCann, 2006). All networks, however, have to cope with structural challenges coming from the internationalization of markets and the changes in knowledge production that were already mentioned in the previous sections. Figure 3.6 illustrates the impact of these changes for local networking.

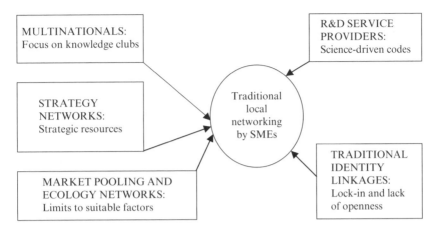

Figure 3.6   Threats to the traditional local networking processes of medium-technology SMEs

1. Firms need to comply with knowledge requirements by multinational firms.

Originally, multinational firms used local networking to organize their supply chain processes within geographical proximity to their production sites to reduce costs for physical delivery (Fisher, 1997). This made it possible to exploit personal linkages between local managers of the OEM and the suppliers for long-term development processes of the production (Maskell, 1999; Dahl and Pedersen, 2003; Harmaakorpi and Melkas, 2005). With increasing internationalization of the process, however, the most important driving force for geographical proximity and intensified cooperation with firms in the same region became the access to specialized and advanced knowledge (Mol, 2005). Thus, OEMs increasingly look for the organization of so-called 'knowledge clubs', where knowledge is kept exclusively within the network and the only access towards this exclusive club is the proof that this new member could offer necessary additional knowledge not accessible in a different way and not competing with any member of the club (Steiner and Ploder, 2008). For medium-technology SMEs, this leads to new considerations on prerequisites for networking with multinationals, as they are used to focusing on personal linkages and social connections outside the business to seal the relationships. Nowadays, only the quality of formal knowledge and the accessibility of cognitive codes open the gates to these kinds of networks. Consequently, SMEs have to adjust their networking strategies, focus on more formal knowledge interactions and the protection of the exclusiveness of their knowledge to become sufficiently attractive for this type of network (Liyanage et al., 2007).

2. Firms need to communicate on more science-driven codes to develop networking with R&D service providers.

R&D service providers are universities, public research institutes or specialized private consultancy firms (UNCTAD, 2005). They become increasingly important in the context of integrative technologies, as they are able to offer knowledge from the more advanced science-driven disciplines and should be able to translate that into the codes for medium-technology industrial problem solutions (Benzler and Wink, 2005). On the other hand, the medium-technology SMEs traditionally develop synthetic knowledge skills to combine more abstract knowledge from new technologies into concrete engineering problem solutions at specific machines. Within new integrative technologies, these two bridging functions have to be synchronized, as the medium-technology SMEs now have to be able to understand the content and limits of science-driven disciplines according to their usual codes (Olk and Young, 1997; Harada, 2003). This adjustment, however, still has to be developed, as the communication routines, relevance of personal linkages and ways to present knowledge in the science-driven and in the medium-technology-driven world of knowledge creation clearly differ (Wink, 2007). For medium-technology SMEs, this implies the need to look for new ways to build up trust with network partners and to select the knowledge needed, as the traditional modes – personal linkages and continuous social contacts – do not fit with the science-driven segments.

3. Firms need to be sufficiently open to knowledge and linkages outside their original networks.

As already explained, traditionally, SMEs use personal linkages to build up common identities and routines to form networks. This takes a relatively long time and depends crucially on personal sympathies and experiences. Thus, these identity networks are typically concentrated on regions with long-lasting firm structures (Hassink, 2005; Grabher and Ibert, 2006). As a result, the ties between the actors can become extremely strong and independent from short-term market processes. The risk, however, refers to the relationship to potential network partners outside the network, as the codes and routines within the network become so idiosyncratic that nobody outside the network is accepted (Gertler, Wolfe and Garkut, 2000). This causes lock-in effects, when no new impulses reach the network and any new idea is immediately denied if it was not invented within the network of insiders (Hassink, 2005). These structures could be kept competitive as long as OEMs as major customers were still restricted to original regions of their supply chain. With increasing internationalization and formalization of knowledge, however, any local network is under constant competitive pressure from outside (see Mazaud and Lagasse, 2007, for the example of Airbus). If they are not sufficiently open and understand which kind of knowledge is available outside the network, they will inevitably lose their competitiveness. Thus, medium-technology SMEs have to look for new management strategies and human capital to increase their openness and to develop their incumbent local network ties (Bathelt et al., 2004).

4. Firms need to be sufficiently flexible to build up network ties regardless of regional network histories.

The weakest form of cluster linkages can be seen in areas where only the sheer availability of locally concentrated production factors for specific sectors or markets causes a competitive advantage (Audretsch and Feldman, 1996; Acs, 2002). These agglomerations allow the exploitation of pooling effects, as firms can select between greater varieties and/ or within a bigger set of production factors (Iammarino and McCann, 2006). In many industrialized areas, foreign direct investors often attract further suppliers in a region and the agglomeration of further production factors, thus decreasing the factor costs for SMEs in the region (Cantwell and Piscitello, 2005; Poon, Hsu and Jeongwook, 2006; Kim and Zhang, 2008). In contrast to the networks mentioned so far, however, there are no direct networking effects, as the firms are not directly cooperating or tied in any other way. Increasing numbers of firms even cause the risk of increasing factor costs if the factor growth does not cope with the growth of factor demand. Additionally, the chance of networking for knowledge creation – joint development of suitable skills or innovative products – cannot be exploited, as any joint code is missing (Ferlie et al., 2005). Thus, the capabilities of every firm crucially depend solely on the firm itself, as it cannot expect any support from other firms. Considering the structural challenges and threats to medium-technology SMEs mentioned in the previous sections, these weak linkages within agglomerations cause the risk that the SMEs cannot compensate for their structural weaknesses, thus losing competitiveness. Consequently, the future competitiveness of these SMEs will depend on their capabilities to build up ties even in such regions without network history.

5. Firms need to develop linkages to other organizations to develop strategy resources.

Traditionally, lack of R&D and investments in knowledge commercialization is seen as a major weakness of innovation structures in medium-technology SMEs. Besides these structural elements, which might be overcome by strengthening the human capital and integration in supply chains, strategy resources by management can also become a crucial bottleneck in SMEs, as the management is usually trapped into short-term daily business processes and often based on restricted international and diversified experience. Consequently, SMEs often do not realize their actual technological market potentials and fail to develop long-term structural adjustments (see the example of the aeronautics cluster, Teichert and Harder-Nowka, 2007). These weaknesses can be compensated for if the SME management can make decisions based on external input of ideas and initiatives. Strategy networks are an example of how to make this support available (Cappellin, 2007). The network partners join together to look for common long-term strategic objectives and transfer the long-term objectives into short- to mid-term projects. To use these kinds of networks, however, it is necessary that the management in the medium-technology SMEs understands these weaknesses and looks for necessary structural support, and that these activities can be bundled within a network where firms trust each other in mid-term projects (see Steiner and Hartmann, 2006, for experiences in Styria).

* * *

The following best practice examples for strategies in local networking again serve to show which ideas could be found in the areas of investigation and which experiences could be observed with different strategic activities. We differentiate three different strategic priorities:

3.3.3.1   From ecology to identity networks

Ecology networks are characterized by market pooling in agglomerative areas (Iammarino and McCann, 2006 characterize this as pure agglomeration). This means that firms with similar needs with regard to production factors gain access to factor markets in the same region. As explained above, this type of relationship is too weak for medium-technology SMEs to compensate for their structural weaknesses in international knowledge production processes. Therefore, firms, political programmes and other organizations in these areas search for additional ties between the organizations. As SMEs traditionally build their linkages on personal and social connections, these initiatives focus on social events and other opportunities for the firm representatives to form these types of linkages. Typical examples of this in our investigation sample are initiatives in Hamburg to connect the firms within the aeronautical cluster by joint events like conferences, presentations by individual firm representatives or visits to other aeronautical clusters (Wink, 2007). The joint identity is based on the idea of a joint production location, which should be sufficiently attractive for other producers with skills so far not available within the region and for highly skilled human capital, which has been recognized as a major bottleneck. Similarly, the cluster in Wales looks for joint events and opportunities so that individual representatives get to know each other and get the opportunity to build trust in the reliability of others. Thus, these activities are seen as a necessary first step to intensifying the linkages of a regional network.

These activities, however, can only be successful if firms actually recognize a specific advantage of the networking. The major barrier to more intensified cooperation in Hamburg is still the mutual assessment of the SMEs as potential partners that do not have enough to offer (Lublinski, 2003). The lack of competitive skills in the other SMEs constantly raises fears by the SME managers that cooperation could only be exploited by the others without necessary return on network investment (Jalabert et al., 2008).

3.3.3.2 From identity to strategy networks dominated by supply chain management

Typical deficits of identity networks include openness to knowledge outside the network and ambiguity of strategic directions. The partners trust each other and build up personal linkages, but the activities are only weakly bundled in one joint direction. As a result, the direct benefits for the participating firms are limited. One strategic option to overcome these weaknesses is to have one overall umbrella or dominant network partner responsible for the joint strategic direction (see Bottazzi et al., 2002, referring to hierarchical clusters). Typical examples are hierarchical clusters formed along supply chains with the OEM or a specialized service provider as the strategy-formulating partner and the other network members as satellites around this central node (Pibernik and Sucky, 2006). Within our investigation, the cluster in aeroplane cabin interiors in Hamburg shows typical characteristics of this type of cooperation. Here, two dominant OEMs, Airbus and Lufthansa Technik, are the only nodes within a network that shows almost no additional bundled linkages between the other actors. The third potential node, serving as a holding of suppliers to the OEM, soon reached its peak in bundling but could not permanently act as a joint system supplier and lost its bundling capacity. We illustrated these network structures with the help of social network management software.[1] Based on a 'snowball approach' (see Box 3.1), we

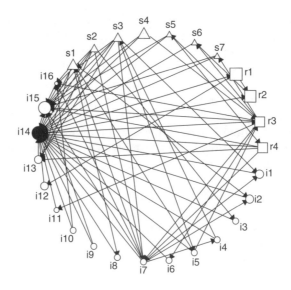

Source: Joanneum Research.

Figure 3.7   Network structure in Hamburg aeronautical cluster

asked the interviewed firm representatives who their most important partners were in the cluster with regard to material or knowledge (R&D and
joint project) interactions. Figure 3.7 visualizes the structure we found in
Hamburg with a clear hierarchy between the two OEMs (i15 and i16), the
holding of suppliers (i14) and the other firms and service providers. The
other linkages only refer to material linkages between service providers
and industrial firms, but without bundling and direct linkages between
industrial firms.

Another example of these kinds of network adjustments can be found
in Silesia, where a network mainly based on joint experiences in a mining
region was changed towards a strategic network according to the rationale of
multinational foreign investors (see Andersson and Forsgren, 2000, on strategic rationales by multinational firms). Here, these strategic adjustments
allow for an increasing internationalization of a hitherto mainly regional
business and the acquisition of knowledge outside the original regional
network, which was mainly dominated by a public research institution.
These adjustments show the strengths of such a strategy. If the dominating
OEM and the regional SMEs have similar interests, it helps the short-term
assertion of joint adjustments and the overcoming of strategic deficits of
the SMEs involved. On the other hand, these adjustments according to the

OEM intensify the dependence within the value chain (Bottazzi et al., 2002). The SMEs are in particular restricted in strategies to look for diversification and extension to potential competitors of the OEM. Thus, this strategy can only be a weak support to compensate for bottlenecks in strategic planning resources of the medium-technology SMEs.

3.3.3.3 From ecology to strategy networks dominated by knowledge management

The third strategic approach also uses external resources to the SMEs within the network to initiate strategic directions. Here, a common service provider or a pool of network members is responsible for the development of a joint strategy within the network and the transfer of the strategy into single projects. A typical example of a concentration of strategic resources at a service provider within our investigation is the Austrian region Styria, where so-called competence centres ('K-centres') focus on the cooperation with firms on knowledge from specific technologies, for example on acoustics, polymers or materials and light metal technologies (Steiner and Hartmann, 2006; Steiner and Ploder, 2008). This cooperation is characterized by a mid- to long-term strategy of the centre to promote knowledge on the technology, primarily within the region, and they use this strategic approach to make available suitable knowledge for the cooperation projects with medium-technology SMEs, but also big firms. Due to their independence, the competence centres are accepted by all participants in the regional economy, as the SMEs do not have to fear becoming increasingly dependent on the strategy of a single OEM. The focus on knowledge as the purpose of interaction also changes the character of networks towards knowledge networks, as the networks based on supply chain management are mainly driven by material linkages (see Fisher et al., 1997, for this distinction).

Other examples for such knowledge-driven strategy networks are the poles of competitiveness introduced and selected in recent years in France. Within our sample, the medium-technology SMEs of the optics industry in Ile de France we investigated are engaged in the SYSTEM@ TIC PARIS-REGION pole, which focuses on embedded system technologies for sectors at the interface between electronics, IT and optics industry. The main rationale of these poles is the formulation of a joint strategy within the global competition and a programme of joint projects to follow these strategic objectives. The drivers in most cases, as also in the case of SYSTEM@TIC PARIS-REGION, are big multinational companies, but the integrated SMEs are also part of the strategic development, as they have the knowledge to assess which strategic options might also be technologically feasible. Therefore, the formulation of a joint

*Table 3.3   Opportunities and limits of strategic approaches in local
            networking*

Strategy	Opportunities	Limits
Forming identity networks	Intensifying linkages between regional firms, strengthening personal and social linkages, forming trust as necessary premise for further cooperation	Connection to knowledge and strategy resources, limits to openness outside the region, dependence on single individuals in the network
Strategy networks in supply chain management	Strengthening strategic view of SME investments, improving reliability of cooperation, strengthening local engagement of the OEM	Dependence on dominant OEM, lack of compatibility between the strategies of OEMs and SMEs, lack of openness to members outside the value chain
Strategy networks in knowledge management	Strengthening the basis for knowledge interaction, decreasing the dependence on single actors or OEMs, openness to members outside the region with suitable knowledge	High entry barriers, as SMEs need to show suitable formalized knowledge, need for strategic leadership, either by a pool of members or specific service provider

strategy – and not only of a supply chain dominated by one or few single firm(s) – and the focus on knowledge are the main characteristics of this third group of strategic approaches. The focus on knowledge also determines the limits to this approach, as for many incumbent SMEs the entry barriers to becoming a member in the strategy networks are too high. They are not able to show necessary formal knowledge capabilities and have only limited resources to engage in cooperation projects with competence centres, where formal R&D equipments are needed (see Giuliani, 2005, on these strategies within knowledge club clusters). This underlines that only a part of the medium-technology industrial SMEs will succeed in implementing the structural change towards new local networks.

Table 3.3 serves as a summary of the strategic approaches we observed in the context of local networking. The strategy networks seem to be able to compensate for several shortcomings of medium-technology SMEs in global competition, but they also require additional formal knowledge resources of the SMEs. In the following section, we look at the relationship between the local and the international networking activities.

3.3.4 International Networking

Traditionally, medium-technology industry SMEs concentrate on national or even regional markets, as they can use here their specific strengths in intensifying long-term personal relationships and continuity within their strategic outreach (von Tunzelman, 1998). Internationalization has always been seen as a potential threat, because most of the SMEs' management lack the necessary experience and skills to implement suitable strategies. Examples of a gradual internationalization process, for example explained by the Uppsala model or integrated into eclectic explanations of location choices (Dunning, 1988; Johanson and Vahlne, 1990), mainly referred to strong independent SMEs with clear market leadership within niche markets, and even within these cases the domestic markets still dominate the strategic processes. For most of the incumbent SMEs in medium-technology industries, the integration into regional supply chains served to protect them from further internationalization (Carbonara et al., 2002). With the change towards global and modular sourcing, however, suppliers are increasingly forced to look for international partners in developing knowledge for whole modules or to take the risk of relocation of standardized production to cut costs (Mol, 2005). For the medium-technology SMEs, this means overcoming their traditional weaknesses in international networking. Figure 3.8 illustrates some of the negative effects of international networking.

1. Firms need more international contacts and experiences to be able to identify suitable partners for networking.

In most of the incumbent medium-technology SMEs the management has almost no or only a little early experience with foreign companies. In some cases, in particular in spin-offs, they at least had experience with big – multinational – firms, but only at lower management levels or in specific executive functions. As a result, they only have a few contacts with firm representatives from other countries and are only weakly informed about the cultural norms and routines in networks in other countries. As a consequence, if SMEs try to internationalize their networking, they tend to follow other firms from their regions in their international movements (Chetty and Agndal, 2008) or try to exploit all contacts available without clear focus on needs and perspectives (Chiarvesio et al., 2004). Thus, they need to extend their information base and to link the internationalization process with their overall strategic processes.

2. Firms need to overcome language barriers to increase the share of foreign employees and to intensify international contacts.

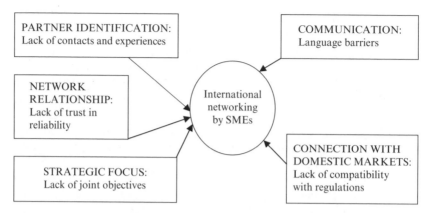

Figure 3.8   Threats to medium-technology SMEs by being forced into international networking

One specific problem that is closely related to the lack of experience and contacts refers to language barriers. Due to the low share of employees with work or other experience in other countries, the SMEs fear a lack of control and reliability within international transactions, as they do not completely understand the exact content of communication. Even communications in the English language are not a regular standard for incumbent SMEs used to concentrating on domestic markets. Again, this can lead to inefficient decisions on suitable partners – guided by expectations that the partners might speak the mother tongue of the SME management – and restrictions to the exploitation of the full potential of international cooperation.

3.   Firms need to build up experiences in international relationships and to develop new forms of network cooperation to increase the reliability of networking activities.

As already explained in the earlier sections, a special characteristic of networking by incumbent medium-technology industry SMEs is their strong dependence on personal and social linkages. They need these close linkages to have necessary trust in the reliability of partners, as they have less formal and legal options to protect themselves from default within cooperation (Dupuy and Torre, 2006). In international relationships, however, the opportunities to build up these kinds of relationships are restricted, as frequent F2F contacts and social control outside professional contacts as typical instruments to intensify personal linkages are less available (Wink, 2008). Thus, managers in medium-technology SMEs either need more time to develop these types of linkages within international cooperation and learn to consider the specific networking culture in other countries via a longer period with several short-term contacts at conferences, fairs or other forms of temporary geographical proximity (Bathelt and Schuldt, 2005; Torre, 2008) or they need to use other forms of linkages, for example more formal agreements via contracts or cognitive linkages via cooperation on very specific topics.

4. Firms need to adjust their strategic objectives to common goals in international networks.

Strategy networks on a regional level help SMEs to overcome their specific scarcities in management resources for strategic processes. Here, common goals within a supply chain or the use of common technologies without competition enables firms to cooperate on strategy formulation and transfers from mid-term strategies to single steps and projects (Mariotti et al., 2008). In an international environment, these processes are more difficult, as often the strategic objectives of partners in different regions are distinct or even competing with each other. For example, the cooperation between medium-technology SMEs in the incumbent EU countries and partners in Central and Eastern Europe can help both to exploit their short-term competitive strengths (tacit knowledge capabilities on one side and cost advantages on the other). With time, however, the partners in Central and Eastern Europe look for improvements of their productivity and knowledge, while the SMEs in the incumbent countries fear losing competitive advantage or are forced into further relocations of production (Michna and Kalka, 2006). Strategic cooperation needs mid- to long-term benefits for both partners without fear of unfair distributions.

5. Firms need to consider compatibility of international linkages with domestic regulation.

Often, industry and firm norms in supply chains require the proof of specific qualifications of employees or standards for production processes and products (Wink, 2009b). These formal requirements, in particular if they are included in the most advanced safety and environmental standards, for example in aeronautical production, are hardly met in some of the low-cost countries. For SMEs being forced by the OEM to cut costs and to relocate parts of the production processes or to look for cheaper workforces, the compliance with these formal requirements becomes an increasing problem.

* * *

Our investigation has showed that so far, the internationalization of production in medium-technology industries by SMEs has only slowly begun in recent years due to the problems described above. They are forced to accelerate the speed of these adjustment processes due to pressures by OEMs intensifying their outsourcing processes, but it is still a small adjustment compared with the activities of big multinational firms, for example in the automotive industry. Our investigation revealed two major strategic directions of these internationalization processes, when they include transnational networking activities:

3.3.4.1 Exploitation of gatekeeper functions

Due to the specific problems for medium-technology SMEs in finding suitable partners for international networking in building up suitable codes for communication and cooperation, in synchronizing the strategic objectives with partners and in adjusting the activities to existing standards and requirements, most SMEs only indirectly participate with international networks. The easiest way of being affected by international networks is the integration into a value chain with a multinational OEM, which exploits its international networking experience within the regional network as well (Piscitello and Rabbiosi, 2006). Here, the SMEs receive the information from international markets via their customers and look for suitable solutions to new requirements. For a long time, these connections were almost the only linkages for the SMEs to international markets, as they did not have to adjust their cooperation with other (regional) partners and were not directly confronted with the international relationships. This focus on the existing linkages, however, increases the dependence on the OEM acting as a gatekeeper.

As in the case of the strategy networks, the gatekeeper function can also be executed by a service provider. The K-centres in Styria, for example, cooperate closely with firms and research institutes in Germany and transfer these experiences into cooperation with the regional firms (Steiner and Ploder, 2008). Again, this has the advantages of relying on the existing relationships and preventing the necessity of adjustments in the networking behaviour of the SMEs. Although the dependence of the SMEs on the K-centres is not as economically threatening as in the case of the OEM acting as a gatekeeper, the gatekeeper approaches always limit the strategic options of the SMEs, as they have to adjust to the experiences and rationales of the gatekeepers in internationalization and cannot act as flexibly as might be necessary (see in general for the relationships between gatekeepers and proximities, Wink, 2008). These shortcomings might be avoided by the second approach: utilization of specific events and initiatives.

3.3.4.2 Utilization of specific events and initiatives for internationalization
This approach considers the lack of information and experience of the
management in many incumbent medium-technology SMEs. Therefore,
specific events like fairs, conferences or presentations and visits by groups of
SMEs are used to offer at least temporary geographical proximity between
potential international partners to find out whether a possible basis for
further cooperation can be identified (Bathelt and Schuldt, 2005). A typical
example of this is the activity within a joint regional initiative of the aeronautical cluster in Hamburg, which supports the organization of an annual
fair on cabin interiors, where most of the regional medium-technology
SMEs have their specific focus, and single trips to firms at other aeronautical clusters or one-day conferences on specific topics (Wink, 2007; Torre,
2008). These activities are supported by the regional public administration,
which developed a joint qualification programme on vocational training
for aeronautical firms in Hamburg and the French regions Midi-Pyrénées
and Aquitaine. All these activities offer opportunities to the firm managers
to get to know entrepreneurs from other regions, their visions and attitudes
and to look for common projects and interests (Amin and Cohendet, 2000).
Time will tell how far these opportunities will be exploited but the approach
shows that it is possible to overcome the specific scarcities of resources for
international networking in medium-technology SMEs.

Table 3.4 summarizes the opportunities and limits of the approaches
described. International networking still seems to be the most advanced

*Table 3.4   Opportunities and limits of strategic approaches for
international networking of medium-technology SMEs*

Strategies	Opportunities	Limits
Gatekeeper functions	Exploitation of already existing linkages on the regional level, use of the regional actors with the best international expertise, low risk for the SMEs of being trapped in inefficient specific relationships	Dependence on the gatekeepers, lack of flexibility according to the single SME's need, lack of potential for the SME to learn within international contexts
Specific events and initiatives	Preconditions for the SMEs to look for their own specific interests and experiences in international networking, openness to different topics, connection with different topics and countries	Dependence on the willingness and capabilities of the SMEs to exploit the opportunities, restriction to temporary geographical proximity requires adjustment of networking codes

structural challenge for knowledge creation in medium-technology SMEs. The experiences in our case studies, however, show that it is possible to overcome existing barriers and that strategies can be developed that consider the specific needs of the SMEs.

3.4   CONCLUDING REMARKS

This chapter serves to show some empirical evidence of how medium-technology industry SMEs can succeed in adjusting to the turbulences and changing environments of their markets.

In contrast to many studies stating that the scarcity of resources in incumbent SMEs makes it too difficult for them to cope with new requirements of knowledge creation in integrative technologies, global and modular sourcing strategies by multinational OEMs and increasing competition by firms located outside the EU, this overview reveals that the firms can actually be prepared for this new and intensified competition and that the firms and regions find different strategic solutions according to different preconditions and needs in single cases. As general strategies, we observed the growing role of science-driven spin-offs as SMEs are being integrated into new knowledge value chains. Besides this relatively new phenomenon for medium-technology SMEs, other firms diversified their markets of applications or – as a contrast – focused even more strongly on very specific niches or looked for a more formalized way to cooperate with other firms, even up to the formation of a joint holding by former individual firms.

Furthermore, new strategies to adjust the traditional ways to organize knowledge creation within the SMEs could be observed. As an extension to traditional strengths of knowledge creation in SMEs, more investments in further education could be observed. These activities help to increase the – generally shrinking – loyalty by employees and to formalize the knowledge base of employees, which was hitherto more based on tacit knowledge and hardly connected with expectations in multinational OEMs. Other strategies focus on new ways of cooperation between SMEs or between SMEs and other partners to cover the deficits so far identified for SMEs to be integrated in global knowledge value chains. Finally, new financial instruments are used by entrepreneurial SMEs to overcome the capital gap while still maintaining independence.

Within all clusters of investigation, changes in local networking could be observed. Strategies range from the formation of identity networks to connect personal and social linkages with the more formal and organizational requirements of industrial value chains to the emergence of strategy networks in material value chains, where OEMs play a major part in formulating a joint strategy, which also covers SMEs within the value chain, and the emergence of knowledge-driven strategy networks, where not only OEMs are responsible for the development and assertion of strategies on knowledge generation and exploitation, but also intermediaries like knowledge-intensive business service companies or R&D providers.

Reactions by the SMEs to the growing importance of interregional networking could be only rarely observed. Those best practices to be identified are driven by gatekeepers like OEMs or R&D service intermediaries or by specific events like trade fairs and joint initiatives. It becomes obvious that interregional linkages will only be intensified after an intensified diffusion of the new business strategies by successful SMEs.

The empirical insights presented in this chapter cover the strategic reactions by SMEs in medium-technology sectors. These developments are initiated, supported and framed by political programmes and instruments in the regions, which will be presented and discussed in detail in the fifth chapter. In the next chapter, however, we first of all provide a theoretical framework to understand the changes in the specific medium-technology markets presented in the empirical study, the differences to the often studied high- and low-technology markets and the rationales the SMEs follow within their networking.

NOTE

1. We thank Michael Steiner and Michael Ploder from Joanneum Research in Graz, Austria, for providing the network illustrations based on the data collected in the empirical part of the IKINET project.

4. The analysis of regional knowledge networks

Riccardo Cappellin

This chapter aims to increase the understanding of the process of knowledge creation and innovation in medium-technology sectors and to identify characteristics of innovation networks within regional clusters and barriers to their enlargement at the European level. Medium-technology sectors have achieved high success in industrial restructuring and play a key role in European competitiveness as they represent the largest share of European export in manufacturing industry and indicate the highest growth rate in European exports toward global markets.

4.1 THE PROCESS OF INNOVATION AND KNOWLEDGE CREATION

Innovation is promoted by factors operating both on the supply side and on the demand side. Among the first are the costs and the quality of labour, the use of new machinery embodying modern technology and the accessibility to qualified suppliers. Among the second are the access to a specific market, the level of demand, the forms of competition and the existence of specific barriers to potential competitors such as intellectual property rights (IPR), which insure a temporary rent. These complementary factors define the opportunities or the challenges in the external environment and they have to be complemented with the individual capabilities internal to the firm (see Figure 4.1). In fact, the viability of a new process or product represents a necessary but not sufficient condition. Innovation also requires the existence of subjective capabilities or immaterial factors. These latter are represented by the capability of the firm and the entrepreneur to elaborate an original long-term project (that is, a 'business plan') and a positive evaluation of the risk by the potential investors. Thus, internal knowledge and internal or external financial resources are two additional necessary conditions for the adoption of an innovation and they indicate the subjective capabilities/weaknesses existing in the firm

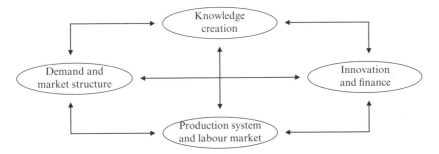

Figure 4.1   The relationship between knowledge creation and innovation

that may lead to the exploitation of external opportunities or to facing external threats.

In particular, the adoption of innovation requires a greater effort by the firms in the creation of knowledge. Firms should search, evaluate and adapt new technologies from external sources or develop them internally. These search activities require that firms invest in R&D and especially devote time and resources to the technical design of the new product or process and to the organization of the innovation projects. Thus, while most innovation studies focus on the process of adoption of technologies, we focus on the various factors of the process of knowledge creation, as knowledge represents the necessary precondition for innovation, in particular in the case of medium-technology industries, where tacit knowledge, labour capabilities and creativity of the firms represent the key competitiveness factors.

4.2   THE INTERNAL AND EXTERNAL CONDITIONS FOR INNOVATION

The process of knowledge creation depends on the capability to combine different pieces of previous knowledge in an original way. This requires a high connectivity, which may be defined as a positive combination of both a high accessibility to different knowledge sources and an adequate receptivity, in order to be capable of interpreting and using them in an appropriate way. Accessibility depends on geographical distance, but also on the existence of other obstacles that may increase the transaction costs between the firms or the regions. These latter may be related to the differences in the organizational structures or in the institutional framework. On the other hand, receptivity depends on the internal capabilities of the firms and the regional economy considered, on the level of education, previous

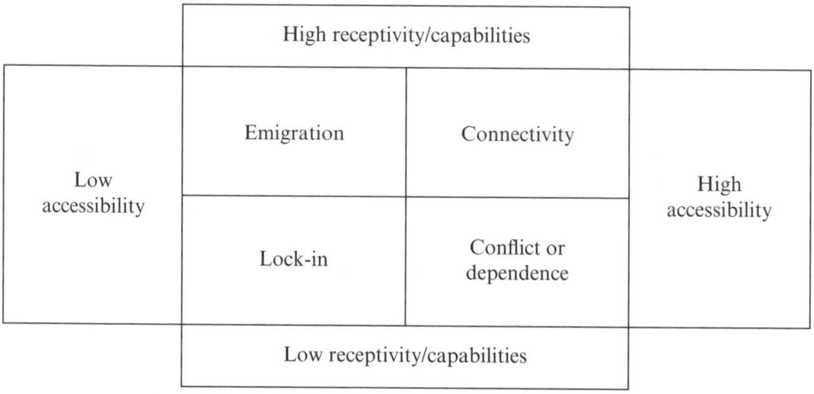

	High receptivity/capabilities		
Low accessibility	Emigration	Connectivity	High accessibility
	Lock-in	Conflict or dependence	
	Low receptivity/capabilities		

Figure 4.2   Connectivity as the result of accessibility and receptivity

experience and the availability of specialized know-how. Thus, receptivity is linked to the capability to attract external qualified resources or also to retain these resources and to avoid them moving to other firms and regions. A positive combination of accessibility and receptivity is a prerequisite to achieving economic integration and synergy between firms and regions. And the lack of both accessibility and receptivity leads to a situation of closure and stagnation, which may be defined as a 'lock-in' effect (Figure 4.2). If regions or firms are characterized by highly receptive or qualified human resources, but also by a low accessibility to other complementary capabilities, emigration or 'brain drain' could be the consequence. In the opposite case, a low receptivity by the human resources and a high exposure to external technology could lead firms and regions to a situation of technological dependence or even to a conflict situation between the external investments and the prevailing internal traditional culture.

A further element in the process of knowledge creation is creativity, or the capability to sustain the continuity of the process of knowledge creation. According to the model of interactive learning, creativity is closely related to connectivity, as defined above. In fact, creativity implies both a high interaction between different actors, firms and regions, through intense and frequent meetings and exchanges of information and knowledge, and also the original combination of different and complementary pieces of knowledge (Figure 4.3). Without sufficient connectivity, neither interaction nor combination would be possible and a low interaction with other local and external actors and the sole use of traditional know-how would lead to a situation of stagnation or a 'lock-in' effect. A high interaction, but only between actors who have very similar competencies, may lead to only marginal improvements or incremental innovations, while the

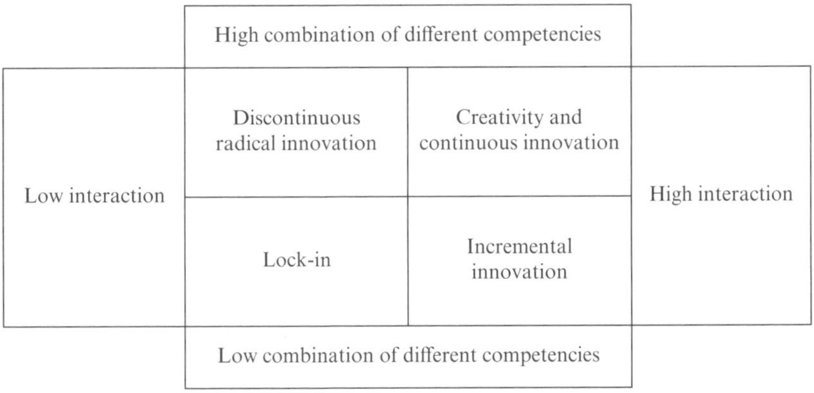

	High combination of different competencies		
Low interaction	Discontinuous radical innovation	Creativity and continuous innovation	High interaction
	Lock-in	Incremental innovation	
	Low combination of different competencies		

Figure 4.3   Creativity as the result of interactivity and combination

opposite case of the combination of different complementary competencies, but with too low frequency of interaction, could lead to no results or to discontinuous radical innovation.

A third characteristic of a process of innovation is that internal capabilities such as creativity should be combined with the stimulus of opportunities or challenges by the external environment (Figure 4.4). In fact, innovation is mainly driven by the need or aim to solve urgent problems, which may represent either a risk for the survival of a firm or a condition in securing the growth of the firm. Opportunities or challenges may be represented by the evolution of market demand, such as the opening of new markets or an increase of competition. Otherwise, the stimulus may be represented by the availability of new technologies that compel the abandonment of less efficient traditional technologies or facilate the production of new products and services, satisfying existing or new needs by final or intermediate users. In particular, a high creative capability of the local human resources and entrepreneurs coupled with the lack of market stimulus or the lack of appropriate production technologies may lead people to emigrate or firms to invest abroad. In the opposite case, exposure to international markets and pressure by technological change may endanger the competitiveness and lead to a crisis for the firms and the local economy if local creative capabilities or knowledge are too limited.

Creativity within individual firms should be combined with good local governance in order to lead to innovation and regional growth and promote the transformation of industrial clusters into a 'learning region' (Figure 4.17). Therefore, innovation in medium-technology sectors may be interpreted not as the linear effect of an R&D investment, but rather as the result of a process of interactive learning, where various factors

	High creativity		
Low external stimulus	Emigration	Innovation and competitiveness	High external stimulus
	Lock-in	Crisis and lack of competitiveness	
	Low creativity		

Figure 4.4   Innovation requires external stimulus and creativity

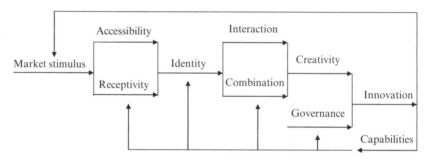

Figure 4.5   The process of interactive learning and innovation

are combined and represent necessary but insufficient conditions (Figure 4.5). Moreover, innovation leads to a process of learning and the development of new capabilities that improve the various factors indicated above. Finally, innovation is going to change the external environment and that may represent the stimulus to innovation for other firms. This indicates that innovation is a dynamic and cumulative process.

4.3   THE PROCESS OF INNOVATION IN SMES AND MEDIUM-TECHNOLOGY SECTORS

While most of the literature and policy debate on innovation focuses on high-tech sectors, the innovation process in medium-tech sectors has rather different characteristics and it is explained by different factors: Machinery and transport equipment production represents a typical example of a medium-technology sector. Different from high-tech sectors such as the biochemical, pharmaceutical or information technology sectors, the production process in mechanical industry may be distinguished by many different phases and the final product is the result of the assembly of a very large number of intermediate components.

Medium-technology sectors are based on technological paradigms that started centuries ago but have been improved by engineering expertise and by integrating experiences from other technological disciplines like material sciences or nature sciences. Technology in medium-technology sectors is characterized by high complexity, as products are made from a large number of heterogeneous physical components that require a variety of agents, competencies and pieces of knowledge for their production. Thus, medium-technology sectors are highly dispersed, fragmented and characterized by a high modularity, specialization of the firms, forms of vertical quasi-integration between the firms, which are organized in complex and continuously changing supply chains. Firms in medium-technology sectors mainly produce intermediate products for other firms rather than final products for the consumer market. The fragmentation of the production process and the high specialization of the firms explain why economies of scale are less important, firms are of small size and why the firms develop a very strong interaction with their external local environment, characterized by a great diversity of private and public, local and non-local actors.

These circumstances cause high competition between the SMEs and also the need to promote cooperation between the various producers. In fact, the large number of SMEs existing in medium-tech sectors calls for a different approach in innovation policy, which should aim to exploit the potential of complementarity between widely dispersed components and actors. SMEs in the medium- and low-technology sectors do not invest in routine R&D activities, as they cannot recuperate the high cost of these investments and they also often lack the necessary human capital resources to maintain continuous interaction with basic research institutes and researchers from disciplines different from their own field of specialization. Thus, in contrast to large firms and high-tech sectors, innovation processes in SMEs working in medium- and low-technology sectors do not depend on formal R&D, but on tacit knowledge or on combinatorial capabilities and interactive learning processes within networks of firms. Innovation is gradual in nature and consists mainly in improvement of existing products, services and processes. In particular, the process of innovation in medium-technology sectors is driven by an intensive interaction between the suppliers and the customers, due to the high specificity of the needs of the customers, who require solutions made by different complex combinations of many specific components.

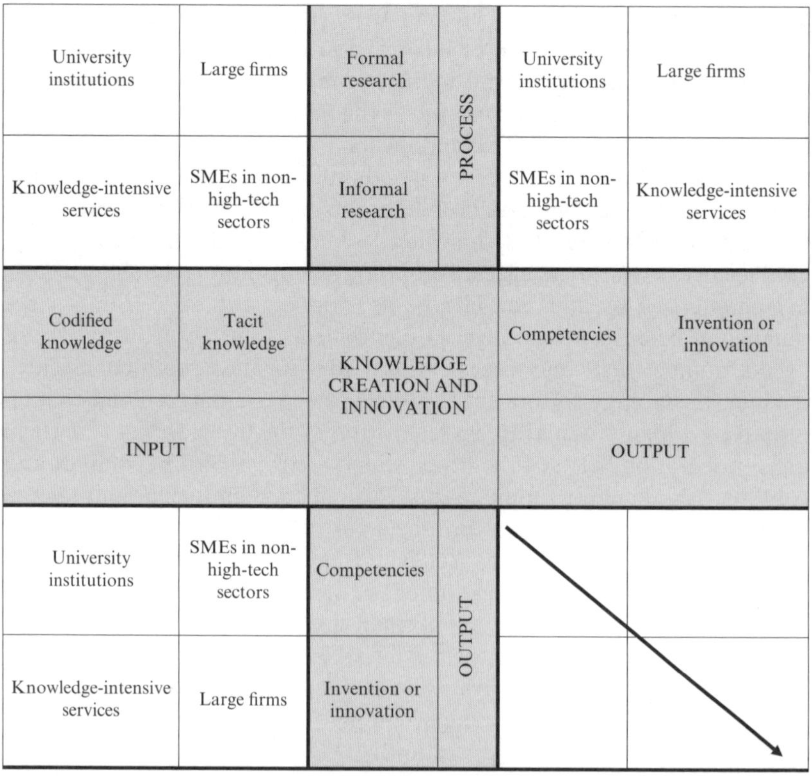

University institutions	Large firms	Formal research		University institutions	Large firms
Knowledge-intensive services	SMEs in non-high-tech sectors	Informal research	PROCESS	SMEs in non-high-tech sectors	Knowledge-intensive services
Codified knowledge	Tacit knowledge	KNOWLEDGE CREATION AND INNOVATION		Competencies	Invention or innovation
INPUT				OUTPUT	
University institutions	SMEs in non-high-tech sectors	Competencies	OUTPUT		
Knowledge-intensive services	Large firms	Invention or innovation			

Figure 4.6   Input, processes and output of knowledge creation in different organizations

The characteristics of the innovation process in SMEs as opposed to those in large firms, in knowledge-intensive services and in research institutions (Figure 4.6) can be clarified by comparing the characteristics of the inputs, the processes and the outputs in the innovation process within these four organizations. In particular, inputs may be distinguished between codified and tacit knowledge. The processes may be distinguished between formal research activities and informal research activities. The output may be distinguished between innovation/inventions and internal competencies:

- Innovation processes in SMEs working in medium-technology sectors are characterized by tacit knowledge, informal research processes and development of competencies, which represent the competitive assets of SMEs.

- Innovation processes in large firms are characterized by tacit knowledge, formal research activities and development of inventions/innovations.
- Innovation processes in the modern knowledge-intensive services are characterized by codified knowledge, informal research activities and development of inventions/innovations within the users of these services.
- Innovation processes in the academic institutions are characterized by codified knowledge, formal research activities and development of students' and researchers' competencies.

Moreover, innovation processes within SMEs should be analysed not within the individual firm, but within the system or network to which the SMEs belong. In fact, within the individual firms, problem-solving may be achieved by decomposing a problem into sub-problems through the 'ex ante' coordination by a superior authority. On the other hand, a decentralized economy is typically characterized by incomplete and scattered information or by bounded rationality. No single individual can solve all problems. Thus, in a decentralized economy, problem-solving is the result of marginal improvements made by various individual actors through an 'in itinere' coordination or according to heuristic and recursive processes and mutual interactive learning. These characteristics of the process of knowledge creation and of innovation are particularly evident in the case of the local production systems of SMEs.

The individual parts of the networks of SMEs seem to change in an almost coordinated manner. Technological progress is implicit or of an involuntary type, as opposed to R&D projects guided by a unique decision-making body as in the large firms model. It follows technological trajectories and evolutionary processes that are not optimizing but have an interactive character and are based on recursive adjustment processes of the various actors involved. SMEs' systems are characterized by multiple incremental product and process innovations. It is often difficult to distinguish the management of the process of daily production aimed at responding to the needs that result from the orders of the customers, and the process of product development and innovation. In particular, local production systems of SMEs are characterized by a systemic process, within which different phases may be distinguished (Cappellin and Orsenigo, 2000):

- the phase of knowledge creation, characterized by learning processes based on emulation and the close interaction of actors with different competencies;

- the innovation phase, characterized by a 'problem-solving' approach that makes expert use of a combination of different and complementary knowledge;
- the production phase, characterized by the joint work of various specialized suppliers.

SMEs develop vertical flows of tacit knowledge within their respective 'filière' or value chain. Moreover, they are also increasingly developing horizontal linkages with different technologies and sectors, which are crucial in order to promote structural changes and a productive diversification of the cluster through the creation of new fields of production (Cappellin, 1998). A close complementarity emerges between the 'soft' cognitive networks, which organize the learning and innovation processes, and the 'hard' networks that are based on real and monetary flows of goods/services or on financial funds. In fact, the development of innovation and competence within SMEs is related to the subcontracting relations that promote tight 'client–supplier' relationships of technological collaboration. Moreover, the relations of financial control among SMEs, within groups of several firms and often controlled by an intermediate leader firm, are often the results of spin-offs in innovative sectors from the mother firm or of the acquisitions of other firms, which allow the diversification of the traditional productions of the controlling firms. This process explains the evolution of knowledge in the small and medium-sized firms as the result of the combination of complementary capacities in the framework of widespread interactive learning processes. In fact, the development of new productions requires the innovative combination of the different types of technologies characterizing different sectors. Technology spreads across industries and the new knowledge indicates a higher level of flexibility.

In conclusion, the case of the local production systems of SMEs indicates the following new dimensions of the process of innovation (Cappellin and Orsenigo, 2000):

- The integration of different and numerous technological and organizational knowledge inputs, derived from other sectors and regions, which enable the renewal of know-how and solutions to new problems. External knowledge should be combined with the knowledge and technologies internally available, since the frontier of technology is increasingly at the crossroads of two or more disciplines or traditional cultures.
- The interactive character of the learning process, which involves groups of individuals both within the individual firms and outside

('social networks') and that requires the development of linkages, networks and cooperations between the most different actors, also outside the channels of the existent institutional structures.
- The gradual and cumulative character of the innovation process, which develops in a gradual way and proceeds along trajectories or development paths that are based on the continuous learning process by the entrepreneurs, the technicians and the workers engaged in the productions.

Thus, the innovation process in medium-technology sectors can be interpreted according to a 'systemic approach'. This approach is different from the 'linear approach' that is based on R&D investment and just promotes the transfers of information and modern technology or provides customized expertise to individual firms. This new and alternative concept of innovation as an interactive learning process allows a broadening of the regions and sectors and firms that may be considered as innovative, as they are not only represented by those organizations where massive investment in R&D is made. From a policy perspective, the traditional linear model of innovation is based on a rational process of optimization by the individual firms and it has a technocratic character in distinguishing the decision-making phase and the execution phase within the production processes. On the contrary, medium-technology sectors seem to require a systemic approach based on promoting knowledge networks and cooperation between the various local and external actors and on the development of the internal capabilities of these actors.

4.4 THE COMPLEX NATURE OF TACIT KNOWLEDGE AND CREATIVE CAPABILITIES

Tacit knowledge plays a key role in the process of innovation by SMEs in medium-technology sectors, where innovation is based on the capability to informally search for a solution to local problems together with other partners. This process is different from the formal research activities in the high-technology sectors. Codified knowledge can be interpreted as a stock or a resource that can be transferred between the persons through language and between the firms within the market. While the concept of tacit knowledge is often defined only according to a residual perspective with respect to the concept of codified knowledge, the key characteristic of tacit knowledge or 'know-how' is its idiosyncratic dimension or the fact that it is embedded in the people and linked to the process of learning. Thus, tacit knowledge can be interpreted not as a resource, but rather as a complex set of competencies or capabilities to use the available resources (Cohen and Levinthal, 1989; Abramowitz and David, 1996; Nonaka and Konno, 1998; Lawson and Lorenz, 1999; Rizzello, 1999; Cohendet and Steinmueller, 2000; Howells, 2002; Akbar, 2003; Wink, 2003; Grabher, 2004; Zook, 2004; Ferlie et al., 2005; Handly et al., 2006; Amin and Roberts, 2008; Duguid, 2008). That explains why tacit knowledge or 'know-how' is linked to the process of action. While codified knowledge is of an objective nature and it relies on language, symbols and signals, tacit knowledge is subjective and it is closely linked to perception, interpretation and action. Tacit knowledge is related not to the knowledge of 'what' and 'why', as is codified knowledge, but rather to the knowledge of 'how' (that is, know-how), 'with whom' and 'when' or according to which procedure or routine. Tacit knowledge is embedded in human beings and should therefore be considered for its impact on the future actions of the subject. Tacit knowledge is not a stock that is the result of technology transfers, as is codified knowledge, but rather a competence that is the result of a learning process, which is usually of a collective nature.

In particular, tacit knowledge is essential both in explaining the capabilities of an individual actor to think and to act and in explaining his or her capabilities in the interaction with different actors. Tacit knowledge may refer both to the internal capabilities, which explain the process of how an individual actor behaves, and also to the relational capabilities, which explain how he or she interacts with other actors, and facilitate his or her close integration with these actors. The internal capabilities of an individual or of an organization may refer to their capability to select and interpret information, to their cognitive frame and system of values, to their attitude to risk-taking and entrepreneurship, to their creative capabilities and to their learning capabilities. The relational capabilities may consist in the 'automatic' coordination between actors when they react to external stimulus following specific 'routines', in the capability to learn together through a process of interactive learning, in the leadership and governance capabilities necessary for joint action. In fact, actors may be capable of coordinating their action with that of other actors when they react to external stimuli in an automatic way according to specific routines that have been interiorized, have often not been explicitly codified and are only based on experience. Moreover, through interactive learning processes and building new connections, actors learn how to learn together with other actors and jointly modify the rules of the learning process and the common schemes of interpretation of external information. Tacit knowledge may also be represented by the rather implicit esteem and thrust that an individual firm or entrepreneur enjoys in the local business community, as the organizational and managerial capability to govern or steer the action of other actors is more of an art than codified knowledge.

Tacit knowledge is more ambiguous, redundant and fungible than codified knowledge and it allows the definition of transversal associations or metaphors through imagination or intuition, such as is typical of 'lateral thinking', which may lead to scientific breakthroughs. Tacit knowledge plays a key role in the process of knowledge creation. Various forms of interaction between SMEs occur in the process of innovation and lead to the sharing of information, codified knowledge and 'tacit' knowledge. Internal tacit knowledge has to be combined with others' tacit knowledge and with codified knowledge. Through a socialization process with the other actors, tacit knowledge generates collective tacit knowledge and it may also be transformed into new codified knowledge. Tacit knowledge is related to the capabilities to create specific 'patterns', 'frames' and 'mental models' for interpreting the world. These capabilities also define the receptivity of an actor to external information, some of which will be 'understood and accepted', while other fragments will be rejected because they are incompatible with the prevailing mental frame. As indicated by Loasby (2003, p. 20), 'the actual generation of new ideas is necessarily tacit. What has not been thought cannot yet be codified'.

Tacit knowledge represents the background from which codified knowledge emerges. In particular, the creation of knowledge is the result of a cognitive process, which may be represented as a cumulative cycle made of different phases in which the role of tacit knowledge is crucial. In fact, tacit knowledge ensures the comprehension of codified knowledge, which was imported from outside (phase 1), the capability to combine codified knowledge in an original way (phase 2) and also the capability to apply the codified knowledge to the solution of specific problems in different localized contexts (phase 3). On the other hand, codified knowledge is crucial in the process of development of the individual competencies as in formal education activities (phase 4), which lead to the development of tacit knowledge. The availability of tacit knowledge by the individual actors represents the base for the development of interactive learning processes between these actors (phase 5). These interactive learning processes lead to the development of tacit collective organizational and technological knowledge (phase 6), which characterizes specific groups of individuals, firms and organizations. The socialization of tacit knowledge within the groups, firms and organizations is preliminary and instrumental to their codification and transformation of tacit knowledge into codified knowledge (phase 7). This codification allows knowledge to be more easily organized, maintained and diffused within the firms and organizations and also between the various firms and organizations (phase 8). Finally, the diffusion of knowledge and the transformation of local knowledge in diffused knowledge and their access should be accompanied by the development of the receptivity of the involved actors, which requires the development of understanding capabilities or the availability of tacit knowledge (phase 1), thus returning to the first phase of this cyclical process of knowledge creation.

A key form of tacit knowledge in the process of innovation is represented by creativity (Florida, 1995, 2002; Asheim and Clark, 2001; Wink, 2007; Asheim, Boschma and Cooke, 2007; Florida et al., 2007). In fact, 'architectural competency' or the capability to recombine different fragments of knowledge in an original way is in itself tacit. Creativity requires 'combinative' knowledge or the original combination of different 'specialized knowledge', which may be represented by information, technology, tacit and codified knowledge, in the framework of an iterative process of experimentation of failure and success. Creativity is based on imagination and pattern-making that establish new connections between pieces of information and knowledge. The human mind reacts to external stimulus according to the previous knowledge and structures, and changes cannot be easily accepted unless they are framed. An environment in continuous change creates challenges that make human beings feel uncomfortable as they prefer to live in a stable environment organized by specific routines. Routines, order and sense of place are a psychological need of the human mind, as they help in pattern-making and in orienting oneself, which is crucial for survival. There is balance between order and creativity, as order facilitates creativity and successful knowledge creation determines new routines. Thus, creativity is the result of a process of selection and of association and simplification ('pattern-making') that allows the combination of different and complementary information, technology and knowledge borrowed from various sectors, disciplines and regions in the solution of a specific problem, which stimulates action and that usually requires the joint contribution of the various interested actors. Creativity requires exploration, social interaction and a wide set of connections, allowing sharing, transforming, retaining and creating knowledge. It is based on joint work and it implies reflexivity, contestation, negotiation and problem-solving. It may be hindered by the lack of required competencies within the local economy, leading to a situation of lock-in.

Creativity is not only the capability of an artist; it is also crucial both in the elaboration of new theories by a scientist by combining in an original way existing codified knowledge, and within the firms, where it indicates the ability to combine different information, technologies and capabilities in a creative way to solve specific problems in different localized contexts. This complex connection of different parts of knowledge is characteristic of innovation in medium-tech firms, as they need to connect new ideas and existing knowledge to solve new specific problems hitherto unknown and often exclusively emerging in the relationship with a single customer. Science-driven knowledge in high-tech sectors on the other hand advances through the marginal extension of the existing analytical or abstract knowledge base and through a logic or mathematical thinking and it leads to discoveries characterized by a more general applicability to different problems in various productions.

Creativity requires the combination of knowledge in different fields and the interaction between actors having different competencies. The creative process is a fundamental component of a cognitive process through which various sets of knowledge are first searched, identified, understood, analysed for similarities and finally brought together by adapting and extending their significance, leading to the creation of a new set of knowledge. As combinations of the three basic colours: red, green and blue, create all different colours, creativity requires the combination of previous knowledge. However, it also requires an enlargement of the cognitive distance, which is indicated by the arrows in the Figure 4.7. Openness, connectivity, increased accessibility and receptivity are key conditions for knowledge creation. New ideas always develop at the frontier of different established knowledge fields, which are extended into new directions. In fact, the growth of knowledge is always at the margin (Loasby, 2003). The model in Figure 4.7 is analogous to the concept of Weber's 'critical isodapane', which explains the spatial agglomeration as an effect of a decrease of transport costs. It also indicates that the three firms, A, B and C, which master three specific fields of knowledge, do not need to merge or geographically

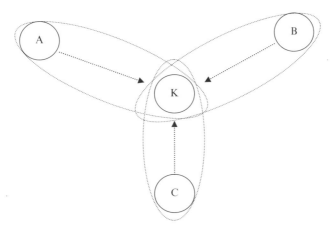

Figure 4.7   Creativity as combination of diverse accessible knowledge

agglomerate, leading to the creation of a geographical cluster, in order to create new knowledge, while they may only develop some forms of inter-action by reducing the cognitive distance that has previously separated them. Thus, geographical concentration into a cluster can be substituted by cognitive interaction within a network.

Moreover, innovation emerges by breaking established links and creat-ing new links. This process is similar to Schumpeter's ([1942] 1975) process of 'creative destruction'. Both exploration and exploitation are compo-nents of the creativity process. Exploration is the search for diversity, while exploitation is the search for homogeneity and compatibility. This process of extension and combination of existing knowledge is facilitated in the case of tacit knowledge. In fact, tacit knowledge might be more easily recombined than codified knowledge, as it is more implicit, ambigu-ous and flexible. Thus, recombining knowledge from different agents, sectors, disciplines and countries may be easier when the tacit component is very strong. On the other hand, the codes inherent in different bodies of codified knowledge may be excessively stringent and they can impose uni-vocal interpretations and rigidities in the use and modification of knowl-edge itself. Thus, these codes may be incompatible with each other.

This process is cumulative, as creativity or knowledge creation leads to the development of new technical and organizational competencies that increase receptivity. In fact, creativity is both a factor of a learning process, as it allows the creation of new knowledge, and also the result of a learning process, as the new knowledge being created improves the crea-tive capabilities and then the capabilities to further develop the learning process. Learning and competencies are linked by a bi-directional rela-tionship, as learning feeds into competencies, and these latter act on the process, the direction and speed of learning.

Policies aiming to promote creativity are different in the various sectors. Creativity in high-tech sectors requires large investments in R&D, while in medium-technology sectors creativity requires networks and informal interaction, leading to interactive learning between SMEs. However, crea-tivity also requires a sustained effort in innovation by SMEs. In fact, the purchase of a new machine or a patent represents a shortcut, and it is not enough for a sustainable innovation and competitiveness strategy unless it is accompanied by an adequate investment by the SMEs at the time and the human resources required for the design of innovative productions and the organization of these latter in cooperation with other firms.

Creativity does not only consist of the adoption of specific product and process innovation within an individual firm, but also of the design of medium-term projects having a collective nature with the participation of various SMEs and large firms. In fact, regional innovation policies should promote large innovative common projects in the existing clusters and the various regions rather than aiming at the creation of new clusters. The enhancement of creativity requires the facilitation of not only the vertical relationships along the supply chain between client and suppliers, but also the horizontal relationships between different sectors both locally and with external partners such as international research institutions and large international firms.

The most appropriate characteristics of a governance structure for the relationships to promote creativity seem to be a low level of formalization of the relationships, not too high a specialization, a network organization, autonomy and responsibility, the trust that all workers are capable of giving a creative contribution to the firm, the measurement of results and rewards, self-regulation and adjustment focusing on the exploitation of the actual results rather than on the strict adherence to previously defined guidelines, and the creation of various channels of communication between the units, firms, institutions and workers interested in the same area of production. In fact, a linear process of diffusion of technology seems to be closely related to the sequential characteristics of the 'fordist' production chain and of the logistic supply chains, where the flows of information circulate in a specific direction. On the contrary, networks are models of governance of the relationships characterized by feedback relationships in the flows of information and by a cumulative and incremental process of interactive learning.

Tacit knowledge is more difficult to be transferred between distant agents, as it requires personal contacts and a deep reciprocal knowledge and trust. However, in some cases, the lack of geographical proximity may be compensated by an adequate organizational or institutional proximity, which may allow transfer of tacit knowledge over large distances within organizations and institutions. Thus, networks may represent the appropriate organizational structure to organize diversity, facilitate the sharing and combination of tacit knowledge and stimulate creativity. In fact, tacit knowledge is not 'transferred' as in the case of codified knowledge, but rather it represents a capability that can be learned or 'thought' as the result of a process of interactive learning through which the actors develop internally with the collaboration of external actors' specific new creative competencies, which will allow them to adopt process and product innovation. Tacit knowledge cannot be 'transferred' internationally as in the case of codified knowledge, through better communication, but only through the organization of networks of international collaboration. These networks enable the organization of processes of interactive learning between the firms of different countries and the promotion of the development of new competencies in the economic lagging regions through the creative combination of internal traditional competencies and external specialized competencies. Thus, the so-called 'interregional transfers' of tacit knowledge may be the result of a European regional and innovation policy that develops and governs this process of collaboration and interactive learning between different regions.

4.5   THE GEOGRAPHICAL CONCENTRATION OF INNOVATION ACTIVITIES

Economic literature has often underlined both the role of innovative firms and sectors in explaining economic disparities between regions and also the spatial concentration of the innovative activities, by focusing the analysis on the effect of innovative sectors on the development of their respective territory and on the effect of specific location factors in concentrating the innovative firms and sectors in specific geographical areas.

Clusters may be defined as 'geographic concentrations of interconnected companies, specialized suppliers, service providers, firms in related industries and associated institutions . . . in a particular field that compete but also co-operate' (Porter 1998, p. 77). It is also widely believed that industrial clusters can help to improve the performance of regional economies by fostering innovation and strengthening the competitiveness of firms, thereby generating growth and employment.

The basic idea refers to the expectation of positive effects of geographical proximity of firms belonging to the same sector on their innovative behaviour and performance. However, despite the frequent assertion that clusters raise competitiveness and innovativeness, the theory does not distinguish sufficiently between different kinds of forces that promote the spatial concentration of related activities and it may yield misguided policy prescriptions. Ambiguity and silence still prevail on the specific processes and factors that encourage innovation in industrial clusters and also on the various spatial scales on which clustering processes can operate.

Innovative activities are highly spatially concentrated. That is usually explained by the existence of various forms of agglomeration economies that enhance the development of innovative productions in specific central areas (Cappellin, 1988, 2002, 2007; Karlsson, 1997; Almeida and Kogut, 1999; Rosenthal and Strange, 2001; Simmie, 2001; Bottazzi et al., 2002; Dumais, Ellison and Glaeser, 2002; Fujita and Thisse, 2002; Lublinski, 2003; Torre, 2003, 2008; Torre and Gallaud 2004; Boschma, 2005; Torre and Rallet, 2005; Dupuy and Torre, 2006; Antonelli, 2007; PRSA, 2007;

Andersson and Hellerstedt, 2008). Among the factors of agglomeration are economies of scale, the access to spatially concentrated demand and the existence of external economies. These latter refer to the existence of easy intermediate relationships within and between industrial sectors in a specific cluster, to the availability of local pools of qualified workers and in particular to the existence of 'localized knowledge spillovers' (LKS) (Audretsch and Feldman, 1996; Zucker, Darby and Armstrong, 1998; Breschi and Lissoni, 2001; Bathelt et al., 2004; Davenport, 2005; Iammarino and McCann, 2006; Antonelli, 2007).

In fact, the industrial economics literature on the relationships between technology, geographical distribution of innovative activities and international specialization has usually focused on the process of geographical diffusion of innovation and on the accessibility by innovative firms to 'knowledge spillovers' emanating from universities, research institutions and other firms. These analyses adopt a linear model of technology diffusion, which implies a clear distinction between the producers of technology and its users.

On the other hand, the regional economics literature has explained geographical concentration of innovative activities on the basis of a systemic approach to innovation and as the result of a process of interactive learning between different complementary actors within a cluster or a regional innovation system (Vázquez Barquero, 1990; Nelson, 1993; Cooke, 1998; Cooke and Morgan, 1998; Steiner, 1998; Acs, 2002; Crevoisier and Camagni, 2000; Paniccia, 2002; Cooke, Heidenreich and Braczyk, 2004; Brenner, 2004; Simmie, 2005; Cooke et al., 2006; Geenhuizen and Nijkamp, 2006; Steiner and Hartmann, 2006; Brenner and Mühlig, 2007; van Geenhuizen, 2007). This has led to the identification of various channels through which technology can diffuse, such as vertical production linkages between suppliers and clients, mobility of qualified labour force, spin-off and financial control between firms, informal and formal technological collaborations (Capello, 1999; Capello and Faggian, 2005).

The collaborative nature of innovation processes has reinforced tendencies towards geographical clustering because of the advantages of locating in close proximity to other firms in specialist and related industries. According to this approach, SMEs should not be considered individually, differently from large firms, but rather as part of a complex regional production and innovation system. Thus, as the result of an endogenous development process determined by the adoption of innovation within specific localized innovation networks, innovative firms and activities emerge in a given region, rather than that they are attracted or move to that region.

4.6 THE LOCALIZED CHARACTER OF COGNITIVE PROCESSES

The literature on cognitive economics highlights a third approach in explaining the spatial agglomeration of innovative activities, different from those indicated by the industrial economics and the regional economics literature. In fact, the spatial concentration or diffusion of innovative activities has a more fundamental reason than the existence of 'localization factors' working on the attraction of innovative firms. This reason is rooted in the intrinsic spatial nature of the process of knowledge creation. In particular, our study aims to come to a better understanding of the processes of knowledge generation, transfer and absorption within and between firms and other organizations within a region, by focusing the attention on innovation as the result of an interactive process involving the sharing and exchanging of different forms of knowledge between regional actors. This perspective is clearly important when analysing the relationships between small and medium-sized firms in the process of innovation adoption.

In synthesis, knowledge creation is the result of pattern-making or of the classification and reclassification of exogenous stimulus. Thus, the process of knowledge creation has an interactive and a combinative character, and a closer geographical proximity and/or a greater cognitive proximity facilitate the interaction between various complementary actors and the combination of complementary pieces of knowledge. Knowledge can only develop in a localized or specific framework and calls for a geographical and cognitive proximity of the various actors, which participate in an interactive learning process. Knowledge creation apparently only has an a-spatial character and cognitive sciences clarify on the basis of theoretical considerations that the process of knowledge creation works in a localized framework. Thus, the agglomeration of innovative productions can be explained on the basis of the spatial or localized nature of the processes of knowledge creation.

The analysis of the relationship between the process of cognition and space can be based on the psychological theories of those economists who first investigated the problem of knowledge creation and who provided contributions that have later been confirmed by recent advances in neurosciences, such as neurobiology and psychology (see also Table 4.1 for a summary). According to cognitive theories, a brain operates, as in Smith's ([1795] 1980), Hayek's (1952) and Marshall's (1994) theories, by forming selective connections. According to Adam Smith, it is characteristic of human nature to be uncomfortable when unable to make sense of a particular phenomenon, especially when that phenomenon is repeated; people therefore try to invent 'connecting principles' that will collect unexplained phenomena into categories and provide an acceptable explanation of these categories. In fact, Adam Smith pointed to the role of those 'specialised philosophers and men of speculation, who are often capable of combining together the powers of the most distant and dissimilar objects' (Smith [1776] 1976, p. 11). Satisfactory explanations are a source of positive pleasure, especially if the solution is aesthetically pleasing, and are likely to be widely adopted by those encountering such phenomena (Loasby, 2003).

According to Marshall and Smith the brain works by linking the idea of an initial impression received by the body with the idea of an action that the body performs in response, and then linking the latter with the idea of an impression that is interpreted as a consequence of that action (Smith, [1795] 1980, Marshall 1994; Loasby, 2003; Raffaelli 2003). In fact the brain is a selective system and it works not according to logic and mathematical thinking, but rather according to the recognition of configurations. This pattern-making activity performs the vital function to allow to the brain to orient itself in the surrounding space: a function that is crucial for survival and has been developed through human evolution. In fact, cognitive activity seems necessarily to represent the result of a reaction to the stimulus coming from the local environment. Connections clearly imply a spatial framework and proximity enhances connections.

The spatial dimension of the process of cognition is also clarified by the fact that the local environment and the aim to respond to new needs and to solve the problems of local users is the most important stimulus to innovate for the firms. Cognition and innovation are related to the stimulus of a problem emerging in a specific field or to the opportunity to satisfy an emerging demand in a specific market (Gallouj and Weinstein, 1997). The local environment is the source of challenges and risks for the individual actor and it is related to the national and international economy. Firms should respond to the new needs and demands (as indicated in the TKM approach to be illustrated below) in local markets and aim to solve problems of local users. The strength of the stimulus and the possibility of perceiving it depends on the spatial accessibility (as in the TKM approach). Moreover, cognitive proximity and a low geographical and cognitive distance facilitate the identification of weak signals and enhance collaborations.

A second key concept in the process of cognition is that of routines and path dependence (Loasby, 2001, 2002). According to Marshall, over time the brain may develop a range of closely connected impressions and actions, which we might call routines. In fact, the application of solutions or the repetition of new actions develops new connections between different parts of the brain (Marshall, 1920, p. 252), which gradually take over the maintenance of these activities, leaving the conscious brain activity free for new initiatives, including those that utilize these now-automatic connections. According to Rizzello (2003), 'neurognosis' is the phenomenon, according which, when an organism faces new information, its capacity to give significance to this information depends on its previously stored experience and on its neurognostic structures. Thus, the human brain and mind evolve by following a path that strongly depends on pre-existing structures, as it adapts to external challenges while searching to maintain consistency and integrity. This implies time irreversibility and that experience matters. This concept implies that spatial and cognitive proximity are a key condition in order to promote frequent and strong connections between different actors.

Activities are mostly strongly linked or embedded in their local environment. Firms and actors respond by aiming to survive and to preserve the integrity of the local environment. This process explains the 'receptivity' to external stimulus by local actors (as in the TKM approach). In particular, external stimulus should be compatible with the internal integrity of the local production system and should lead to a gradual process of adaptation. In fact, firms and actors respond and adapt in order to survive and to preserve the identity and integrity of the local environment facing the threats of external competition. The process of knowledge creation in a given location is characterized by switching costs and rigidities, inertia or stickiness and it evolves according specific paths.

The concepts of local endogenous development and of complex adaptive systems imply some form of immobility of resources and of internal integration and coherence, as is implied by the neurognosis concept. The territory represents a resource in economic development and it is characterized also by a specific identity (as in the TKM approach), which increases internal cohesion and synergy, but it may also determine a form of spatial dependence, as the specific characteristics of the local selection environment may create obstacles and lead to lock-in effects. For example, in local industrial clusters (Steiner, 1998) specialized in medium-technology sectors, knowledge creation is tightly related to the sectoral specialization, the industrial culture and know-how existing in the innovation systems to be considered. These factors may facilitate the early identification or the design of new patterns, combining previously existing ideas and pieces of information and knowledge. At the same time, however, they also constrain the discovery of a new pattern in the attempt to ensure the consistency and compatibility with existing solutions, causing path dependency and in some cases 'lock-in' effects.

A third concept elaborated by cognitive theories is that of 'exaptation' (Rizzello, 2003). While new knowledge, which is corroborated by apparently successful application, is consolidated into new routines, if directed action fails to achieve its objective, the recognition of failure leads either to a modification of existing routines or to experimentation resulting in new routines. Thus, knowledge that is already organized into routines facilitates the creation of new knowledge, especially that which builds on the old. That introduces imagination and the possibility of trial and error within the mind, as in modern practices of research and development. Problems in the economy require combinations of routines and novelty, and these combinations are themselves modified by evolutionary processes of trial and error. This sequence of creativity against a background of routines, leading to new routines that provide a more advanced basis for further creativity, is a dialectical process. Each resource, instead of constituting a well-defined input into one or more production functions, is a multi-specific asset, the potential uses of which have to be discovered, invented or imagined.

It is indeed a most important characteristic of knowledge that it can be reused, but in a way that is not simply deducible from current uses. As indicated by Rizzello (2003), 'exaptation' is the phenomenon through which previous neuronal structures built and developed to solve problems of interpretation of the external world effectively reveal their capacity to co-opt new configurations and functions when individual faces new problems. In fact, new neuronal structures emerge from old ones, in order to give significance to the sensorial data. Coase (1992) explained the firm as a set of incompletely specified contracts, which provided resources to be deployed at some date yet to be chosen and within a domain that could be broadly envisaged, thus avoiding the cost and time of making the necessary arrangements at that date. It is an investment in creating capabilities that provide options. A Coasean firm is a combination of purpose and capabilities that retain sufficient degrees of freedom to allow people to take decisions that may make a difference.

The concept of exaptation is tightly related to that of creativity and to variations. In fact, the growth of knowledge is always at the margin (Loasby, 2003). The generation of variety across organizations is a natural consequence, as imperfect specification is a condition of those experiments at the margin on which Marshall relied for the variations that were a chief cause of progress (Marshall, 1920, p. 355). In particular, a movement is easiest to adjacent states, but typically there are many states that are adjacent to each current position, so that even individuals or organizations with identical current positions may develop in different ways. In practice, individuals and firms will not have identical positions, even those with similar experiences and engaged in similar businesses, and this increases the potential for variation, as Marshall noted. Marshall believed that this process tended to result in ever greater differentiation of function, matched by closer coordination (Ibid., p. 241). The concept of specialization is related to the division of labour and Adam Smith suggested that the most fundamental aspect of the division of labour is the division of knowledge (Metcalfe and Ramlogan, 2005) as: 'each individual becomes more expert in his own peculiar branch, more work is done upon the whole, and the quantity of science is considerably increased by it' (Smith [1776] 1976, p.11). According to Marshall and Hayek, the same stimulus may generate a variety of responses due to the differences in initial perceptions and the selective connections that are due to the reinforcement of what appears to work (Loasby, 2003). According to Hayek, any impulse is a 'representation', which is itself interpreted in terms of the relationships that have already been established within the brain (Hayek, 1952). Similarly spatial dependence is related to the fact that the same external stimulus may lead to different 'creative' responses according to the casual combination of the actors involved in the process of interactive learning or the connections established with them, as is characteristic of a complex, adaptive system (Metcalfe and Ramlogan, 2005).

Clearly space matters in the process of knowledge creation. Innovation requires the search and the integration of complementary resources and capabilities and that is enhanced by the existence of network relations with other local actors. In fact, Hayek argues that instead of direct connections between particular stimuli and particular sensory qualities, the effect that is produced by any stimulus depends on the location of this impulse in relation to other impulses within the network of connections (Hayek, 1952). From a spatial perspective, tacit knowledge explains why clusters are faster in adoption of innovation. It is perhaps because of this double threat to initiative and variety that Marshall was so impressed with the virtues of an industrial district that seemed to ensure the automatic organization (Marshall, 1919, p. 600) of highly specialized activities while facilitating both the generation and the active discussion of novel ideas, including ideas for constructing new patterns of relationships between firms. The spatial dimension of these concepts elaborated by the cognitive economics literature is indicated by the fact that reconversion of existing capabilities to new uses is possible only within a limited domain and it implies geographical or cognitive proximity, as firms initially look for the support of local suppliers and for the demand of local customers.

However, inventions and innovations are increasingly the result not of individual creative activity but of a collective process of searching and learning. Innovation requires the sharing of tacit knowledge, which is more ambiguous, redundant and fungible than codified knowledge, but it requires direct personal contacts. Complex adaptive systems (CAS)

(Holland, 2002) are highly innovative and are also necessarily localized in geographical space. In particular, regional innovation systems (RIS) can be interpreted as evolutionary networks made by interacting brains, which through explicit collaboration or through spontaneous market selection generate systemic innovation. Network externalities emerge in a territorial framework and local networks facilitate interaction and flows of information and knowledge. Interactive learning is the key process in knowledge creation and the links and the frequency of the contacts are constrained by spatial distance. The process of interactive learning within a regional innovation system leads not only to imitation, but also to an increasing specialization and differentiation of the individual pre-existing firms into new productions and to the spin-offs of new firms. Thus, creativity is enhanced and limited by local capabilities (as in the TKM approach).

For example, the development of the thought of individual scientists has been affected by their respective local cultural environment. The various schools of thought are often related to specific cities or countries and not only to a historical period. Moreover, learning together is often a characteristic of the professional communities and know-how is often collective and localized. In fact, the urbanization economies and the Jacobs externalities (Jacobs, 1969) related to the diversity of metropolitan areas, or the localization economies related to the specialization of industrial clusters, enable the easy identification of local complementary capabilities in the process of innovation. The concentration of firms in large metropolitan areas facilitates innovation, both because this concentration decreases transaction costs between the actors (Cappellin, 1988) and because this diversity enhances business opportunities and entrepreneurship capabilities, due to the high diversity of origins, sectors, competencies existing in these areas and the easy access to a wide scope of new emerging needs and complementary resources.

A further key concept in cognitive theories, when applied to the analysis of the economy, is the concept of institutions. Smith's, Marshall's and Hayek's psychological systems rely on routines and institutions that economize on cognition. Institutions play a key role in the process of knowledge creation. Rules and organic institutions standardize the world and in so doing they simplify the ambit in which humans use their limited cognitive capabilities. In fact, routines facilitate the connections and create free time to be devoted to the explicit thinking on innovation (Hayek, 1952). Thus, following rules and codifying them in institutions is an 'economic way' to act successfully. The routines and institutions within Smith's, Marshall's and Hayek's psychological systems allow us to focus attention on the issues for which they are inadequate at any particular time. According to Loasby (2001, 2002, 2003), the maintenance of stable baselines within particular domains is a prime function of formal organizations, and the appropriateness of the baseline is a major determinant of organizational success or failure. Order makes room for creativity, which is stabilized in a new order that combines newly established expectations and beliefs into a patterned performance. Thus, in the brain, conscious attention is reserved for problem-solving or the introduction of novelty. Cognitive processes indicate an evolutionary sequence made by variety generation, selection and the preservation of selected variants in the form of modified or novel routines and institutions (Loasby, 2003).

The spatial dimension of the concept of institutions is clarified by the fact that coordination by institutions is a necessary process when knowledge is spatially dispersed between different actors and for solving the problems of information asymmetries. Moreover, it is impossible to refer to institutions without considering the territory on which they exercise their power, the geographical or sectoral borders with respect to other institutions and to the political participation by the people living or working in a given area. In fact, institutions are linked to the concept of territorial sovereignty and to the concept of legitimacy, which implies a local constituency. The spatial dimension of institutions is clearly indicated by their relations to local history, to the memory of centuries of interdependence between local actors, to the existence of a common culture, to the distinctive characteristics of the individual places and the existence of a place identity, to common visions of the future, common values, specific norms and routines and reciprocal trust. The process of economic development in specific regions depends on the existence of 'intermediate institutions' and on the local 'social capital' (Coleman, 1988; Maskell, 1999; Scott, 2000; Field, 2003; Sorensen, 2003) and they facilitate the connections and decrease the cognitive distance between the local actors. In particular, strategic dedicated organizations and institutions seem to be required for the management of knowledge and innovation networks of SMEs in intermediate technology sectors within a given territory (as in the TKM approach).

The focus on the specific phases of the cognitive process, highlighted by the cognitive economics literature, allows us to identify their close correspondence with specific territorial factors and process and the role of space and geographical distance in the creation of ideas and new knowledge (Table 4.1). Moreover, the theoretical concepts indicated above correspond to a large extent to the various phases of the 'territorial knowledge management' approach (TKM), to be illustrated later in this chapter (Cappellin, 2003b, 2007). In particular, the concept of connections corresponds to that of external stimulus. The concept of neurognosis corresponds to those of receptivity and common identity. The concepts of exaptation and variation correspond to the concepts of creativity and interactive learning within a

Table 4.1   The spatial/localized dimension of cognitive processes

Components of the Cognitive Processes	Territorial Factors and Processes
According to cognitive theories, a brain operates by forming selective connections	Cognition and innovation are related to the stimulus of a problem emerging in a specific field or to the opportunity to satisfy an emerging demand in a specific market
Human brain and mind evolve by following a path that strongly depends on pre-existing neurognostic structures	Spatial and cognitive proximity are key conditions in order to promote frequent and strong connections between different actors and the specific characteristics of the local selection environment may create obstacles and lead to lock-in effects.
'Exaptation' is the phenomenon through which previous neuronal structures built and developed to solve problems of interpretation of the external world effectively reveal their capacity to co-opt new configurations and functions when individual faces new problems	The reconversion of existing capabilities to new uses is possible only within a limited domain and it implies geographical or cognitive proximity
The same stimulus may generate a variety of responses due to the differences in initial perceptions and the selective connections that are due to the reinforcement of what appears to work	Complex adaptive systems (CAS) are highly innovative and are also localized. Network externalities emerge in a territorial framework and local networks facilitate interaction and flows of information and knowledge
Following rules and codifying them in institutions is an 'economic way' to act successfully	Institutions are linked to territorial sovereignty and political participation and to local history, common culture, place identity, values, norms, visions, trust

local network. The concept of institutions is clearly related to the concept of governance of knowledge and innovation networks.

Thus, the previous analysis highlights that space is relevant not only in order to examine the process of territorial diffusion of innovation and/ or to examine the impact of innovation on the structure of the territory and on regional disparities. On the contrary, the focus on the localized dimension of cognitive processes allows us to highlight the fact that space and territory affect the process of knowledge creation. In fact, that is the fundamental reason for the spatial agglomeration of innovative activities that are based on the knowledge creation processes occurring in specific geographical areas. The specific characteristics of these areas, both the central and most developed areas and also the peripheral and less developed areas, lead to different characteristics of the processes of knowledge creation in these individual areas and this affects the innovation and the competitiveness of local firms. Therefore, the relationships between the space economy and knowledge are clarified not only by the uneven spatial diffusion of different types of knowledge, such as codified and tacit knowledge, or analytic, synthetic and symbolic knowledge, or by the existence of urbanization or localization economies explaining the agglomeration of innovative activities in specific geographical areas. On the contrary, what seems more relevant is the role that space directly plays on the process of cognition or on the generation of knowledge and innovation.

In conclusion, it is possible to underline the difference between a temporal or evolutionary perspective and a spatial or territorial perspective in the analysis of the knowledge creation process. From a temporal perspective, individuals classify new stimulus and associate patterns of stimulus to patterns of response on the basis of previously experience successes. The exchange of ideas, information and knowledge activate a creative process of re-elaboration of own knowledge and of increasing specialization by connecting existing elements in new ways within the mind of the considered person. A spatial perspective on the analysis of the innovation process also introduces the interaction between various local and external actors as a new element to the combination of different pieces of knowledge within an individual mind or firm, as indicated by a functional or temporal perspective. Knowledge creation is the result not only of the combination of a new stimulus with the individual previous experience, but also of the combination of different competencies between the various actors who are interacting in a learning process occurring within a given network or local area.

This explains the different spatial pattern of creativity and the effect of lock-in. In fact, from a spatial perspective, the same stimulus may determine a different pattern of response in each regional innovation system according to the different form of network of local actors, as the way an innovation system responds to an external stimulus depends not only on the existing individual capabilities of the actors who interact in the learning process, but also on the level of integration and the forms of the links that have been built between them. Not only does the plurality of the individuals allow a plurality of responses as an individual combines the stimulus with his or her own experiences, but also the stimulus to an individual actor may be combined with the different complementary competencies of the various actors who are directly or indirectly linked to him or her. This leads to differences in the pattern of innovation within diversified communities or systems of SMEs.

The increasing integration within a regional innovation system leads to an increasing specialization of the various local actors. In particular, the knowledge that is shared between the various actors usually has a different meaning for the donor and the receiver, as its significance depends on its combination with their respective specific internal capabilities. This increased knowledge leads them to specialize in order to perform a specific or rather unique function within an innovation network. Thus, the processes of the interaction between regional actors and of the combination of different pieces of knowledge specific to different scientific or production fields are related to the process of adaptation, greater specialization, selection and greater integration of the actors within a knowledge and innovation network. These processes in a local production system of SMEs occur in a rather informal or automatic way, rather than being planned by a superior coordinating authority, such as within an individual large firm.

Moreover, cognitive theories explain that the building of mental frameworks, connections or routines in our mind leads to linking in an automatic way patterns of stimulus with patterns of responses. This combination of the external stimulus with previous individual knowledge leads to the phenomenon of 'path dependence'. Similarly, from a spatial perspective, the success in solving previous problems leads to strengthening the particular links between specific actors and to creating soft infrastructures such as routines, norms, intermediate institutions, trust, common identity and sense of belonging, which facilitates the future interactions between these same actors. In other words, the external stimulus may lead to the combination of the individual competencies of an actor with the competencies of other selected actors in the same local community and that may lead to 'embeddedness' or to 'spatial dependence'. From a functional perspective, a lock-in effect may be the result of the lack of capability by an actor to perceive and to adapt to a new stimulus that is too different from his or her individual capabilities. However, from a spatial perspective, a lock-in effect may also be the result of the exclusion of some external actors who appear too different, and a too strong internal homogeneity within a local innovation system may hinder the receptivity to diversity and the interaction with external actors.

Thus, we may conclude that the time and the space dimensions are both relevant in the process of innovation. While the 'evolutive approach' clarifies the 'path-dependent' character of the innovation process, a 'network approach' clarifies the 'spatially embedded' character of the innovation process, as this latter depends on the interaction between various local actors within a collective learning process.

4.7   THE ECONOMIC CHARACTERISTICS OF LOCAL PRODUCTION SYSTEMS

At the present time the organization of production is experiencing a profound transformation process in which the hierarchic models are giving way to more flexible and decentralized forms of organization. This has produced multiple interpretations such as industrial districts (Becattini, 1990), flexible specialization (Piore and Sabel, 1984), industrial clusters (Porter, 1990, 2000), the knowledge economy (Lundvall, 1992; Florida, 1995), the new economic geography (Krugman, 1991; Fujita and Thisse, 2002), the theory of the innovative milieu (Maillat, 1995; Maillat and Kebir, 1999; Crevoisier and Camagni, 2000) and regional innovation systems (Cooke, 1998). Thus, a single unique interpretation of how production is organized within the territory does not exist.

4.7.1   Industrial Districts

According to Becattini (1990), an 'industrial district' is the result of the combination of the specific sociocultural characters of a community, of the historical-naturalistic characteristics of a geographical area and of the technical characteristics of the production process, and it is the result of a process of dynamic integration (a virtuous circle) between the division of labour in the district and the widening of the market for its products. In particular, the Marshallian industrial district would be made up to a population of independent small and middle-sized firms, mostly coincident with individual production phases, supported by a myriad of units supplying production services, and of cottage and part-time workers, which are all oriented by an open group of pure entrepreneurs through the market of the production orders. Although there is no single definition of industrial district in the very large number of empirical and theoretical studies devoted to the analysis of this modern form of territorial organization of firms, a wide consensus seems to exist on the following characteristics of an industrial district (Steiner 1998):

- a high specialization in a specific product;
- a population of small and medium-sized firms;
- production processes decomposed in different phases with low optimal technical sizes;

- a presence of external economies for the individual firms, but internal in the local territory;
- the development of subcontracting agreements and of cooperative behaviours between the firms;
- a high mobility from employee to self-employment status and high birth and death rates of the firms;
- the development of a common production and organizational know-how embodied in the skills of the local labour force.

4.7.2 'Innovative Milieu'

With respect to the concept of industrial district, the concept of the 'innovative milieu' is focused not only on the efficient and decentralized organization of the local productions, but also on the role of innovation processes. These could take different forms, like the processes of imitation and of development of specific technology or the ability to reallocate local resources from the sectors in decline to new emergent sectors when the local production system is stricken by a crisis and by external shocks. Two typical elements of a milieu are (1) a 'logic of interaction' that is revealed by the creation of 'innovation networks' and by an explicit cooperation between the different local, private, public and collective actors (Maillat, 1995), and (2) a 'dynamic of collective learning', which implies the ability of the local actors to gradually modify their behaviour according to the change in the external environment and to activate the internal resources of the milieu in order to create solutions that are appropriate to a new situation.

4.7.3 'Regional Innovation Systems' (RIS)

The approach of 'regional innovation systems' (RIS) emphasizes the systemic dimension of the innovation process, which derives from the fact that a regional innovation system is made by a plurality of actors, for example large and small firms working in a production sector where network relationships exist or could be economically foreseen, institutes of research and of superior training, private laboratories of R&D, agencies of technological transfer, chambers of commerce, enterprise associations, professional training organizations, specific governmental agencies and appropriate offices of public administration. This sense of belonging represents the basis of an 'associative approach' or of an 'associative governance', which leads to the creation of clubs, forums, consortia and different institutional schemes of partnership (Cooke, 1998; Cooke and Morgan, 1998). A regional innovation system could be defined as a system in which the firms and the other organizations are systematically engaged in interactive learning through an institutional environment characterized by local embeddedness.

The concept of RIS certainly appears to be broader than the traditional concept of industrial district and able, also like the concept of innovateur milieu, to analyse different types of local production systems. From this perspective a typology of RIS could be built (Cooke, 1998). For instance a 'localist RIS' like Tuscany is characterized by a few large firms both of local and of external origin, by a spectrum of activity of research or by a 'research reach' that is not very broad. On the other hand, an 'interactive RIS' like Catalonia and Baden Württemberg is characterized by a relative balance of large and small firms, both indigenous and external, while the spectrum of research activity includes diversified structures of regional research and the reliance on external innovations. Finally, a 'globalized RIS' like California or North Rhein-Westphalia or Midi-Pyrénées is characterized by the domination of global firms, often supported by a localized supply chain made by SMEs that are rather dependent on the large companies.

4.7.4 The Approach of 'Proximity Dynamics'

The approach of 'proximity dynamics' introduces the notion of territorial proximity given by the intersection/overlap of three different dimensions of proximity that may be classified respectively under the names of 'geographical proximity', 'organizational proximity' and 'institutional proximity' (Bellet, Colletis and Lung, 1993; Rallet and Torre 1998). While organizational proximity deals with the links in terms of production organization, geographical proximity deals with the links in terms of distance. Organizational proximity is based upon on the logic of organizational membership and intrinsic similarity of the actors. Geographical proximity refers to the natural and physical limits and includes the effect of transport infrastructures. An industrial district combines in its definition these two components, since the firms that constitute an industrial district are tied up among themselves at the same time in terms of reciprocal similarity or of common membership and they are also located at a short functional distance from each other. Finally, institutional proximity means the belief in representations, models and rules of thought and of action by the agents belonging to a common territory. It consists of the development of relationships of intentional nature, like the relationships of cooperation, trust, exchange of technological information and partnership that determine the strategy of the actors. It implies forms of collective action and the creation of institutions both formal and informal that perform an often fundamental role in the mechanisms of operation by the economic agents.

Interaction through the price mechanism is not the only interaction and it could be accompanied by a series of non-market interactions or by forms of reciprocal coordination, like the relationships of cooperation or the relationships of trust or technological interaction. Geographical proximity allows the development of knowledge interactions, if it is complemented by an appropriate organizational and institutional context. However, the experience accumulated in the international transfers of technology has demonstrated that geographical distance is less important as an obstacle to international cooperation than organizational and technological distance. In fact, cooperation is greater between firms with similar technology, even when they are localized in different regions, than between organizations of the same region that do not share the same problems and objectives.

4.7.5 'Learning Regions'

According to the approach of 'learning regions', 'knowledge represents the fundamental resource in the contemporary economy and the process of learning represents the most important process' (Lundvall and Johnson, 1994, p. 23). This strategy is based on the belief that the opportunities of development and the exogenous risk factors, which have an objective character, do not determine automatic results but that, in order to be valorized or opposed, they require the development of local technical, organizational and entrepreneurial abilities, which must be built through a process of learning and have a subjective character. The objective of a 'learning region' refers to the integration of tacit or implicit traditional knowledge, which is bound to the local context, with codified knowledge available at the world level, in order to stimulate the regional endogenous potential. The creation of new knowledge implies an intense process of interaction (Nonaka and Konno, 1998), which is characterized by transfers both of tacit and explicit knowledge and requires face to face contact and a physical proximity, as well as contact through ICT over greater distances.

The concept of the learning region (Florida, 1995; Asheim, 1996; Morgan, 1997) is very similar to that of the regional innovation system and it indicates that the presence of a plurality of actors within the same local production system favours the diffusion and the accumulation of knowledge. The knowledge networks are based on vertical customer–supplier relationships, which are a crucial tool for the development of incremental product innovations, and also on horizontal relationships that could promote the development of the innovation process through the offer of information on technological opportunity and the process of imitation and adaptation of success innovations adopted by other firms and organizations (Maillat and Kebir, 1999). The concepts of regional innovation systems and learning regions appear to be more general than that of industrial district and are suitable both for the less developed regions and for more developed regions, which now appear to have overcome the phase of narrow specialization. They are based on the concept of evolutionary learning, which makes them suitable for interpreting the continuous changes in the internal structure, in the geographical dimension and in the relationships with the exterior of a local production system.

4.7.6 'Institutional Thickness'

The approach of 'institutional thickness' is based on the idea that the economic development process is not the result of a completely endogenous dynamics of the economy, but that it rises from the interaction between the economic and the social system, which are to be considered in their different and also institutional aspects (Rullani, 1998). The 'institutions', as understood according to the approach of 'neo-institutional contractualism', represent the framework that the social and political action creates for ordering the individual behaviour of the economic operators in more or less organized and coherent forms. Therefore, the institutions are not confined in the public sphere, but they emerge in the complex interaction between the individual subjects. Therefore, the institutional thickness has a definite evolutionary character, since the institutional fabric is the result of a long and gradual process of learning or of 'institutional learning'. Moreover, this constant evolution and creation of the different organizations and institutions that integrate and guide a local production system, correspond to the dynamism of the organizational forms in the system of the private firms.

Typical examples of institutions that offer a new decisional infrastructure to the post-fordist economy are the 'collective actors' performing a fundamental role in the implementation of the principle of self-organization. In fact, in the post-fordist stage, public regulation must be, at least partly, transformed into self-government of the (individual and collective) actors, by adopting on a wide scale what, in the institutionalist debate, is called the principle of subsidiarity (Cappellin, 1997; Rullani, 1998). These recent theoretical approaches in the analysis of regional economic development define some important characteristics of a modern regional industrial and innovation policy. The theories of industrial districts and territorial networks underline the development of the territorial 'embeddedness' of production activities. The theories of innovation milieu, regional innovation systems and learning regions underline the importance of promoting the development of interactive learning at the regional level. All these theories underline the importance of the institutional thickness, the development of intermediate institutions and various forms of informal and formal association between the firms and between these latter and the regional institutions.

4.8 THE ROLE OF PROXIMITY AND THE CHANGING NATURE OF LOCAL PRODUCTION SYSTEMS

Given that geographical agglomerations allow different types of networks and different patterns of behaviour and also different forms of learning, knowledge sharing and knowledge creation, geographical proximity per se is not sufficient to generate knowledge between firms. The forms of organized learning differ remarkably between clusters, as the diffusion of knowledge within clusters is highly selective and strongly depends on the position of firms within networks and their absorptive capacity. Geographical proximity alone is only a facilitating factor, and it is neither a sufficient nor necessary condition for promoting cooperative relationships in innovation. Thus, regional policy-makers need to orient the policies aiming at the promotion of learning and innovation in a specific cluster or territorial network in order to enhance the factors associated with various types of proximity, which are different from traditional geographical proximity. A related concept is that of temporary geographical proximity, which is determined by the movements and meetings of the actors when participating in working groups, scientific conferences, industrial fairs and so on, as these movements may be a substitute for the permanent concentration of the actors in the same geographical area (Torre, 2008).

Geographical distance may also represent an obstacle to the interaction between two firms or other economic and social collective actors. However, it may be compensated by organizational proximity (Torre and Rallet, 2005; Dupuy and Torre, 2006; Gherardi, 2006), when these individuals are linked by belonging to the same organization, such as the same firm, characterized by internal routines and procedures, which may facilitate their relationship. Moreover, it may be compensated by institutional proximity, when these firms are linked by the existence of a common institutional framework, made by procedures, contracts, norms, and intermediate institutions that perform the role of soft infrastructures facilitating their relationship.

While these three concepts of distance or proximity refer to external obstacles hindering the relationship between individuals, firms or actors, the internal characteristics of these individuals, firms or actors determine the concept of receptivity. In fact, the existence of objective framework conditions facilitating or hindering the interaction, as indicated by the concepts of geographical, organizational and institutional proximity, should be complemented or compensated by the existence of subjective capabilities leading to the exploitation of these opportunities. Receptivity may also be defined as 'cognitive proximity', since it refers to the similarity of the subjective mental frame of the individual actors considered and of the tacit and codified knowledge owned by these actors, as these characteristics may facilitate the process of interactive learning between them. In particular, cognitive proximity represents a key factor for the extension at the international level of the cooperative relations in the process of interactive learning between the various firms. Thus, while the concept of accessibility refers to that of distance (that is, geographical, organizational and institutional proximity), the concept of receptivity refers to that of similarity (that is, cognitive proximity). The first refers to external obstacles. The second refers instead to internal characteristics.

Accessibility and receptivity represent two complementary conditions that allow the interaction. As indicated by Figure 4.2 in Section 4.2 above, a low accessibility may at least partially be compensated by a high receptivity. On the other hand, a high accessibility or proximity may lead to positive interaction and interactive learning when the receptivity is also adequate, but to a situation of blockade or lock-in and even to conflict, when the receptivity of the two individuals, firms or actors is very low, due to their very different characteristics or due to the high cognitive distance between them. In particular, organizational factors play a different role in the concept of accessibility and in the concept of receptivity, as the analysis shifts from the level of individuals to a higher level of aggregation. In fact, when the analysis focuses on the relationships between individuals, organizational factors are an external condition to these latter and they may determine their organizational proximity, facilitating the relationships between two individuals within a specific organization. On the other hand, when the analysis focuses on the relationships between two organizations such as two firms, organizational factors explain the internal characteristics of these firms and they may be a factor of similarity, which may facilitate their reciprocal relationships or their reciprocal receptivity and cognitive proximity.

Regional innovation systems and territorial networks ensure the advantages of closer geographical, organizational and institutional proximity between the firms belonging to the same regional innovation system. On the other hand, regional innovation systems and territorial networks also ensure the advantage of a higher receptivity or closer cognitive proximity, as the actors may become more similar due to the long-term effect of more frequent interactions. Both the accessibility and receptivity evolve in time and are the result of previous actions. The continuous investment in soft and hard infrastructures is increasing the accessibility between two actors, while their reciprocal receptivity is affected by the gradual development of competencies, which are a result of the processes of interactive learning between these actors.

Thus, regional production systems should be analysed against a historical background and are the result of an evolutionary development. Regional production systems in many countries have evolved from the stage of pure geographical agglomeration of similar firms, working in the same industrial sector and competing with each other, as indicated by the cluster concept. They also often do not correspond to the traditional industrial districts characterized by close production and social linkages between the various firms. Regional production systems have transformed themselves into territorial networks made by specialized and complementary firms and are characterized by a greater sectoral diversification, a greater integration of the various sectors of the local economy and also by an increasing internationalization. In fact, a modern regional production system is not characterized by the geographical concentration of many specialized firms in the same sector, but rather by an increasing diversity and complementarity of the various firms and by the development of external relationships with other regions and countries.

While the models of clusters and industrial districts were characterized by the concepts of sectoral specialization and geographical concentration, the model of territorial networks is characterized by the concept of integration, both between various sectors and between various regions. Key concepts in the model of territorial networks are those of openness, connectivity, integration, synergy and cooperation. Second, the model of territorial networks implies a greater formalization of the relationships between the firms, which were based on trust and personal links in the traditional geographical clusters and industrial districts. Third, the cluster concept has evolved from a predominantly material linkage and agglomeration-based concept to the concept of the innovation network, where the key process is the creation of tacit or codified knowledge in traditional sectors and its diffusion into new fields of production. Fourth, according to evolutionary and institutional economics, innovation networks also represent an institution that supports knowledge generation and the sharing of knowledge or a form of governance enabling the generation and diffusion of knowledge between various local and external actors.

An innovation network is a set of many actors linked by stable, frequent, intense, direct and indirect relationships, which allow flows of intermediate products, human and financial resources, information and knowledge and is facilitated by different forms of proximity and by different forms of soft infrastructures or bridging institutions. In particular, an innovation network is the result of a process of collective learning and of flexible forms of cooperation between many different private and public, regional and international actors, such as large firms, SMEs, suppliers, knowledge-intensive services, higher education and research institutions, financial intermediaries, public administration and many other partners such as professional associations and media. Moreover, the actors of an innovation network may belong to the same or different regions and to the same or various other sectors and they may develop a sense of common identity and a common development strategy. The structure of an innovation network is highly flexible and continuously evolving on the basis of a principle of negotiation between the various actors participating in the network, rather than on a principle of hierarchy or a principle of competition.

Regional production systems in medium-technology sectors are not made only by SMEs, as they are characterized by close relations between large firms and SMEs. Moreover, firms are often different from the traditional SMEs, which only adopt innovation by imitation and adapt to technology transfers from larger firms. Indeed, an increasing share of SMEs consists of innovative and highly specialized SMEs, which closely cooperate with large firms in the framework of highly integrated supply chains and are introducing innovation for adoption by the large firms. Regional production systems are characterized by high mobility and also by high stability. The first is demonstrated by the high turnover within the firm demography, related to the births and the closures of firms, while the second is indicated by the fact that subcontracting arrangements between the various firms require a high interaction and are rather stable when compared with normal commercial relationships.

Innovation is not adopted by SMEs in isolation. Innovation is not the result of the individual inventor or entrepreneur. Innovation requires the combination of different competencies within processes of collective learning. Thus, firms are forced to cooperate in order to increase and diversify their knowledge base. The focus on regional innovation networks rather than on the individual firm in the analysis of innovation processes, highlights new factors that relate to the links between the various firms in a local economy and are crucial in a long-term perspective. In particular, the development of know-how, the transformation of tacit knowledge into codified knowledge, the collective learning processes, the development

Table 4.2   The characteristics of innovation networks

Key Elements and Focus	Innovation Networks	Clusters	Industrial Districts	RIS
Firms	+	+	+	+
Geographical proximity	+	+	+	+
Material relationships	+	+	+	+
R&D and technology transfers	+	–	–	+
Knowledge creation processes	+	–	–	–
Intermediate institutions	+	–	+	+
Strategy	+	–	–	+
Intersectoral character	+	–	–	+
Interregional character	+	–	–	–
Evolution paths	+	–	–	+

of new competencies or skills of the people, the level of switching and adjustment costs in the process of change are all factors that have to be interpreted not only within an individual firm but also from a territorial perspective within a specific network of various firms.

The similarities and differences between the concept of innovation networks and other related concepts in the literature of regional economics are described in Table 4.2. Thus, all these concepts are based on the existence of various firms, of geographical proximity and of material linkages. However, different from all other related concepts, clusters focus on material relationships and do not explicitly consider the role of intermediate or bridging institutions, as does, for example, the concept of industrial districts. Moreover, different from clusters and industrial districts, networks and regional innovation systems consider the existence of R&D investments and technology transfers between the firms. They may have an intersectoral character. They may be capable of developing a common strategy and have an explicit dynamic nature, allowing evolution along specific paths. Finally, the concept of innovation networks differs from all other concepts in the fact that it explicitly considers the cognitive processes of knowledge creation and may have an interregional character. Thus, it perfectly fits into the context of medium-technology industries, as the intersectoral and interregional linkages of knowledge play a major role for the evolution of these industries. The empirical sections in Chapter 3 illustrated that successful medium-tech SMEs typically make use of systemic linkages to other firms or intermediate institutions.

4.9   THE MODEL OF KNOWLEDGE AND INNOVATION NETWORKS

The relationships between the firms become more complex, risky and need to be redesigned in a long-term perspective. This has compelled firms to devise new organizational forms and contractual arrangements, which may be capable of managing these new and more complex relationships. The role of the interactive learning process for knowledge creation and the access to tacit knowledge underline the importance of the concept of knowledge and innovation networks (Powell, 1990; Karlsson, 1997; Scott, 2000; Cappellin, 2002, 2003a; Holland, 2002; Krätke, 2002; Gay and Dousset, 2005; Cantner and Graf, 2006; Grabher and Ibert, 2006; Karlsson and Ejermo, 2006; Wink, 2007, 2008; Van Geenhuizen, 2007; Steiner and Ploder, 2008). In fact, networks are an appropriate form of organization, facilitating the interaction and the flows of information and knowledge. Knowledge circulates within networks through formal and informal institutions. Explicit or codified knowledge may be exchanged on technology markets. Conversely, tacit knowledge requires allocation mechanisms, which are different from the markets, since it has an asymmetric character, implies high risks and requires reciprocal trust, identity and shared values leading to collaborations. Only specific organizations and institutions and not traditional markets are capable of ensuring those connections that allow the exchange and the close interaction of tacit knowledge and competencies.

The structure of a network can be illustrated by the relationships between various actors, which can be classified into six groups: large industrial firms, industrial SMEs, knowledge-intensive business services, financial services, research institutions and public institutions, as indicated in Figure 4.8. These actors correspond to those considered in the empirical analysis of the IKINET project (Cappellin, 2004a). The network relationships between these groups of actors have different intensity and they are mostly hierarchically organized around the large industrial firms. Each group of actors is characterized by very close internal relations and it may represent a sub-network within the overall network. The theoretical model illustrated within this section aims to explain the general characteristics of those networks observed in the empirical analysis and described in Section 4.3. In particular, the structure of a network is characterized by:

- nodes, which may be firms and other private and public actors;
- links, which connect directly or indirectly the various nodes;
- flows, which may be material or immaterial, such as product, services, financial, labour, power, information and knowledge flows;

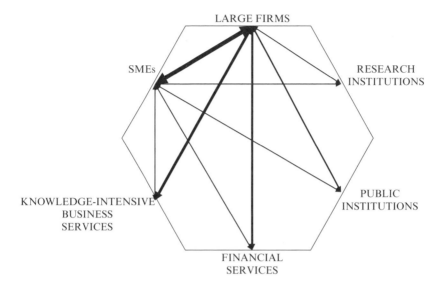

Figure 4.8   Information and knowledge links in a regional innovation system

- distances, which may be geographical but also technological, organizational, cultural, institutional and determine obstacles or transaction costs in the circulation of the flows;
- infrastructures, which may be material or immaterial, such as norms, institutions and social capital, and reduce the transaction costs, thus facilitating the circulation of the flows between the nodes.

Network relations present five characteristics. First of all, the relationship between two nodes is characterized by a precise direction that identifies a relationship of control or of dependence of a node with respect to another node. That implies that the relationships within a network usually have a hierarchical character. Second, each node has a specific function, which depends not only on the relationship with another individual node, but also on its position in the overall network. Third, the various networks are interconnected between themselves, and the relations existing between two nodes in a specific network are normally linked to relations between the same nodes in other networks. In fact, different dimensions of the process of local interaction and of geographical agglomeration can be observed.

Regional production systems are a complex web of different but also interlocking networks, such as the economic networks of flows of intermediate products, networks of labour and capital flows, but also social or friendship networks, institutional or power networks and spatial or physical networks. The networks where tacit and codified knowledge and information circulate are closely related to the networks of material flows ('value chain'), labour flows (professional mobility) and financial flows (credit and equity), and also to the network of power or institutional relationships (multilevel governance). These networks are different in respect of the involved actors, in the spatial extension and therefore also have a different significance in explaining the factors of geographic agglomeration. Some of these networks may be more efficient in some regions than in others. In fact, the failure of many artificial clusters seems to be related to the fact that policy initiatives have concentrated on some of these networks, while being incapable of activating the other types of networks.

Fourth, networks have a different geographical reach. Knowledge flows are more important at the regional level, while the supply chains of material flows are becoming international. The network relations observed in the empirical section reveal that the immaterial dimension is increasingly dominating the material one within local clusters. While the firms have extensive international supplier relations, these latter are becoming relatively weak within the individual region. However, the knowledge-oriented relations of firms are to a large degree regionally concentrated. Thus, supplier relations are more or less separated from knowledge-intensive ones. There is no automatic parallelism of different types of interactions. Fifth, the relations existing within a specific network at a particular time are normally related to the relations existing in the previous periods within the same network, due to the existence of cumulative processes of learning and of path dependence. In fact, networks can be analysed from a dynamic perspective and are characterized by their flexibility. Their evolution (Figure 4.9) is related to:

- the change in the capabilities of the various nodes;
- the change in the intensity of the various flows;
- the creation and disappearance of some links;
- the change in the alternative paths linking directly or indirectly the same nodes;
- the creation of hard or soft infrastructures between particular nodes;
- the path of evolution of the overall structure of the network.

The network approach is very different from the neoclassical approach, which represents the traditional base of economic analysis. Within the neoclassical model of perfect competition the firms are all equal and connected through the anonymous mechanism of the market, while in the model of the networks the firms are all different and integrated between

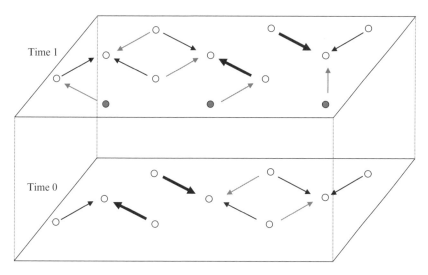

Figure 4.9   The evolution of the network form

them through different types of relations, which have an intentional character. While the traditional neoclassical paradigm underlines the horizontal dimension of the competition between the firms in the market and the process of determination of an equilibrium price, the network paradigm underlines the vertical dimension of the relations of production integration between the firms, which participate in different phases of the value chain. The crucial characteristic of a network of firms is not the concept of equilibrium and disequilibrium, as in the neoclassical model of the market, but rather the concepts of integration, sequential interaction, circulation, diffusion, feedback, recursive processes, symbiosis and co-evolution.

4.10   THE DYNAMIC PROCESS OF INTERACTIVE LEARNING WITHIN NETWORKS

The adoption of a network perspective allows us to highlight some new aspects of the process of technological change. In fact, in a network perspective, technological change may be interpreted as the result of the continuous or gradual search by each node for the most appropriate level and form of integration or cooperation with the other nodes or actors within the network. Technological change is similar to a process of iterative adaptation of the direct and indirect links between any couple of nodes in order to maximize their respective interaction and integration.

As in the model of neural networks, an innovation is the result of an adaptive learning or searching process, which leads to new synaptic connections of various nodes. A scientific breakthrough and an innovation occur when the joint impulses or signals coming from other nodes are not only compatible with the node considered, but also overcome a certain threshold of intensity. That allows the considered node to perceive this stimulus. The node may then decide whether to conflict with it or to adapt to it. If the stimulus is compatible with the existing cognitive system, an interactive processing may lead to identifying an incremental solution to an existing problem and that stimulates the act of innovation. Clearly, time is also a crucial factor as it facilitates perceiving a continuous stimulus or absorbing and adapting gradually to it.

Networks promote interactive learning and evolution. Networks are a form of learning organization that ensure a greater overall dynamic efficiency. While competition and monopoly are static models, networks promote dynamic processes of adaptation, specialization and selection both within individual firms and at the aggregate level between firms. The process of adaptation of the innovative firms to the external stimulus occurs in a gradual form first when the individual firm abandons traditional solutions that are not adequate any more ('creative destruction'). Then, the process of adaptation occurs at the aggregate level through the process of diffusion of the most innovative solutions that have been experimented with success by some innovative firms and are later adopted by the firms lagging behind, leading to the complete abandonment of the most traditional productions.

In particular, the processes of innovation diffusion and adaptation are closely linked to a process of increasing specialization rather than to increasing homogeneity between the actors belonging to an innovation network. In fact, the individual firms have access to external knowledge and transfer their knowledge to other firms. Each firm is led to re-elaborating the new knowledge obtained through the interaction in a different way from the other actors and can focus on a different selected field and generate an innovation. Firms gradually differentiate the products, the areas of overlap between firms decrease and each firm becomes more effective and innovative. The process of selection occurs first ex ante within the individual firms as the result of the explicit technological and organizational choices of the individual firms, which choose temporary solutions to the individual problems through the iterative processes of research and experimentation based on successes and failures. Then, ex post, the success or failure in the market selects the most innovative individual firms. Finally, the process of diffusion of innovation through imitation by the more traditional firms selects the most efficient productions of the considered regional economy, until the less efficient productions have disappeared.

In a dynamic environment the creation of value and of new knowledge depend on the integration of the knowledge acquired from many other firms and the speed of innovation depends on the interaction between a plurality of actors. Due to their flexibility, networks represent the most effective form of organization to promote a fast speed of innovation. In fact, the major advantage of the network model of organization is to ensure to the firms a faster access to a wide scope of complementary competencies existing in other firms and to remove the barriers that are hindering the operation of new products, processes and markets and that could lead to a lock-in situation. Through network integration, firms are capable of decreasing the resources and time for adopting an innovation with respect to the situation where they would be required to develop internal capabilities. This high flexibility is a key competitive factor in a dynamic market, where innovation has to be adopted faster than by competitors.

Thus, networks are characterized by lower 'adjustment or switching costs' (Cappellin, 1983) in the choice of new possible partners. Weak ties or indirect links can easily be transformed into strong ties or direct links when the need to respond to external opportunities and threats makes that necessary. For example, networks allow even SMEs to have access to the global markets, as through indirect links or cooperation with large local or foreign firms it is possible to export and also to produce in remote areas without a direct investment of the firm concerned.

Networks also imply less 'transaction costs' (Williamson, 1981; Cappellin, 1988) in interfirm relationships than a competitive market made by isolated producers and users. Within networks firms can easily change the level of cooperation with previous partners, as implicit contracts can more easily be adapted than formal contracts. Moreover, networks lead the various actors to invest in the creation or strengthening of soft and hard infrastructures and routines linking them. That makes the relationships between firms more intense or increases the speed of the flows between the firms.

From a governance perspective, networks enable that 'ex ante coordination' that is needed for long-term investments and major innovation. Networks facilitate the solution of conflicts between the various firms, which are inevitable in a purely competitive market, thus reducing the costs and risks and the waste of time related to these conflicts and lack of coordination. However, the network model limits the autonomy in decision-making of the individual firm, compared with a competitive market made up of isolated firms, or in a hierarchical organization, such

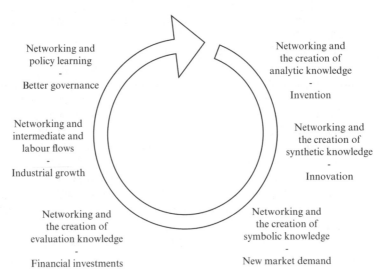

Networking and
policy learning
-
Better governance

Networking and
the creation of
analytic knowledge
-
Invention

Networking and
intermediate and
labour flows
-
Industrial growth

Networking and
the creation of
synthetic knowledge
-
Innovation

Networking and
the creation of
evaluation knowledge
-
Financial investments

Networking and
the creation of
symbolic knowledge
-
New market demand

Figure 4.10   The different complementary networks in the innovation process

as a single large integrated company or an autonomous state. Clearly, within networks decisions depend on an interactive process of negotiation between the various firms and other actors and often develop in time in an iterative way.

The process of innovation may be interpreted as the result of the sequence of various forms of networking, as indicated in Figure 4.10. In particular, the discovery of inventions requires immaterial flows of codified or 'analytical' knowledge. Then, the exchanges of engineering-based or 'synthetic knowledge' facilitate a timely adoption of a technological innovation. Then, the exchange of 'symbolic' knowledge, such as in the creation of new brands, allows a tighter integration with the culture and needs of the users and the growth into new markets and the exploitation of the latent demand in new market niches. Moreover, any innovation requires a greater investment and access by the firms to financial networks, where more evaluation knowledge is needed in order to overcome the asymmetries of information between the firms and the financial institutions. Production innovation requires a restructuring of the traditional flows of intermediate products and services between the firms and implies access to new qualified human resources and a higher labour mobility. Finally, innovation requires the creation of policy networks between the various local actors and flexible institutions and procedures to manage the decision-making process characterized by many interdependent stakeholders.

4.11 THE ROLE OF NETWORKING AND KNOWLEDGE CREATION IN REGIONAL DEVELOPMENT

According to the model of territorial networks, a local production system of firms is similar to a 'complex adaptive system' made by a large number of actors, firms and institutions, which interact in non-linear ways and adapt or learn (Holland, 2002). In particular, as indicated in Figure 4.11, the process of economic development is the result of the close interaction between the following eight blocks of variables (Cappellin, 2003):

- growth of regional output and employment;
- interregional and international networking and competitiveness;
- local networking between the various sectors and firms;
- birth, growth and closure of local firms;
- investments, product and process innovation, productivity increase;

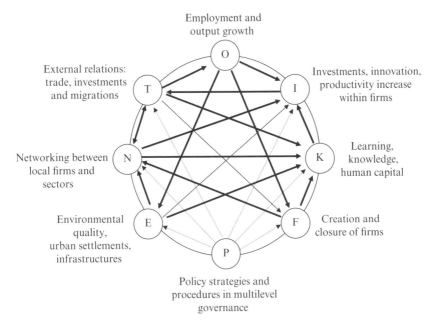

Note: O= output; I = investment; K = knowledge; F = firms; P = policies; E= environment; N = networking; T = trade.

Figure 4.11   Factors and key links in the process of socioeconomic development

- knowledge creation, learning processes, competencies and human capital;
- quality of the physical environment;
- policy framework and multilevel governance.

Increased networking between local firms and sectors promotes interactive learning, knowledge creation and the growth of human capital. These latter processes promote investments, innovation and then productivity increase within firms. That promotes international competitiveness and exports, which determine output and employment growth. This latter promotes the creation of new firms, which further increases the local networks and the process of interactive learning and the growth of local know-how. These latter processes are also stimulated by international openness and contacts with actors external to the region. Environmental quality is affected by the growth of the regional economy and it facilitates the networking between local firms through the provision of infrastructures and it facilitates the growth of knowledge creation by attracting qualified workers in the region. Finally, policies adopted in a multilevel governance framework through the negotiations between the various local actors may affect directly and indirectly all the above indicated variables and processes.

This model may also be used to explain why the openness to the international economy may determine the crisis of a local economy and a spiral of cumulative decline, as often indicated by the critics of the globalization process and exemplified by the case of the old industrialized regions (Figure 4.12) facing a problem of sectorial reconversion. In fact, the withering of the local know-how, due, for example, to the lack of a strong effort in research and professional education may decrease the innovation, the growth of productivity, the competitiveness of regional exports and the production capacities of local industry. It also decreases the birth rate of new firms and increases the death rates of firms, which determine an increase of the financial concentration of the local firms and the weakening of the process of local networking.

The process of globalization and increased international competition may also determine the crisis of some local firms and constrain the surviving firms to deep restructuring processes, with negative effects on local employment. This initial effect may determine a cumulative decline of the local subcontracting networks and of service and industrial firms that are oriented towards the local demand. That decreases the diversification of the local production system and limits the development of the local know-how as well as increases the technological dependence on outside knowledge. Moreover, the crisis of large exporting firms determines a

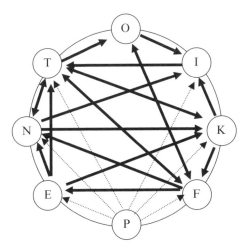

Figure 4.12   Factors and key links in the process of socioeconomic decline

rupture of the links with the international economy, which will make it more difficult to develop forms of international technological cooperation between the firms. This may have a negative impact on the development of the local know-how and innovation capabilities. The closure of firms determines the creation of huge industrial derelict sites and that decreases the capability to attract external investments.

In the case of many economic lagging regions (Figure 4.13), the external financial flows sustain the revenue level and the local demand. This determines the development of local production systems made by service and industrial firms mainly oriented to the local demand rather than to the national or international market. However, the dependence on public resources determines an increase of employment in the public sector, a distortion in the sound financial evaluation of the investment projects and negative effects on the labour ethic and on saving capabilities, spreads at the local level an assistance mentality and patronage practices, and hinders the sense of responsibility of the local institutions and the development of their internal capabilities. This hinders the development of local networking between local firms and institutions and determines a lower cohesion in the local community. In particular, the abundant flows of financial resources transferred to the firms discourage the stimulus to increase productivity and to introduce innovation and determine a decrease of the labour mobility and flexibility. These effects also determine a low sensibility to the problem of the quality of the urban and natural environment and a negative impact both on the capability to cooperate between local actors and on the attractiveness of external private investments. External public

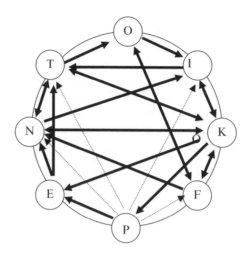

Figure 4.13   Factors and key links in the stagnation of economic lagging regions

funds strengthen hierarchical relations with central authorities, hinder the development of horizontal relations with foreign regions and determine an attitude of closure and international isolation.

The prevailing of a bureaucratic and conservative culture hinders the development of innovation and entrepreneurial capabilities and the creation of new firms. The lack of production diversification of the local economy and the difficulties in cooperation between the local firms hinder the development of interactive learning processes, the development of the local know-how, competencies and technological and organizational capabilities within the firms. The low development of local networks, the limited forms of cooperation with other local firms or organizations and the frequent internal local conflicts and political instability lead to a lengthening of decision-making processes and decrease the pace of innovation adoption and productivity and competitiveness.

From the perspective of the knowledge economy, it is important to facilitate the reciprocal interactions between the process of learning and knowledge creation and all the other variables indicated in Figures 4.11, 4.12 and 4.13. In particular, increased knowledge promotes greater international openness through participation in international innovation programmes and international technology transfers. Increased knowledge promotes regional networking through the diffusion of technology spillover, and it is promoted by the creation of local innovation networks. Increased knowledge promotes the turnover of firms, as it stimulates the creation of science start-ups, while these latter increase the diversity of the industrial environment and stimulate the creation of new knowledge. Finally, increased knowledge promotes investments in structures and the adoption of innovation, as it provides the capabilities to design new projects and it is promoted by the investments in R&D and the demand of new competencies.

4.12 THREE TYPES AND PHASES OF A REGIONAL INNOVATION NETWORK

Regional production systems evolve from the model of industrial clusters and industrial districts based on many rather homogeneous firms linked by flows of knowledge spillover to the model of territorial innovation networks made by complementary specialized firms, which are linked by formal forms of cooperation in production, commercial and technological fields, not only locally but also increasingly at the interregional and international level. Territorial networks may be classified into three types of networks: 'ecological networks', 'identity networks' and 'strategy networks', which have different characteristics, as indicated in Table 4.3. Regional production systems have usually evolved from the form of a simple agglomeration of similar SMEs, such as in so-called ecological networks, to the form of community characterized by intense processes of interactive learning, such as in so-called identity networks, and they may finally evolve to form strategy networks, characterized by an explicit governance of knowledge interactions between the various firms.

In particular, ecology networks are characterized by strong unintended interactions between various actors and facilitate various forms of traded and untraded technological interdependencies or technology spillover, as it occurs in geographical agglomerations. Ecology networks may be assimilated to 'agglomeration economies'. They are made by relationships of objectively observable stable interdependence. They are also based on behavioural adaptation, strong specialization, complementarity and idiosyncratic relationships. Basically, ecology networks are the result of geographical agglomeration and they characterize the areas of concentration of the firms belonging to the same sector, such as an industrial cluster, or also widely diversified areas, such as urban areas (Cappellin, 1988, 2007; Acs, 2002). Information and communication technologies may favour the creation of these types of networks. Ecology networks are the result of external economies, which are also defined as 'localization economies' or 'urbanization economies' and spread in a rather automatic and casual way between the various firms and actors living in a specific local environment.

Table 4.3   Types and phases of a regional innovation network

	Ecological Networks	Identity Networks	Strategy Networks
Type of relationship	External economies	Exchange	Joint investment
Form of interaction	Interdependence	Cooperation	Strategic coordination
Self-consciousness	Objective homogeneity	Subjective factors, intended relationships, sense of identity	Subjective factors, intended relationships, joint aims
Formalism	Informal relationships: imitation	Informal relationships: trust relationships	Formal relationships: contracts
External support	Geographical proximity	Common infrastructures, intermediate institutions and social capital	Joint decision-making and policy-making
Key knowledge base	Symbolic/ synthetic knowledge	Synthetic/ symbolic knowledge	Analytical/ synthetic knowledge
Key knowledge phase	Exploitation	Examination/ exploitation	Exploration/ examination
Knowledge interaction	Knowledge spillover	Interactive learning	TKM and R&D
Differentiation process	Homogeneity	Autonomous specialization	Division of tasks
Innovation	Process	Organizational	Product
New firms	Imitative	More specialized	Innovative
Sectors	Low tech	Medium tech	High tech

Identity networks are based on the sense of identity and common belonging, on the existence of trust relationships and specialized inter-mediate institutions ('social capital'). They may be defined as places of collective learning, where the development of common production know-how occurs. Typical cases of such community networks are the industrial districts or the regional innovation systems. This subjective element distinguishes them from ecology networks. Thus, community networks require the sharing of a homogeneous culture, common values and the development of common production know-how. However, they lack the capability of central coordination and strategy-making.

Strategy networks are based on intended relationships and cooperative agreements between firms and other organizations. They are the result of negotiations, agreements on specific strategies and the creation of formal and explicit joint ventures by the participating actors. Strategy networks also imply the reciprocal commitment of specific resources, which are invested in order to achieve common goals and future but uncertain benefits. They imply forms of central coordination, the creation of procedures for the exchange of information, the codification of individual implicit knowledge and the joint investment in the creation of collective codified knowledge. Strategy networks may be represented both by widely geographically dispersed strategic alliances made by a pool of large and small firms in different regions or by local clusters and regional innovation systems that explicitly want to become a 'learning region'.

These three types of networks are characterized by different forms of knowledge interactions. In fact, knowledge spillovers characterize the ecological networks, interactive learning processes characterize the identity networks and explicit governance of knowledge relations between the various local and non-local actors is a characteristic of strategy networks. Moreover, it is useful to distinguish three types knowledge (Asheim and Coenen, 2005; Asheim, Boschma and Cooke, 2007), such as: (1) the science-based or 'analytical' knowledge that is important in high-tech sectors, (2) the engineering-based or 'synthetic' knowledge that is most important in medium-technology sectors, and (3) the creativity-based or 'symbolic' knowledge that is most important in low-technology sectors. In fact, each of these three types of knowledge is important in each of the three types of territorial innovation networks indicated above, as indicated in Table 4.4. However, the governance of knowledge interactions within the various types of networks implies an appropriate balance of the different types of knowledge.

In ecological networks, such as the traditional clusters in their initial phase of the life cycle, both the synthetic and the analytic knowledge circulate in a rather automatic way or without any explicit design. This may be facilitated by the existence of general infrastructures and services, such as the proximity to universities, and by the imitation of the best practices in contiguous firms. In the case of identity networks such as the most developed industrial clusters, the firms are intentionally participating in interactive learning processes, aiming at the creation of synthetic knowledge such as in the framework of traditional subcontracting relationships of a supply chain. In this case, specific types of analytic knowledge may diffuse from some technological and scientific infrastructures such as technology transfer centres for the industrial SMEs. Identity networks can improve the innovative capabilities and international competitiveness of European medium-tech SMEs, as they can promote informal forms of cooperation

Table 4.4   The knowledge flows in different types of networks

	For ecological networks	For identity networks	For strategic networks
Symbolic knowledge	Localized knowledge spillover, labour mobility, competitors imitations	Interactive learning within professional communities	Interdisciplinary integration and collaboration
Synthetic knowledge	Localized knowledge spillover, labour mobility, competitors' imitations	Interactive learning between SMEs and with clients	Technological collaborations within the supply chain
Analytic knowledge	Localized knowledge spillover, university education	Technology transfers from universities and service centres to SMEs	Joint R&D projects and networks of centres of excellence

with universities in order to combine the characteristic strong base of synthetic knowledge with elements of analytical knowledge.

Finally, the shift to the model of strategy networks implies the design and creation of specific infrastructures, institutions and procedures that may facilitate the knowledge flows. These policy measures may be represented by the 'territorial knowledge management' (TKM) and the 'competence centres', in the case of synthetic or engineering-based knowledge, and by international integrated projects and networks of excellence, in the case of analytic or science-based knowledge. Specific joint projects can facilitate the medium-technology firms in organizing the partnership and knowledge flows with institutions and organizations having strong competence in symbolic and analytical knowledge. Thus, politics and public institutions have a crucial role in enhancing the exchange of knowledge between different industries, the universities and other R&D organizations and in promoting the evolution of a cluster from the form of an ecological network to that of an identity network or a strategic network, which is in fact characterized by the identification of common aims and culture.

4.13   THE ROLE OF INSTITUTIONS IN KNOWLEDGE INTERACTIONS

Development processes do not take place in a vacuum but rather have profound institutional and cultural roots (North, 1990). The central issue of economic history and of economic development is to account for the evolution of political and economic institutions that create an economic environment that induces increasing productivity. Institutions define and limit the set of choices of individuals. They include any form of constraint (formal and informal); they can intentionally be created or they may simply evolve over time. Economic development is stimulated in those territories with highly evolved, complex and flexible institutional systems. Barriers that hinder self-sustained growth processes frequently appear due to deficiencies in and poor performance of the institutional network. Training and research institutions, entrepreneurial associations, unions and local governments can more efficiently use available resources and improve competitiveness when firms are integrated into territories characterized by thick relational networks. New institutional theory argues that the strategic significance of institutions in development processes lies in the economies that their functioning provides, as institutions:

- generate external and internal economies of scale;
- reduce transaction and production costs;
- increase trust among economic and social actors;
- favour economies of scope;
- improve entrepreneurial capacity;
- increase learning and relational mechanisms;
- reinforce networks and cooperation among the actors.

A nation can be maintained only if there is interposed a whole series of secondary groups, called 'intermediate institutions', between the state and the individuals, which are near enough to the individuals and are capable of attracting them strongly in their sphere of action. The diffusion of knowledge and the creation of innovation in a specific network or sectoral/regional/national innovation system depend on the 'institutional thickness' of the innovation system to be considered. In particular, a wide range of institutions is required in the process of innovation:

- Regional governments are required to attract external investments, to coordinate large strategic projects and to promote the birth of new firms and entrepreneurial capabilities.
- Local governments are required for effective territorial planning and for the creation of efficient transport and logistics infrastructures.
- Local credit institutions are required for the financing of innovative projects by existing firms and to enhance the creation of new firms.
- Local education institutions, such as vocation training and university institutions, are required for the identification of the labour

skills required by new technologies and for maintaining the traditional productive skills in a given territory.

- Labour agencies or trade unions are specialized institutions that are required for an effective management of the local labour markets and to facilitate the interaction between the supply and the demand of labour, the wage negotiation procedures and the management of the 'welfare' system.
- Chambers of commerce and industry associations are major partners in promoting a regional innovation system and in the identification of the strengths and weaknesses as well as of the strategic lines of competitiveness and development.
- Finally, the local and regional authorities may encourage constructive interactions between firms and discourage opportunistic behaviour by supporting institutions that promote their collective interest. They may provide financial and technical support to companies, specialized infrastructures, information systems or training programmes for particular industries.

Institutions have a key role in the process of innovation. In contrast to traditional linear innovation models, modern theorists argue that the process of innovation is highly interactive and is dependent upon social and cultural institutions and conventions (Morgan, 1997). The stock of knowledge grows through learning processes that are interactive and influenced by the institutional set-up regarding their content, rate and direction. Thus, institutions have a key role in the process of innovation and in the generation and working of 'knowledge and learning networks'. Institutional arrangements are important for the generation of knowledge and learning networks as they (Lawson and Lorenz, 1999; Maskell, 1999):

- reduce the uncertainty about the experiential knowledge of others (of other companies, research institutes and so on);
- raise the specificity of development, processing and diffusion of knowledge within the network to strengthen incentives for the participants to concentrate their investments in the network and protect new knowledge against competing networks;
- increase incentives for medium- and long-term investments into diffusion channels – for example, common codes, products, fora – between the different participants in a network;
- develop and adapt research, production, distribution and after-sales strategies and increase the absorptive capacity of new information by the other participants.

Cognitive theories underline the fact that creation of new connections or the reinforcement of existing connections implies compatibility with other actors, success in the adaptation and the development of appropriate routines and institutions. The role of institutions is to create new routines or baselines that ensure the adaptability of connections between actors (Hayek, 1952). In fact, the speed of the information flows and decision-making processes is closely connected to the stability of the organizational forms, rather than to the flexibility of labour. The existence of a well-developed institutional system made by various structures and infrastructures facilitates relationships and decreases transaction costs. The stability of the networks is ensured by the existence of adequate hard and soft infrastructures representing a public good and being not only created by the individual actors themselves but also by the public authorities. Rules, procedures, organizational forms, norms and routines constitute the foundation of organizational behaviour. In a way it is paradoxical that the focus on economic change goes hand in hand with a growing interest in institutions. Therefore, a central concern of policy should be the creation of institutions that may enhance the connectivity of knowledge.

In general, the challenge of the emerging 'knowledge economy' (Lundvall, 1992; Lundvall and Johnson, 1994; Abramowitz and David, 1996; Foray and Lundvall, 1996; OECD, 1996; Morgan, 1997; Maillat and Kebir, 1999; Karlsson and Johansson, 2006; Karlsson and Andersson, 2007) indicates the need to design new institutions capable of governing the relationships between the various actors. In fact, the main argument of the approach of institutional economics as indicated by Ronald Coase and Oliver Williamson can be summarized as follows: the market is not the optimal mode of coordination for each and any economic transaction, because there are other modes of coordination that may produce lower transaction costs. The exchange of knowledge cannot be effectively coordinated by conventional markets. In particular, whereas, in principle, explicit and codified knowledge may be traded on markets, tacit knowledge is non-tradable and requires non-market allocation. Knowledge is channelled within networks by formal and informal institutions, for instance within the firm, in the context of interfirm networks or forms of cooperation between private agents and public institutions. Because of the specific character of technological knowledge, its asymmetric and tacit character transactions between organizations and individuals have to be mediated by non-market methods, primarily through networks and other forms of arrangement and procedures, which build trust and work to limit the damaging consequences of asymmetric information. So policy may support clusters by reducing transaction costs (Williamson, 1981).

The role of institutions refers to the reinforcement of identity and reciprocal trust. These factors limit the disadvantage related to the asymmetric circulation of information by reducing uncertainty and the risks that are due to the impossibility of foreseeing the effects of innovation, and increase the incentive for medium- and long-term investments. Clear examples are the creation of various forms of communication channels, such as the norms, technical standards, protocols, associations between the participants in a network and also the investments in continuous education, which increase the receptivity to new technologies by the various local actors.

Besides formal institutions the concepts of trust and social capital are increasingly being applied in attempts to understand the underlying institutional features of clusters and networks. Social capital (Putnam, 1993, p. 196) according to one popular definition:

> refers to features of social organization, such as trust, norms and networks, that can improve the efficiency of society by facilitating co-ordinated actions. Social capital can be seen as a conceptualization of the glue that facilitates transactions, cooperation and learning in an uncertain world.

Social capital represents an asset that may become increasingly important in the emerging context of the learning economy. In fact, the generation and transmission of new forms of tacit knowledge is facilitated and may even be conditioned by a certain level of social capital. Moreover, in a globalized world of freely moving capital and increasingly freely moving people, only social capital remains tied to specific locations. In fact, the 'learning economy' is characterized by the 'hypermobility' of the information and knowledge and the local character of the social capital.

In particular, clusters and networks should be interpreted as learning organizations and among the non-market devices by which firms seek to coordinate their activities with other firms and other knowledge-generating institutions. They can be regarded as economic clubs acting to internalize the problems of effective knowledge transmission and are a substitute both for formal markets and organizational integration. Thus, clusters and networks can be regarded as a form of Coasean institution (Coase, 1992) that tries to integrate the positive external effects of innovation, technological knowledge and development activities (Coleman, 1988; Keeble et al., 1999; Lagendijk and Cornford, 2000). As the connectivity of knowledge is particularly decisive for synthetic knowledge, which is typical of medium-technology industries, the institutional settings contribute in a very specific way to the emergence and growth of medium-technology sectors. It is no wonder that countries with a long-lasting national and regional institutional framework like the Scandinavian countries, Germany or Austria (Hall and Soskice, 2001) reveal a continuously strong performance in medium-technology industries, while the United Kingdom or the United States with their strong focus on markets and individualistic decision-making lost huge parts of their medium-technology sectors.

4.14 GOVERNANCE AS A DISTINCT MODEL OF REGULATION

In a developed market economy, many economic relations are not regulated by the market competition between firms producing the same products (Williamson, 1981; North, 1990). Neither are they regulated by the norms defined by the state or by the internal rules within a large company. In fact, many economic relations are regulated by negotiations, agreements and forms of partnerships between the firms working in different sectors and between various economic stakeholders characterized by different capabilities. Thus, market competition, state norms or internal corporate organization and networks or multilevel governance represent three different and complementary forms of regulation of economic relations in a market economy, and innovation policies can adopt these three forms of regulation in order to promote international competitiveness of a modern industrial economy.

The multiplication of the players and the layers of negotiation at the international, national and local levels demands a different model of regulation, called governance, based on organizational structures of interaction and partnership and this model increasingly characterizes national economies and even more local societies. In fact, the relationships between the national and the regional public administration, and between them and the various private actors, may be interpreted according to the organizational paradigm of the network. In general, the design and implementation of innovation policy needs to tackle the problem of the architecture of the institutional framework and to solve those policy issues that occur in the organization involving: relationships between the centre and the periphery, the public and the private sector, the firms and the workers and the various external stakeholders, the world of production and that of financial intermediaries, the public centres for technology transfer, private knowledge-intensive services and last but not least the integration of the economic and technological perspective with a social and institutional perspective. On the one hand, within the firms the governance of the innovation processes consists in the decisions on the integration or the outsourcing of specific activities, and also on acquisitions of other firms, on the sale of specific internal non-core activities and on the creation of alliances with other firms. These decisions by the firms do not usually depend on the policies of public authorities, while they are affected by the investment strategies of large corporations, banks and private equity funds. On the other hand, governance at the collective level consists of promoting changes in the connections within regional or sectoral innovation networks, allowing the participation of new actors to the decision-making processes, the empowerment of individual actors and assigning to them specific responsibilities and the development and organization of the human and financial resources needed for the innovation process.

There is a variety of governance concepts in the field of economics, spatial planning and political science. Governance is a general concept for the management of interdependencies among individuals, collective and corporate actors (Van Kersbergen and Van Waarden, 2004; Kaiser, 2008). First, governance as a descriptive term denotes the fact that collective decision-making in modern Western societies is taking place today less frequently in the form of hierarchical order by governmental authorities, but increasingly by network arrangements of public and private actors who negotiate cooperative solutions. This indicates that there has been a shift from 'government to governance' (Boyer, 1990) as non-hierarchical modes of governing characterized by the involvement of non-state actors in the formulation, decision-making and implementation of public policies gain importance. The literature on governance explores how the informal authority of networks supplements and supplants the formal authority of government. The governance concept addresses the need to manage interdependent activities of a variety of actors vertically across different territorial levels as well as horizontally across different decision-making arenas (Héritier, 2002). Rhodes (2008, p. 1246) defines governance as follows:

1. Interdependence between organizations. Governance is broader than government, covering non-state actors. Changing the boundaries of the state meant the boundaries between public, private and voluntary sectors became shifting and opaque.
2. Continuing interactions between network members, caused by the need to exchange resources and negotiate shared purposes.
3. Game-like interactions, rooted in trust and regulated by rules of the game negotiated and agreed by network participants.
4. A significant degree of autonomy from the state. Networks are not accountable to the state; they are self-organizing. Although the state does not occupy a privileged, sovereign position, it can indirectly and imperfectly steer networks.

Thus, governance refers to governing with and through networks (that is, 'network governance'). In fact, some governmental action or a 'shadow of hierarchy' may be a precondition for prompting industry to engage in self-regulation or sectoral governance (Héritier and Eckert, 2007).

The increasingly close linkage between organizations in civil society and the state and the development of policy networks (Marsh and Smith, 2000) is an important element of the 'shift' towards governance and it characterizes almost all countries. This new multistakeholder dialogue in most modern economies, not only in continental European countries but also in the United Kingdom and United States, may include not only individual companies, employers associations and trade unions, but also a wide variety of civil society organizations, alliances and networks, operating locally, nationally and across borders. This includes thematically organized business networks, business intermediaries, NGOs, community groups, think tanks, foundations, research institutes and academic institutions, local, regional and national public institutions, authorities and governments, regional and international multilateral governmental organizations.

In synthesis, we may define governance as a model of regulation of the relationships between the firms and the actors belonging to a network, based on interdependent adjustments decided on the basis of negotiation procedures. Governance differs both from the spontaneous interaction between atomistic behaviours funded on the individual interest and competition, as in the free market model, and also from the changes enforced by a centralized authority as in the government model. Governance is the challenge of steering and positioning complex policy networks made by many different actors at the international, national and local level through complex organizations and forms of horizontal and vertical negotiation. The main challenge of governance is therefore to establish procedures that

> sustain coordination and coherence among a wide variety of actors with different purposes and objectives such as political actors and institutions, corporate interests, civil society and transnational organizations. What were previously indisputably roles of government are now increasingly seen as more common, generic, societal problems which can be resolved by political institutions but also by other actors. (Pierre, 2000, p. 4)

Moreover, governance cannot be considered as a purely local process, but as a multilevel process that develops through territorial and functional networks, transversal policy networks, the proliferation of technical bodies, distributive coalitions and organized economic groups at the international, national and local levels (Hooghe and Marks, 2003), as indicated by the so-called 'open method of coordination' (OMC) (Kaiser and Prange, 2004). Up to now, governance has become especially relevant within the complex negotiation and decision-making system of the European Union.

In the European Commission's White Paper on European Governance of 2001 working group report, governance is defined as the 'rules, processes and behaviour that affect the way in which powers are exercised at European level, particularly as regards openness, participation, accountability, effectiveness and coherence' (European Commission, 2001, p. 8, fn. 1). Thus, in many European and non-European countries, innovation policy does not only consist in the public financing of research activities, it also aims to promote the creation of regional clusters of innovative activities; on the one hand, and to enhance the internationalization of local firms and their links to international innovation networks on the other. According to a multilevel governance approach, industrial policies should not only orient the medium-term strategies of the individual firms and their internal technological innovation; they should also promote organizational innovation in the international relations between the various firms and the development of new relations.

Different aims and policy tools may be relevant at different levels. Thus, at the European level, the increasing interdependence of highly integrated markets leads to the need for a European competition policy and authority. On the other hand, at the national level, new institutions may be represented by national strategies, programmes and laws that mobilize complementary flows of public finance. Third, at the regional level, policy-making may be characterized by the design of specific regional projects, the creation of new 'intermediate' institutions between the state and the individual actors and flexible forms of public–private partnership.

There is a large variety of modes of governance of knowledge relations. These forms of dynamic coordination range from coordinated transactions and constructed interactions to quasi-hierarchies (Antonelli, 2005). For example, the following organizations represent different governance modes:

- large 'networks of excellence' between research institutions and research groups;
- international and interregional agencies;
- large multinational companies and financial groups' cross-participation between firms;
- joint projects between national and foreign firms for new productions and new technologies;
- committees, norms and technical standards between the firms of the same sector;
- vertical sectoral clusters of firms in the same supply chain;
- industry and professional associations;
- cultural and professional associations, scientific associations;

- professional communities of practice;
- local networks, communities or industrial districts;
- local stakeholders' coordination tables and territorial pacts with local actors;
- regional innovation strategies (RIS) and territorial knowledge management;
- forms of public–private partnership and strategic planning contracts with large firms;
- poles of competitiveness and centres of competence.

According to an evolutive approach the policy-maker should not optimize a specific objective function, but rather promote the variety, diversity and creativity, the adaptation to the market stimulus and the exploitation of technological opportunities through the creation of an innovation system made by various institutions and open to the external world. A new innovation policy should not be based on a 'prescriptive' approach but rather on a 'transactive' approach, as the most important problem is not 'what to do' but rather 'how to do it' and 'with whom'. The policy-makers should identify key stakeholders and act on the transaction costs in order to promote the best internal integration in the relations between the various local actors and a greater openness toward the external actors. Innovation policy does not only concern the development of technologies but also the role of institutions and organizations. Rather than to optimize a specific goal, policy-makers should focus on the promotion of creativity, the adjustment to the market stimulus, and the exploitation of technological opportunities through the creation of a national or regional innovation system made by a set of various institutions and open to the international economy.

In particular, the governance of an innovation network, especially in a regional and urban framework, requires that the policy-makers search for a flexible balance between the apparently contradictory characteristics and processes of the 'identity networks' and the 'strategic networks', such as the choice of:

1. homogeneity between the various actors within the network versus diversity and specialization of the complementary competencies and characteristics of the individual actors;
2. thickness of the network or tight integration between the various actors versus leadership and relative isolation of the nodes characterized by outstanding excellence;
3. hierarchical coordination between the various nodes versus preservation of the autonomy of the various actors, characterized by

distinctive competencies and roles, to avoid forms of collusion and ensure flexibility;

4. explicit top-down cooperation between the various actors versus complex negotiation procedures, which aim to mediate recurrent conflicts of interests between the actors.

Hall and Soskice (2001 and 2003) in their edited volume, *Varieties of Capitalism*, contrast the case of so-called coordinated market economies, such as the Scandinavian countries, Germany, Austria and Switzerland, France, Italy and also Japan, with liberal market economies (United States, United Kingdom, Australia, Canada, New Zealand and Ireland). They argue that the technological specialization patterns of developed countries are largely determined by the varieties of capitalism prevailing in these countries. They hypothesize that 'liberal market economies' (LMEs) specialize in radical innovation, while 'coordinated market economies' (CMEs) focus more on incremental innovation. In CMEs:

> [F]irms depend more heavily on non-market relationships to coordinate their endeavours with other actors and to construct their core competencies. These non-market modes of coordination generally entail more extensive relational or incomplete contracting, network monitoring based on the exchange of private information inside networks, and more reliance on collaborative, as opposed to competitive, relationships to build the competencies of the firm. . . . the equilibria on which firms coordinate in coordinated market economies are more often the result of strategic interaction among firms and other actors. (Hall and Soskice, 2001, p. 8)

While this approach can be criticized on many grounds (Akkermans, Castaldi and Los, 2007), our research illustrates that since the exchange of tacit knowledge cannot be effectively coordinated by conventional markets, the density of intermediate institutions plays a major role in the concentration of medium-technology sectors in coordinated market economies, and also in the progressive de-industrialization from these sectors in liberal market economies.

The management of interdependencies among individual, collective and corporate actors in coordinated market economies or in corporatist societies is different from the government and also the market models, as actors are entitled to autonomously regulate important aspects of sectoral and economic development according to principles of vertical and horizontal subsidiarity. In particular, neo-corporatist arrangements (Lehmbruch, 1977; Schmitter and Lehmbruch, 1982; Streeck and Kenworthy, 2005) are based on social groups that are entitled to various forms of collective participation and self-government. Corporatism has the distinction of generating 'institutionalized patterns of policy formation in which large interest organizations cooperate with each other and with public authorities' (Lehmbruch, 1977, p. 92). In highly coordinated market economies, the state and intermediary organizations play an important role in processes of exchange between economic actors. In some cases those actors are entitled to autonomously regulate important aspects of societal and economic development (that is, technical standardization) and thus establish 'private interest governments' (Streeck and Schmitter, 1985). Moreover, the debate on corporatist versus market systems, or coordinated versus liberal market economies can be related to the fact that all LMEs are common law countries and all CMEs are civil law countries (Pistor, 2005), as this link between legal and economic systems is due to social preferences, basic norms or ground rules, found in substantive and procedural laws of different countries.

Sorge and Streeck, for example, identified this influence as the main reason why German industry reached a comparative advantage in the field of 'diversified quality production' (1998). Thus, the sectoral specialization in medium-technology sectors organized in the form of networks of SMEs is closely related to the existence of a complex system of intermediate institutions made up of local chambers of commerce, territorially and sectorally specific industry associations, trade unions, professional associations, public vocational schools, local universities and research organizations, local banks, and so on, and to the adoption of the governance model of social and institutional relations, which characterizes specific regional innovation systems in so-called coordinated market economies. On the contrary, the adoption of a free market model rather than a governance model is closely related to the lack of significant clusters in medium-technology sectors and the large trade deficits in these sectors, which characterizes most 'liberal market economies'.

4.15 THE DIFFERENCE BETWEEN THE GOVERNANCE, FREE MARKET AND GOVERNMENT APPROACHES

Multilevel governance depends on complex policy networks. It is different both from the free market model and also from the traditional top-down planning approach. Thus, multilevel governance is the most appropriate form of regulation of the complex relationships in the innovation and knowledge networks of medium-technology sectors. The three different models focus on three different instruments for the organization of the economic relations between two actors, such as the mechanism of

Table 4.5   Forms of organization and regulation of economic relationships

	Government	Free Market	Governance
Principle	Authority	Competition	Partnership
Aim	Order	Equilibrium	Agreement
Information provided	Regulations	Prices	Contracts
Instruments of organization	Control and adaptation	Price-taking	Negotiation and leadership
Individual motivation and behaviour	Respect of authority	Autonomy, exit or conflict	Trust and bargaining
Complexity	Hierarchy	Individualism	Interdependence
Factor of efficiency	Economies of scale	Perfect mobility and flexibility	Transaction costs and adjustment costs
Interdependence	Vertical integration	No external economies	External economies
Number of actors	Individual actor	Infinite number	Limited number
Level of integration	Maximum integration	Minimum integration	Intermediate integration
Field of action	Sectors	Markets	Policy networks
Problems addressed	Authoritarianism	Monopoly	Conflicts of interest
Corrections to problems	Democracy	Antitrust policy	Specialization and dynamic coordination
Political ideal	Egalité	Liberté	Fraternité
Juridical base	Civil law	Common law	Self-regulation and subsidiarity
Area of relevance	Any state and corporations	Liberal market economies	Coordinated market economies
Goods	Scale-intensive goods	Commodities	Specialized goods
Factor of competitiveness	Economies of scale	Lower prices	Time advantage
Type of innovation	Radical innovation	Incremental innovation	Systemic innovation
Knowledge base	Basic research	Codified knowledge	Tacit knowledge
Time framework	Static	Static	Dynamic

regulations and top-down coordination in the hierarchical model, the mechanism of prices in the market model and the mechanism of contracts and agreements in the governance model. The differences between these three forms of organization and regulation of economic relationships are indicated in Table 4.5.

In the 'government' model, decisions are taken by a public authority and enforced on the basis of a principle of authority. The hierarchical model explains the regulation of economic relationships by the state but also within the large individual firms. On the other hand, the free market model is based on the principle of competition, and it advocates that 'the best policy is no policy' and public intervention leads to distortion of the efficient allocation of resources automatically insured by the market (Bianchi, 1995). Third, the governance model is based on the principle of partnership and agreement between various actors, which, reciprocally, are recognized and legitimized.

Moreover, different behavioural mechanisms and motivations characterize the three models of regulation: norms, control and respect of authority and adaptation characterize the hierarchical model of government; freedom, competition and conflict and exit characterize the model of free market; and trust, negotiation and leadership characterize the model of governance.

While most of the political science literature investigates the comparison between governance and government (Rhodes, 2008), an economic perspective leads to focus on the problem of the respective advantages of the governance model and the free market model in the regulation of economic relationships in a modern capitalist system: an issue that characterizes the current debate on privatization and marketization.

Different from the other regulation models, in a market model the actors refuse to obey and also to agree and they prefer to compete with each other. The actors adjust their willingness to supply and demand goods or services in response to the price signals generated by markets. Markets are self-regulating. The coordination of economic relationships may be indirectly or automatically performed by the market, which assigns production to the most competitive firms as the result of the competition between the many existing suppliers and of the optimal choice by the many possible users. On the other hand, in a governance model, the coordination is the result of the negotiations and explicit agreements between a limited number of individual stakeholders.

The expression 'governance' is used with respect to decision-making systems where the decisions are taken according to open forms of collaboration between a plurality of public and non-public actors, which may differ between the various specific areas of policy intervention and between the various levels of government. The decision-making processes may include forms of horizontal and vertical negotiation, where the exercise of a hierarchical control is only one of the components and most often not the major one. Governance refers to the non-hierarchical model of governing characterized by the involvement of non-state actors in the formulation, decision-making and implementation of public policies (Kaiser,

2008). Governance is about network arrangements of public and private actors that negotiate cooperative solutions. It is a model that may not require the presence of a public institution ('governance without government'). The governance model is also related to the adoption in the public administrations of novel practices and tools or new forms of coordination and cooperation of different levels of government and as private sector organizations and social actors in order to guarantee a more efficient public service or the availability and quality of services (Salomon, 2002).

The governance model represents the result of the adaptation to a continuously changing environment, rather than a deliberate change of strategy. Thus, it is embedded in the ongoing structural dynamics that are largely common to all European countries. It is now widely recognized that the interventionist top-down model ('government') in the innovation policies is neither possible nor desirable, since innovation by its very nature cannot be reduced to command, it has a proactive character and is open to new discoveries. Moreover, the dirigist approach of the 'welfare state' should be changed into an approach based on the concept of partnership and subsidiarity. This is particularly decisive for medium-tech industries, as they are made by many different actors, who would hide their knowledge in the case of a command-and-control approach. Thus, a governance approach is needed to promote the sharing of the necessary information between all participants, as it has already been the experience in the internal coordination through 'knowledge management' within large multinational firms (Gherardi, 2006; van Geenhuizen, 2007).

The governance approach in policy-making is closely related to innovation, as this latter erodes the disciplinary borders and internal hierarchies that characterize the government model. For example, Schumpeter's creative destruction clearly determines conflicts and does not respect consolidated hierarchies. It is also closely related to the internationalization process, as this latter undermines the closure and hierarchies and erodes the regulation capabilities of the states. Moreover, the internationalization of economies insures to the innovators the freedom of exit from those hierarchical organizations, where they cannot accept a dependent role.

However, a free market approach, based on price regulation, is also not appropriate to tackle the issue of innovation. A governance model represents a change from a market-driven model and it seems to correspond to a new phase of development, where technology has an increasing systemic dimension, rather than a single firm perspective and the speed of adoption of innovation has become crucial rather than the decrease of production costs, as in the competition between the firms. These changes require a greater integration of the various actors and the emergence of networks between them.

The distinction between the governance model and the opposite models

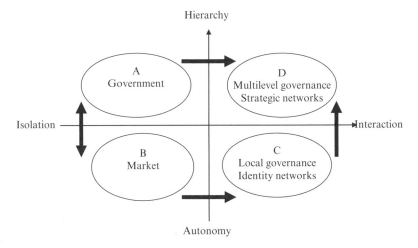

Figure 4.14   The evolution in the relevance of four organization modes

of hierachical organization in the state and in large firms ('dirigism') and perfect competition between many small firms ('economic liberalism') can be interpreted on the basis of their respective position in two major dimensions: 'hierarchy versus autonomy' and 'isolation versus interaction' (Figure 4.14). The first dimension measures the power of the central authorities versus the freedom of the various firms and individuals. The second dimension indicates that the governance model is characterized by a higher level of explicit economic interdependence and it implies the sharing of common values and a sense of belonging. Both the government model and the free market model imply the absolute isolation of each individual: either before the law and regulations, defined and enforced by the state and the directors in a firm, or within the market, as firms are price-takers in a perfect competitive market and no external economies exist. Both the network model and the free market model are based on the principle of autonomy. However, the aspiration for a greater autonomy does not contradict the need for a greater integration, which in fact implies the freedom by the actors to interact with various actors and to make many different combinations of complementary competencies.

Therefore, various recent changes that characterize medium-technology sectors, such as:

- the evolution in technology;
- the increasing complexity of the factors determining the innovation processes;

- the need to integrate complementary technologies;
- the changes in the industrial organization of firms;
- the increasing international competition; and
- the increasing international interdependence of the actors and the firms

seem to indicate the shift from a hierarchical approach to a 'bottom-up' approach that emphasizes individual freedom, as indicated by the arrows in Figure 4.14. At the same time there is also a greater need for a shift from individual innovation to a systemic process of innovation, based on the integration of various and complementary actors and leading to a wider adoption of the governance model. Moreover, the increasing perception of the negative effects of globalization and the unregulated market mechanism advocates a greater role for the state. This determines a cyclical shift between the market model and the state model. Thus, the increasing complexity and interdependence of innovation processes lead to assigning, in various cases, a greater role to national and European initiatives in the governance of knowledge and innovation networks.

In particular, a free market approach advocates measures such as deregulation, privatization, selection of individual projects, autonomy of individual groups of actors and creation of competitive arenas. On the other hand, a governance approach is based on negotiations and agreements between the local and external actors, regional decentralization, the creation of 'communities' and forms of partnerships. The governance model implies the existence of intermediary functions, a greater stability, a long-term perspective and the supply of adequate public investments. This promotes flexibility and innovation. This is particularly decisive in cases of medium-technology innovations, as trust based on long-term relationships and social capital is needed to overcome the fears of the single organizations to be exploited. For medium-tech SMEs, international cooperation would be much harder to handle if they had to continuously consider the risks of losing their secrets and being withheld from the specific tacit knowledge of their foreign partners. Within a governance approach, however, they would be able to assess the risks of international cooperation and look for ways of being protected by institutional frameworks and negotiations.

Industrial activity is certainly enhanced by a favourable local and national environment and it may be hindered by too high taxes and too complex public regulations, as indicated by a free market approach. However, a favourable macroeconomic or external environment is not sufficient to promote innovation, as any innovation depends on knowledge creation and this requires intense interactions between different partners and complex combinations of complementary knowledge. A neo-liberal model advocates a greater wage and labour flexibility and greater competition as the panacea to every economic problem. However, in a modern knowledge economy the concept of innovation seems more important than that of price flexibility, and the concept of integration of the various economic actors appears more crucial than promoting the already high competition in the national and international markets. While the free market model advocates only more competition and more flexibility in any case, the network and governance model focuses on the need for a greater integration between the economic actors and a faster innovation. Thus, the governance model implies the existence of intermediary functions, a greater stability, a long-term perspective and the supply of adequate public investments.

Governance aims to decrease the transaction costs between the actors and the adjustment costs to new technologies (Williamson, 1981; Cappellin, 1983, 1988), thus promoting a higher speed of change. The governance of innovation processes helps to tackle those problems that hinder the speed of innovation, such as bottlenecks, missing links, inertia, resistance, corporate rigidities, collusion, privileges and rents and redistributive inequalities, to overcome fragmented decision-making and to reduce organizational conflicts between the various actors. In fact, regional industrial and innovation policies should aim for a faster speed of innovation and a higher growth rate of the labour productivity. Only the growth of productivity and increasing international competitiveness of regional industrial production may lead to higher production growth and to greater or stable employment.

The free market model leads to competition in a horizontal perspective. However, it does not prevent forms of collusion and quasi-integration in a vertical perspective and between different sectors. In fact, in many modern capitalist economies in Europe, the various forms of collusion between firms, in the bank, insurance, industry, media sectors, through direct and indirect financial links and the exchange of positions between the boards of these organizations, and the tight personal relations between the representatives within the various industry associations and with the world of politics determine pervasive conflicts of interest between the supplier and the user, the controlled and the controller. They are also one of the main reasons for the increasing income disparities and giving specific groups of actors an advantage over other actors. A market that operates freely without rules inevitably leads to collusion and concentration of the economic and financial power within just a few actors. Too free or unregulated market competition leads to mergers, acquisitions, monopolies, increasing disparities between insiders and outsiders, concentration, collusion, corporate rigidities and rents. The free and unregulated market concept is most often an argument for preserving the freedom to collude not only within the same sector but also across sectors, as firms expand externally and diversify into disparate activities and sectors, in industry, service and finance, creating overlapping fields of activity and causing the emergence of conflicts of interests and lack of focus. Forms of intersectoral collusion or integration represent a danger and create a rent situation. Intersectoral integration leads to conflicts of interest and endangers that 'separation of power' that is the basis of a pluralistic democracy, as in Montesquieu's principle of separation between legislature, executive and judiciary power. In fact, totalitarianism occurs when all political and economic power is concentrated within a single group of actors or ruling class. The more developed a society the greater should be the division of labour between sectors and also the division of powers between the different firms and organizations.

These collusions are aimed at short-term financial profits and at defending and exploiting specific rent positions. They represent the major obstacle to long-term systemic or intersectoral innovation and diversification in European industry, as new innovative initiatives could conflict with the incumbent organizations and could undermine the existent power alliances between them. Clearly, SMEs in medium-technology sectors are excluded from these exclusive networks and are hindered in their diversification and growth. In fact, as indicated by the interviews in the empirical investigation described in the third chapter, the relational skills of an entrepreneur in external relations with clients, suppliers, service providers, financial institutions, industry associations and the capability to solve the related economic, financial and legal problems are probably more complex and important factors of success in innovation than the technological and organizational capabilities, the relations with the employees or the relations with the public institutions.

These forms of intersectoral collusion cannot be tackled by traditional competition policies and require a broader governance of the relationships between the various economic actors. Regulation or governance is required in a network in order to prevent vertical and horizontal integration and collusion that may damage other actors. Regulation allows separation of functions and recognition of the respective legitimacy of each actor and avoids confusion of roles. Indeed, the network model is based on the principle of specialization as each node should perform a different function or role within a network. In a network model the relationships between actors are based on monetary or real exchange, negotiation, but also on specialization, division of labour and separation of roles and of activity, in order to avoid conflicts of interest. Governance should ensure the separation of the fields of activity of the different firms and organizations in order to prevent conflict of interests and to ensure a system of checks and balances. Relationships in a network should be based on negotiations and agreements and neither on competition leading to conflicts or to the defeat and exclusion of some actor, nor on hierarchical power relationships leading to integration or collusion. Governance enhances the combination of complementary capabilities on the basis of public and transparent negotiations and agreements. In fact, on the one hand innovation breaks the order of the hierarchy, and on the other it requires close and long-term cooperation between different and complementary actors, which is not ensured by the individualism, the conflicts and also the collusion characterizing a free market.

In conclusion, each model of regulation of the relationships may lead to problematic situations and require adequate instruments to correct them. Democracy avoids the problem of authoritarianism in the government model. Competition or anti-trust policy is required to avoid collusion and monopolies in the free market model. Governance avoids the problem of intersectoral collusion and conflicts of interest in the case of networks. The governance model promotes the integration of the various autonomous economic and institutional actors and enhances the development both of the market relationships and a pluralistic democracy. The procedures of negotiation in a governance model link the major economic and institutional actors through an interactive and sequential learning process. Both market and hierarchies clearly still continue to exist, but they are both working within the framework of decision processes having a negotiational nature.

4.16 THE MAJOR ADVANTAGES OF THE GOVERNANCE MODEL FOR PROMOTING INNOVATION

Both large and small firms cannot easily introduce innovation without cooperation with external actors in medium-technology sectors. Innovation, and also knowledge creation, are not the result of an individual firm or of a single person, but of the interaction between various economic actors or stakeholders, such as the people within individual firms or the relationships between various firms. The most important innovations, which may lead to the creation of new sectors or new firms in the local economy, are the outcome of the joint activity of various actors and not of an individual entrepreneur. Thus, governance or the choice of how to regulate the relationships between the various firms and economic actors has a key impact in determining the success of an innovation network. The systemic character of innovation networks requires a dynamic coordination between the firms based on a gradual and cumulative process of interactive learning. In fact, the adoption of a modern governance approach, based on regional decentralization and public–private partnership, seems more appropriate for promoting knowledge creation, innovation and competitiveness than free unregulated competition or state planning.

The governance approach is closely related to the model of knowledge and innovation networks. Governance also deals with the adoption of organizational arrangements or different mechanisms of regulation to manage the knowledge relationships between various actors who participate in the process of knowledge creation and innovation. Knowledge networks are characterized by a high flexibility and are continuously evolving (Cantner and Graf, 2006; Cappellin, 2002, 2003a; Gay and Dousset, 2005; van Geenhuizen, 2007; Grabher and Ibert, 2006; Karlsson, 1997; Holland, 2002; Karlsson and Ejermo, 2006; Krätke, 2002; Powell, 1990; Scott, 2000; Steiner and Ploder, 2008; Wink, 2007, 2008). The governance of knowledge networks requires the change in the links between the various nodes and the change in the intensity of the flows between the nodes of these knowledge networks. This process of change is similar to Schumpeter's process of 'creative destruction' and it implies the link to new nodes and the exclusion of others for integrating new specific complementary competencies. In particular, knowledge and innovation networks are characterized by an evolutionary process leading both to a greater integration and to a greater specialization of the individual nodes. Thus, the governance of a knowledge network aims to facilitate a continuous change of the internal form and of the borders of the knowledge networks. Both the hierarchical model and the competitive model are static and based on the assumption that demand and technology can be easily foreseen, while the network model is more suitable to the actual dynamic environment, which requires flexibility and a fast adaptability to unanticipated changes both in the demand and in technology. These changes imply the need both for a high autonomy and also for a high integration of the various actors. Neither the dirigist procedures imposed by public authorities nor the price mechanism of a free market can organize the complex relationships between the actors, which are required for major innovation and lead to a cumulative process of increasing specialization and increasing integration between the various actors.

In particular, economic theory illustrates various limits of the free market model and various reasons explain why the model of 'multilevel governance' is more adequate for managing innovation processes than the free market model:

1. Innovation has distributive effects: governance avoids conflicts and promotes inclusion.

Innovation is based on the asymmetric diffusion of information and it creates increasing disparities between insiders and outsiders or between winners and losers, which might cause conflicts. While the market model is based on the value of competition and conflict and leads to an increase of disparities, the governance model aims to facilitate conflict resolution and the inclusion of those who lag in innovation. In fact, governance is the means through which individuals and institutions, public and private, manage their common affairs within a continuous process of cooperation and composition among various and conflicting interests that threaten to undo or upset opportunities to realize mutual gains. Governance enables the achievement of compromise solutions between the various actors and regulates the distribution of costs and benefits of joint complex projects made by several specific measures, thus attaining Pareto optimal solutions through the compensation of the interests negatively affected by some specific policy measure through the positive effects on the same actor of other compensatory measures.

2. Free market competition does not consider actors' interdependence; governance promotes connectivity, specialization and integration.

The market model focuses on atomistic decisions and competition and is based on the hypothesis of complete autonomy of individual actors. However, a firm is an organization and a structure of relationships between shareholders, managers, workers, suppliers and clients. Connectivity is the prerequisite for the division of labour, the specialization and integration of various production phases and labour competencies. The processes of innovation are closely related to the increasing division of labour. In particular, Adam Smith ([1776] 1976) wrote that the most important form of division of labour is the division of knowledge. An increasing labour division requires a framework, such as institutions, that allows the connection of the contributions of different firms and actors. Thus, governance aims to solve the systemic problems of the firms and to promote the connectivity, accessibility and receptivity between the various firms, institutions and the different actors in the economy.

3. The free market approach does not consider information asymmetries and opportunistic behaviours; governance facilitates the flows of tacit knowledge.

Free market competition is based on rational behaviours and on the absence of transaction costs, but individuals only have partial access to information and may take inappropriate decisions. Thus, governance allows better access to information, making it easier for the individuals to develop rational decisions. Moreover, knowledge, which is more complex than information, circulates within networks through formal and informal institutions. Explicit or codified knowledge may be exchanged on technology markets. Instead, tacit knowledge requires allocation mechanisms that are different from the markets such as governance, since tacit knowledge implies asymmetric information and high risks and it requires reciprocal trust, identity and shared values, allowing collaborations, in order to avoid opportunistic behaviours, adverse selection and moral hazard.

4. The model of perfect competition is a static model; governance decreases adjustment costs and promotes higher speed of change.

The neoclassical model of perfect competition is a static model and it may be used to analyse comparative static problems. It focuses on price competition and presupposes complete flexibility and mobility, which are actually hindered by various obstacles and adjustment or switching costs. Instead, in a knowledge economy, competitiveness is based on time and a faster adoption of innovation with respect to the competitors. In particular, time competition requires a higher speed of information flows and of decision-making processes. However, speed of change is closely related to the stability of organizational forms. Thus, governance and a well-developed institutional system, made by immaterial structures and infrastructures, facilitate the relationships between the various actors participating in the innovation process, reduce the switching or adjustment costs and facilitate the adaptation of the economy and the individual firms.

5. The free market approach supposes perfect forecasting capabilities and aims for short-term results; governance reduces risks, enhances trust and long-term investments.

As the free market model is based on the value of competition and conflict, it induces individual firms to maximize short-term advantage and does not consider repeated interactions between the actors of the economy, which justify a collaborative strategy. On the other hand, the approach of multilevel governance is based on the concepts of institutions, identity and trust, which decrease the uncertainty and the risks related to the unforeseeable results of innovations. While the free market model does not take into account the uncertainty of future predictions, governance allows ex ante coordination when the decisions of specific actors depend on complementary decisions by other actors. Institutions and governance are crucial to adopting a long-term perspective and they increase the incentives to invest in medium- and long-term projects such as those in pre-competitive research, the creation of diffusion channels of information or in education, which may increase the receptivity to innovation by the various actors.

6. The model of perfect competition aims to reach static general equilibrium solutions; governance aims to steer the process of evolution of organizational structures.

The existence of a stable equilibrium, as in a perfect competitive model, is challenged by continuous pressures that the external environment exercises on the individual firms and by continuous processes of evolution, adaptation and selection in the economic system. Actors do not choose according to a long-term maximization model; they adopt sequential choices based on reactions of the other actors to previous actions and opportunities occurring in the market. Governance allows escape from completely casual outcomes or from deterministic paths and aims to steer the relationships between the various actors, thus leading to gradual steps towards predetermined general goals.

7. Free market competition leads to concentration and oligopolistic structures; governance aims to remove barriers, conflicts of interests, rents and challenges to established power structures.

Free market competition leads to an excessive diversification of actions by some actors into new disparate fields, thus determining forms of collusion and frequent conflicts of interests between the controlling and the controlled actor or the producer and the user. On the other hand, governance promotes pluralism of actors and a mechanism of checks and balances in the economy and in policy-making. It induces a higher specialization and integration between the various actors in the economy.

In conclusion, the development of the process of interactive learning and knowledge creation requires institutions and governance. However, the evolution of institutions and the various forms of governance in the field of innovation policies at the regional and national level are also the result of policy learning processes. In fact, industrial and innovation policies in the various manufacturing and service sectors, both medium-technology sectors and high-tech sectors, should combine two very different models of regulation, which are not necessarily conflicting with each other, such as the enhancement and regulation of competition between the firms, aiming to decrease market prices on the one hand, and a greater integration of the various actors in the economy to promote the creation of knowledge and a faster adoption of innovation and changes in a wide perspective on the other.

4.17   LEVELS OF INTEGRATION, SPEED OF CHANGE AND THE EVOLUTION OF THE KNOWLEDGE ECONOMY

Free market, governance and government are three different forms of regulation of economic relationships characterized by different levels of integration. The liberal free market approach, which implies atomistic or autonomous decisions by the individual firms and the role of the 'invisible hand' of the market, represents the lowest level of integration. Conversely, the hierarchy model, where the relationships between the actors are very close and have to comply with the indications of a superior power, which may be the state or a large integrated company, represents the highest level of integration. Thus, the networks of firms, which are highly specialized in specific production phases, represent an intermediate case based on a principle of negotiation and cooperation.

The concept of innovation underlines the importance of time advantage, as is indicated by various concepts, such as just in time, lead time, time to market, speed of change, speed in decision-making and coordination and time lags in the adoption of innovation. The level of integration implicit in various forms of regulation and the various speeds of change and creativity may be related as is represented by Figure 4.15. In fact, on the one hand, a too high competition between the local firms hinders the possibility of combining their limited resources. Individual firms, both SMEs and large firms, may have internal creative capabilities, but their speed of innovation can be reduced by the fact that they cannot find internally all competencies required to respond to an external stimulus. That leads firms to create alliances or to merge with medium-sized firms, which may play a key role in steering local clusters and promoting creativity and a long-term strategy.

On the other hand, a too high integration, such as in a large firm or in hierarchical supply chains, which are vertically integrated by a leader firm, may be less capable of exploiting the potential of creativity than a network. In fact, a very large firm created by disparate business areas may be rather closed to external stimulus and external competencies. Therefore, outsourcing of non-core productions and the focus on those areas where the firm enjoys a technological advantage would be the most efficient strategy of the firm. In fact, peripheral technologies may be core

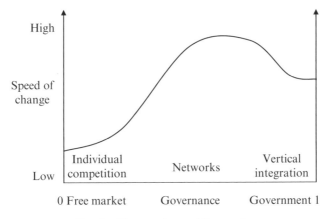

Figure 4.15   The relationship between increased connectivity and creativity

activities for another firm and large firms are increasingly investing in other firms or have created flexible alliances or networks with other firms to accelerate the rate of innovation. Thus, an intermediate level of integration may ensure a higher speed of innovation than the extreme cases of individual isolated firms and a vertically integrated large firm. A network organization allows firms to have easy access to rare complementary competencies of other local firms, thus increasing the capability to respond to external stimuli, to exploit external opportunities and to face external threats, leading to higher creativity and speed of change.

Networks may represent a form of organization or a governance structure that is more effective in promoting creativity or knowledge creation, than both a pure competitive market and a hierarchical organization. Creativity, continuous change and innovation require interactive learning processes between many different actors, and the cooperation between various firms is more efficient than the two extreme situations of the isolation of the individual firms competing one with the other or of the consolidation of all production into a large firm where the relationships between actors are regulated by a central authority. New institutional and organizational structures are needed in order to facilitate the structural adjustment to a knowledge economy, enhance social interactions and accelerate the speed of the process of adoption of innovation. Governance plays a key role in determining the flexibility of an innovation network and in reducing the 'switching costs' or adjustment costs of innovation, thus avoiding the risk of a lock-in effect in territorial clusters and promoting a horizontal and vertical diversification of the traditional productions in these clusters.

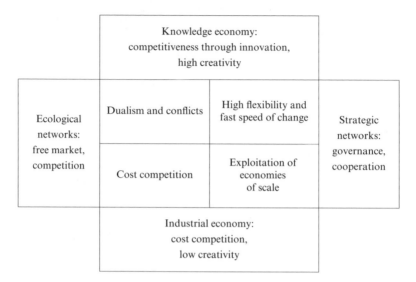

Figure 4.16   High flexibility requires both high creativity and strategic governance

In particular, the shift from an industrial to a knowledge economy implies a change from cost competition to time competition, which is based on innovation and creativity. The governance of knowledge and innovation networks allows a higher connectivity than in a free market framework. That favours creativity and leads to higher flexibility and faster speed of change, as indicated in Figure 4.16. Instead, a pure free market framework would lead to an increasing divide between the insiders and the outsiders and to potential conflicts, which would slow down the process of change. Thus, an inclusive strategy may reveal itself to be more appropriate in order to promote sustainable change in the long term. In fact, the speed of the information flows and the decision-making processes is directly connected with the formalization of the network relationships and the design of contractual forms between the firms, the financial sector, the research and education institutions. Flexibility and innovation speed are related to the stability of the organization forms and the relationships between the various economic actors.

The competitiveness of SMEs in medium-technology sectors depends on (Cappellin and Orsenigo, 2000):

- the process of interactive learning;
- the speed of change and the adoption of innovation;

- the forms of social and economic integration between the local actors ('embeddedness');
- the international and interregional openness of the regional economy;
- the quality of the territory and the investment in the improvement of physical infrastructures and of the institutional framework.

This requires that a modern regional innovation adopts a system approach capable of integrating different policy fields: industrial and innovation policies, research policies, labour policies, social policies, education policies, territorial and infrastructure policies, environmental policies. However, different from a traditional planning approach aiming at 'holistic' plans, a governance approach to innovation policies should be capable of integrating the various regional policies in different but closely connected domains within specific 'action plans'.

A modern regional innovation policy should work on the supply side and aim to improve the capabilities and the receptivity of the firms in participating in the process of competition, rather than work on the demand side and regulate the competition, such as national competition policies. Moreover, innovation policy should also stimulate the demand for new products and services through specific regulations, which may aggregate diffused latent needs, or through procurement by public organizations. It may facilitate the relationships between the demand and the supply, as the process of interactive learning between producers and users has a key role in the creation of new knowledge and innovative products and services. In particular, the perspective of the knowledge economy and a multilevel governance approach seem to imply a change in the policy aims, instruments and decision-making forms with respect to those prevailing in traditional industrial and innovation policies. As indicated in Table 4.6, the key differences seem to be the shift:

- from a strategic top-down to an heuristic bottom-up approach;
- from focus on codified knowledge to the focus on enhancing interactive learning processes;
- from a firm and sectoral perspective to a territorial and institutional perspective;
- from a focus on the supply side to a focus on the demand side and on political and institutional procedures;
- from simple R&D financing to a wider integrated approach aiming to integrate industrial policy with other economic policy domains;
- from a linear approach aiming at the automatic diffusion of technologies to a policy aiming to enhance the innovation capabilities

Table 4.6   The differences between innovation policies and knowledge policies

Innovation Approach	Knowledge Approach
Adopt a strategic approach (top-down: structural, vertical, static, harmonization) in knowledge creation and diffusion	Adopt a learning heuristic approach (bottom-up: system, horizontal, dynamic, evolution) in knowledge creation and diffusion
Focus on codified knowledge/ information and technology diffusion: output indicators	Focus on the development of know-how (tacit knowledge), on enhancing the interactive learning processes, and embedded capabilities (skills, competencies): input indicators
Adopt a firm or a sectoral/ technology perspective	Adopt a territorial/regional and an institutional perspective. Create a 'national/ regional innovation system' and promote institutional building and learning through the creation of new procedures, intermediate institutions and also new forms of relations between public institutions.
Focus on the supply side or the increase of the production capabilities	Focus on the demand side or on the satisfaction of the new needs of society (well-being, welfare, identity, social cohesion, living environment, sustainability, and so on) and on the political/institutional procedures ('how to do' rather than 'what to do', institution building rather than strategy design, the problems of conflict management, consensus, values, identities, ethical issues)
Concentrate only on R&D financing and on financial support to research institutions and high-tech sectors	Adopt a wider policy agenda and an integrated approach aiming to integrate other economic policy domains (labour market, education, industrial, regional, trade policies, and so on)
Promote the diffusion and imitation of the top end actors/ leaders, aiming to decrease the existing divides, according to a 'linear approach' to technology transfers	Promote also the development and inclusion of the bottom end actors/ followers, according to a 'systemic approach', considering also intermediate technologies, SMEs and the enhancement of medium- or low-qualified workers, while focusing on the role of key nodes and links in the knowledge networks

of the actors lagging behind ('outsiders') and to the identification of the key nodes and links ('insiders') in wide knowledge and innovation networks.

4.18   THE EVOLUTION OF INDUSTRIAL CLUSTERS TOWARD THE 'LEARNING REGION'

The factors of competitiveness of a cluster have changed and are no longer the economies of scale external to the firm and internal to the cluster leading to lower production costs, but rather a faster speed of change or rate of innovation. Defining a region as a 'learning region' means that the actors of the system are committed to an interactive learning process allowing the development of knowledge, know-how and other capabilities required for creating innovation and maintaining regional competitiveness (Maillat and Kebir, 1999). The objective of a learning region is the integration of tacit or traditional production knowledge, which is bounded within the local context, with the codified knowledge available at the world level, in order to stimulate the regional endogenous potential. A learning region may represent the final outcome of the evolution of an industrial district, which undergoes an ongoing evolution thanks to the active role of the processes of learning, adaptation and innovation within the network of local actors.

The knowledge base of clusters specialized in medium-technology industrial sectors mainly relies on synthetic knowledge or engineering-based knowledge. However, the increasing complexity of technology requires a broadening of the scope of the technologies to be adopted and indicates an increasing relevance of integrative technologies (von Tunzelmann, 1998; Benzler and Wink, 2005; Bergek et al., 2008; Quintana-Garcia and Benavides-Velasco, 2008). Traditional boundaries between pure and basic research and applied research can no longer hold and medium- and high-technology knowledge should be connected in industrial products. This means the need to connect synthetic or traditional engineering and problem-solving knowledge with analytical or science-based knowledge, through a greater investment in explicit R&D activities (Asheim and Coenen, 2005; Asheim, Boschma and Cooke, 2007). This underlines the strategic value of improved relationships between industrial firms and research institutions. Industry-based and innovation-oriented models of cooperation usually focus on a small number of key companies and research institutions, on the basis of a particular overarching theme. They are highly flexible instruments, aimed at providing short- and medium-term solutions to project-related research and development problems.

However, the transfer of scientific knowledge to SMEs requires a long-term effort for strengthening the multi-dimensional and multi-institutional regional knowledge infrastructure and for increasing the receptivity of firms through job qualifications and further training and education.

Moreover, the increasing complexity and differentiation of needs by the users require that firms improve their cognitive proximity to the users. The more radical an innovation the more important it is to change the cognitive perspective of the customers on needs and solutions so that they will be satisfied by the innovation. Consequently, knowledge exploitation requires a perspective on potential customers, their hidden needs and channels to reach them. This requires investing in the design, the perceived quality and the brand value of the product or services and improving the relationships between the industrial firms and the modern knowledge-intensive business services (KIBS) (Muller and Zenker, 2001). Thus, symbolic or creativity-based knowledge has to be combined with technological excellence or synthetic knowledge.

The limits of the traditional industrial clusters are underlined by the fact that the linkages between SMEs in the process of interactive learning within a cluster are often informal, rather chaotic and time-consuming. This highlights the need for an explicit effort to be devoted to the organization of knowledge networks and knowledge interactions between the firms and specialized suppliers, clients, knowledge-intensive services, research institutions, public administration, other local organizations and many other external actors. The shift from an industrial economy, where competition is based on costs, to the model of the knowledge economy where the key factors of competitiveness are innovation and creativity, can be analysed from the perspective of the shift from a model of automatic free market interdependence, as in 'identity' networks, to a strategic model, as in the 'strategy' networks. Figure 4.17 illustrates this shift.

Traditional industrial clusters, such as the 'identity networks', usually base their competitiveness only on traditional technologies and cost advantages related to spatial agglomerations of firms and informal cooperation between the firms. The spontaneous interaction between firms within the clusters may facilitate the SMEs only in the adoption of process innovation. However, this facilitation causes the risks of lock-in in traditional productions and technologies. From the perspective of a knowledge economy, identity networks at least imply, as indicated above, interactive learning and incremental innovation. However, regional production systems may evolve toward the form of 'strategy networks' that are based on intended relationships and formalized cooperative agreements between firms and other organizations. Strategy networks imply forms of central coordination, the creation of procedures for the exchange of information,

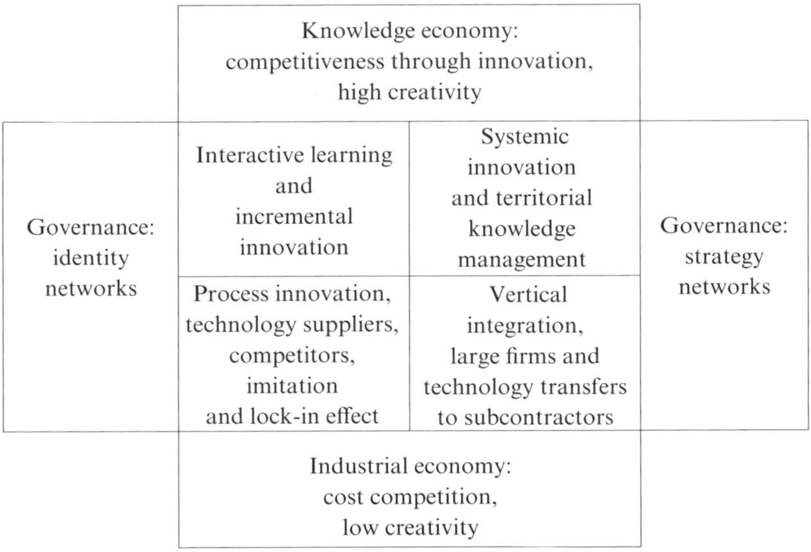

	Knowledge economy: competitiveness through innovation, high creativity		
Governance: identity networks	Interactive learning and incremental innovation	Systemic innovation and territorial knowledge management	Governance: strategy networks
	Process innovation, technology suppliers, competitors, imitation and lock-in effect	Vertical integration, large firms and technology transfers to subcontractors	
	Industrial economy: cost competition, low creativity		

Figure 4.17   From an industrial to a knowledge economy in medium-technology clusters

the codification of individual tacit knowledge and the investment in the creation of collective codified knowledge. In a traditional industrial economy, a more strategic coordination and formal forms of cooperation would lead to a consolidation of the SMEs into larger medium-sized firms or to forms of quasi-hierarchical integration of the supply chain under the control of one single large firm. Within a knowledge-based economy, however, such concentration could diminish the diversification of ideas and creativity of the single parts. Thus, instead of traditional ways of control within a strategic process, strategic governance is needed. The model of 'territorial knowledge management' aims to formulate a theoretical framework for such a governance to enhance the adoption of systemic innovations, which are based on the coordination of the investments made by various SMEs and are focused on strategic joint projects.

4.19   THE APPROACH OF TERRITORIAL KNOWLEDGE MANAGEMENT

'Territorial knowledge management' (TKM) is an operational framework that aims to organize the cognitive relationships between the firms in the process of innovation within a local network or cluster (Cappellin, 2003b,

2007; Wink, 2003; Harmaakorpi and Melkas, 2005). TKM serves to facilitate the flows of tacit and codified knowledge. This approach is highly flexible and can be adapted to various European clusters. Territorial knowledge management aims to make the organization of knowledge interactions more explicit and formal. In a traditional production system, the required information and competencies are often only circulating in a too implicit, complex and slow process. Territorial knowledge management may be defined as the policy that aims to promote the innovation potential, the competitiveness and the development of clusters and firm networks through an appropriate management of the interactive learning processes leading to the creation of new knowledge.

Therefore, TKM represents a new approach to the local innovation policies that represents an evolution of the approach of 'regional innovation strategies' (RIS) and is different from more traditional approaches such as financial incentives to R&D, technology transfer centres, science and technological parks, incubators of innovative firms and venture capital. For medium-technology industries, TKM offers specific advantages, as it serves to overcome the barriers of knowledge interactions caused by the low formality and non-codification of tacit knowledge. These barriers have been so far the main hindrances for many European medium-tech industry firms to gain access to international knowledge networks and pipelines.

While traditional knowledge management focuses on the transformation of individual tacit knowledge into corporate codified knowledge, territorial knowledge management looks for the transformation of the internal knowledge of various firms and regional actors into localized collective knowledge to be shared between all actors of a sectoral/regional cluster. TKM also aims to facilitate the acquisition from outside the region of knowledge, which can be combined with internal knowledge and may be crucial for the competitiveness of the regional production system considered. More generally, TKM aims to facilitate the process of interactive learning through the governance of the cognitive relationships in a network of local actors.

Traditional knowledge management aims to measure the monetary value of the various forms of knowledge existing within a firm through various, mostly quantitative indicators, but the models of knowledge management are neither capable of identifying how the new knowledge is being created nor how from this knowledge value may be created. Knowledge is not a stock or production factor, which can be bought and sold on the market, but rather it is the activity of knowing or a process of learning. Thus, territorial knowledge management follows a cognitive rather than an accounting approach and its aim is to explain the key factors leading to the creation of knowledge and how the firms may create value from knowledge through innovation.

The framework of TKM is rather general and it can be applied to different types of networks and different types of knowledge flows, such as, for example, in the case of the governance of networks of firms in various industrial or service sectors, in clusters with low or medium or high technological levels or also in the case of the professional networks made by skilled workers.

In particular, TKM aims:

1. To promote the creation of the 'territorial knowledge capital' (TKC), by accelerating the speed of circulation of information between local actors and between these latter and external actors, thus avoiding lock-in effects and managing the six levers to be described below. Territorial knowledge capital represents a form of collective tacit knowledge and is the result of the original combination of the 'human capital' of the individual workers and of the 'intellectual capital' of the various firms rather than being the summation of these two components.

2. To extract the value of territorial knowledge capital through the enhancement of innovation, which is the key factor for the competitiveness and growth of a regional economy.

3. To create new innovation networks within the regional innovation system and to guide the creation of new formal and informal institutions, infrastructures, norms, rules and routines, which enable the governance of the innovation networks and the interactive learning processes.

4. To provide a quantitative accounting framework to measure the local strengths and weaknesses from the perspective of the knowledge economy.

The approach of territorial knowledge management is based on the concepts of cognitive economics such as the concepts of networking and integration, interactive learning and knowledge creation. This approach highlights (Cappellin, 2007) that there are six dimensions or drivers that represent key necessary conditions for the development of interactive learning processes within a network and the creation of new tacit and codified knowledge:

- external stimulus;
- accessibility;
- receptivity;

- identity;
- creativity;
- governance.

These six factors allow us to focus the various policy instruments for the governance of the learning networks in a regional innovation system on a limited number of dimensions, which are closely related to the factors of the processes of knowledge creation according to the literature in cognitive economics.

The relationships between these dimensions of the knowledge creation and innovation process are indicated in Figure 4.18. In particular, the external stimulus induced by the opportunities of the demand, the pressure of competition or the change in technologies determines a tension leading to the search for a solution of the problems of the firms. This searching process is facilitated by a higher accessibility to potential complementary partners, and it also requires an appropriate receptivity of these latter. The creation and strengthening of a common identity, made by common values and sense of belonging, is the prerequisite for the cooperation and the search for joint solutions. These latter are the result of creative capabilities and the original combination of different and complementary pieces of knowledge through a process of interactive learning between various local actors. Finally, new ideas can be translated into economic innovations only through an appropriate organization and governance, which implies the commitment of appropriate resources and the integration of the new ideas with complementary production capabilities.

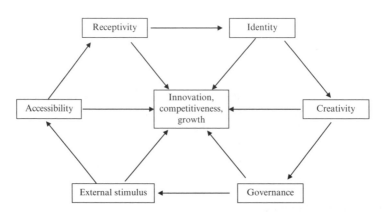

Figure 4.18   Territorial knowledge management as a framework for the governance of regional knowledge networks

The approach of TKM indicates the cumulative nature of the process of interactive learning, adoption of innovation and building of new competencies, as the various phases indicated above feed back on each other. The new knowledge created and the experience developed in previous periods affect the receptivity of the various actors to new ideas and also their capability to understand the emerging needs of potential users. Thus, the development of the internal capabilities of the individual actors is affecting the future evolution path of the innovation system considered.

4.19.1 Promotion of Innovation Stimulus

SMEs are characterized by close user–producer relationships. Innovation is the result of the adaptation to new needs and market demand, to changes in competition conditions and also to breakthroughs in technology. These factors represent external threats to be tackled or opportunities to be exploited and motivate action by the firms. Innovation aims to solve specific urgent problems that call for a solution and motivate investment in the iterative search for different complementary competencies. Firms are stimulated more by the risk of survival determined by the selection mechanism characterizing highly competitive markets than by the explicit aim to find a profit maximization solution on the basis of analytical reasoning. Moreover, innovation in SMEs can be stimulated more by projects aiming to respond to new needs and demands of the user side and to the creation of new 'lead markets' rather than by the aim to commercially exploit new technological discoveries. Tacit knowledge is crucial in this phase since the capability to identify problems, recognize new needs and business opportunities and to identify the appropriate responses to them is based on personal experience and capabilities.

4.19.2 Improvement of Accessibility

Accessibility is related first of all to 'geographical proximity'. Adequate transportation infrastructures, logistics and modern management methods and ICT may favour the development of the relations between the various actors and firms in the local economy, by reducing both the costs of physical mobility and the 'transactions costs'. SMEs are strongly embedded in their territory, which is characterized by the integration of cognitive, economic and social relationships. The role of tacit factors is underlined by the fact that the forms of interaction between the actors are often informal and based on social relationships, rather than on formalized procedures, as within organizations. Thus, the access to external complementary competencies requires not only transportation and communication infrastructures but also 'soft infrastructures', such as knowledge-intensive business services and 'bridging' institutions, which may improve the 'organizational/institutional proximity'.

4.19.3   Management of Receptivity

The 'openness' of the various actors and nodes within the knowledge and innovation networks should be enhanced in order to avoid lock-in effects in traditional competencies and to alert them to the need of accessing complementary external knowledge and assimilating it. Receptivity to external stimulus is related to the specific capabilities of the two partners in a relationship, allowing them to combine internal knowledge with external knowledge. In fact, geographical accessibility or proximity is a necessary but not sufficient condition for interaction or connectivity, and it should be integrated with receptivity or the availability of specific competencies by the two actors of the relationships, thus determining their complementarity, potential synergy and reciprocal attractiveness in terms of exchanging products, services, funds and people. Thus, interaction may be hindered not only by 'geographical distance' or by low organization/institutional proximity, but also by high 'cognitive distance', which is determined by differences in the education level and cultural background, the lack of sharing of mental models, the different sectoral or technological specialization, the lack of broad diversified experiences and low learning capabilities.

Receptivity depends on various forms of 'tacit knowledge', such as the existence of internal tacit 'know-how' within the individual partners of a network, or their reputation, which affects attractiveness and expectation of reciprocity, or by 'relational' capabilities, which enhance the dialogue, the reciprocal understanding and interaction between them. Previous experience, mobility, capability to attract and retain skilled labour and formal education are instruments to promote competencies of the various partners in knowledge networks and their receptivity and ability to use external tacit and codified knowledge in the process of innovation.

Receptivity is not limited to a passive, although favourable attitude. It is a process of learning or a process of adaptation to external stimulus and of re-elaboration of external information and knowledge together with available internal competencies, leading to a feedback effect, which is crucial in order to promote an interactive relationship with the external actors. Therefore, the dynamic or proactive nature of receptivity is underlined by the fact that learning and competencies are linked by a bidirectional relationship, as learning feeds into the building of new competencies, which influence the process, the direction and speed of learning.

In general, a change in the corporate culture is needed in order to promote knowledge sharing and the willingness to collaborate. Human resources should not be considered only for their absorptive capacity and resistance to the adoption of technologies, but rather as the actors who promote innovation and are endowed with specific capabilities. Formal education and life-long learning are instruments that promote the building of competencies of the various partners in localized knowledge networks and their ability to use external tacit and codified knowledge in the process of innovation.

* * *

While these three factors: external stimulus, accessibility and receptivity, are key factors in promoting interactive relationships or the connectivity between the local actors, the territorial knowledge management framework indicates three other factors that are crucial in promoting the original recombination of previous knowledge modules, leading to knowledge creation and innovation.

4.19.4   Building a Common Identity

The acknowledgement of common challenges to survive and develop creates a sense of belonging to the same community or group and is a prerequisite for collaboration in innovation. The motivation by the SMEs in a sectoral cluster to adopt a common action and to exchange their respective knowledge is determined by the sharing of common aims and mental models that induce trust and loyalty. The identity is the sharing of a common culture or a set of values and a sense of belonging to the same entity, as in the case of a company, association, cluster or region, and so on. While the concept of receptivity refers to the similarity of the individual characteristics of the actors, identity refers to their reciprocal relationships and to the explicit subjective feeling existing between them, as indicated by the concepts of trust, sympathy, emotive proximity, sense of belonging and place identity.

The concepts of social capital and relational capital are also linked to that of identity. The sense of local identity and the collaborative attitudes are enhanced by the creation of various intermediate institutions such as industry associations, professional communities or specialized services. Cooperation requires the stabilization of the relationship and defining routines, which promotes trust, avoids opportunistic behaviours and conflicts, as is often the case with asymmetric information such as in innovation processes. These institutions, norms and routines are part of the 'social capital' of the regional economy.

Collaborative attitudes, friendship relationships, the sharing of common values, reciprocal esteem, loyalty, trust and leadership in a sectoral cluster can be considered as a form of tacit knowledge and they affect the 'institutional/organizational proximity' indicated above.

4.19.5   Leveraging Creativity

Creativity is crucial in order to diversify the structure of the local economy into new productions. According to cognitive theories, the creation of new knowledge or creativity is related to pattern-making and to the capability to establish new contacts between different potentially complementary information and technologies, thus leading to new discoveries and inventions. Creativity implies the recombination of subsystems of existing tacit and codified knowledge in order to generate new knowledge and processes of simplification, selection and exclusion of information and knowledge to be combined in an original way. Creativity is also the result of experience and the gradual development of a tacit 'architectural' knowledge capable of combining in an original way different modules of information, technologies and abstract and applied knowledge, often as the result of an iterative process of experimentation, failure and success.

Clearly, creativity cannot be planned in advance, being the capability to discover original solutions, but it requires an appropriate organization. While the 'fordist' approach leads to the utopia of a fully automated firm without workers, a cognitive approach indicates that the generation of new ideas and innovation is not possible without the interaction of the people within the firm and with other external actors and it requires a modern internal organization by the firms. Thus, creativity is the result of the capability by the firms to leverage and combine the professional skills in their internal human resources and to attract and retain qualified workers, raise their morale, promote their empowerment, grant to the potential inventors autonomy and security and stimulate their commitment to risky exploratory analysis and lengthy process of systematic search.

Creativity in large firms or high-tech sectors may be related to explicit investments in R&D. On the other hand, within SMEs, creativity is the result of networking and informal and formal processes of interactive learning. SMEs select and combine in a flexible and original way internal competencies with external competencies of other firms, and the outcomes of this creativity process may be shared by the local actors. In particular, the socialization, sharing and combination of tacit knowledge within a network of firms and local actors are preliminary and instrumental to its codification, which facilitate its diffusion, and also to its transformation into new collective tacit knowledge. This interactive learning process leads to the creation not only of new codified knowledge, but also of new collective organizational and technological knowledge, which is clearly tacit and characterizes specific groups of individuals, firms and organizations.

Creativity requires that SMEs devote more resources, people and time to the activity of systematic searching, exploration and exploitation. The generation of the idea is the result of close interactions between the firm and its clients and suppliers and it emerges after the explicit identification of a specific urgent problem. This idea can often only be developed further through the planning of a joint project, and sometimes even only through the creation of new start-up or spin-off firm. That requires an explicit cooperation within a network organization by clients, suppliers and other firms and organizations, such as knowledge-intensive business services or public research institutions. The flexible use of capabilities of other partners overcomes internal bottlenecks and saves the time and the R&D costs required to internally build these capabilities and thus accelerates the lead time in the elaboration of a new product or process and achieves a dynamic competitive advantage over international competitors.

Finally, within a regional cluster or innovation system the focus on the process of knowledge creation, rather than on the adoption of technologies, should lead to the promotion of diversity and close interaction between different and dispersed actors and the capability to establish new connections between different pieces of information and knowledge. Networks organize diversity and facilitate the combination of information and knowledge. Creativity may be hindered by the lack of needed competencies in the local economy and indicates the need for cooperation with international universities and major international companies.

4.19.6 Building Governance Capabilities

The implementation of innovative ideas and projects requires private and also public 'entrepreneurial' capabilities or the capability to manage the complex relationships between many different actors and to mobilize them to transform knowledge into action. Moreover, the governance activity should promote through the creation of routines, rules and institutions the working of all other, above indicated, phases of the territorial knowledge management framework and reorient existing public investments and subsidies.

Policy-making in knowledge and innovation networks should be based on multilevel governance and intermediate institutions, rather than on the traditional planning or free market approaches. In fact, the working of knowledge and innovation networks requires organizational routines, norms and the support of intermediate or 'bridging' institutions, which may be created by national or regional public authorities or by associations of private actors to organize these networks.

Multilevel governance first implies the choice of the relevant nodes in the networks or the choice of 'how' and 'who'. The steering of relationships between the various actors can facilitate their cooperation, mediate conflicts, create missing links between existing actors, promote the involvement of new actors, define the form and borders of the networks and promote an ex ante coordination, which helps to adopt a forward-looking perspective. Appropriate governance can minimize the 'adjustment or switching costs' in the transition from old to new organizational solutions and accelerate the 'time to change'.

The governance of innovation processes requires an explicit effort in institution building and institutional learning, as the creation and maintenance of 'social capital' or 'public goods' depends on adequate investments by all partners belonging to a given innovation system. However, the governance of knowledge and production relationships between firms is not always facilitated by public institutions, while knowledge-intensive business services and modern financial intermediaries, such as 'private equity', are going to play an increasing role.

Thus, institutions have a clear importance in the innovation process. The creation of institutions and governance of the knowledge creation process are key factors according to the territorial knowledge management framework, as they increase the accessibility and receptivity of the actors in a cluster and develop their sense of belonging and creativity. However, the negative experience of those industrial clusters that have been artificially created in various regions is related to the fact that the creation of an institution, such as a consortium of an 'industrial district', cannot compensate for the lack of intervention on the other various specific dimensions or drivers indicated by the TKM approach and facilitate the interactive learning processes as it spontaneously occurs in natural clusters. Some cluster initiatives have been based just on the spatial concentration of similar activities and focused only on spatial accessibility. Other initiatives have only concentrated on financing local firms and supporting their local identity. Clearly, these initiatives have overlooked the other key dimensions of a territorial process of knowledge creation and have not been capable of replicating the complexity of the factors that characterize spontaneous and successful clusters. In particular, they seem to have missed the need to promote the market orientation or identification of innovation stimulus, the creativity and governance capabilities of a new cluster.

The approach of TKM represents a theoretical and operative framework based on the concepts of cognitive economics and focusing on the factors leading to knowledge creation. This means enlarging on the factors traditionally considered in innovation policies, such as technology transfers, R&D investment and labour training, and also considering other factors that enhance the process of interactive learning within knowledge and innovation networks in the various regions. This approach is especially suitable in the case of networks of SMEs in intermediate technology sectors. However, it is also useful in regions specialized in high-tech or in low-tech sectors, where knowledge creation is still, together with others, a key factor of international competitiveness. Table 4.7 illustrates that

Table 4.7　Policy areas according to the territorial knowledge management approach in selected knowledge and innovation networks

	Type of Knowledge and Innovation Network		
Characteristics and factors	Ecological networks	Identity networks	Strategy networks
Regions, sectors and firms	Peripheral regions Low-tech sectors Traditional SMEs	Industrial clusters Medium-tech sectors Innovative SMEs	Urban areas High-tech sectors Large enterprises
Knowledge base	Symbolic/ synthetic knowledge	Synthetic/ symbolic knowledge	Analytical/synthetic knowledge
Knowledge interaction	Knowledge spill-over	Interactive learning	KM and R&D Joint projects
Innovation stimulus	Cost competition in the global market	Customer needs and high supply chain integration	Product innovation in specialized markets and technology push
Accessibility	Low international accessibility – low local accessibility	Low international accessibility – high local accessibility	High international accessibility – low local accessibility
Receptivity	Low qualification of human resources	Specialized skilled workers	High internal sectoral diversity
Identity	Fragmentation and external dependence	High local embeddedness and local identity	Low cognitive proximity and common identity
Creativity	Technology adoption	Networking and interactive learning	High investments in R&D
Governance	Public infrastructures and finance and deregulation	Multilevel governance at the regional level and bridging institutions	National industrial strategies and firms alliances in specific fields

the TKM approach can be flexible enough to consider the differences and specific characteristics of three different types of regions and sector specialization.

In fact, many innovations in medium-tech sectors have to integrate science-driven (analytical knowledge) or creative (symbolic knowledge) elements that characterize either high-tech or low-tech activities, which may be concentrated in the same region or geographical cluster. In fact, integrated innovations not only require connections between medium and high technologies, but also the comprehension of innovation processes in high-tech and in low-tech sectors. Technologies like the development of composites as new materials are a typical example, where knowledge from high technologies have to be connected with medium-technology productions (where the new materials are used, such as in aeronautics and the car industry) and low-technology productions (where the new materials are integrated, such as textiles).

4.20 THE INNOVATION PROCESS IN MEDIUM-TECH SECTORS

Major factors of weakness of clusters specialized in medium-tech sectors are: (1) a low international accessibility, (2) lack of creativity and product innovation instead of the hitherto focus on process innovation, and (3) need for formal instruments of governance of knowledge relations to enhance the emergence of more formal cooperation between the firms. Innovation policies in the modern industrial clusters specialized in medium-technology sectors should take into account the nature of their knowledge base mainly consisting of synthetic and symbolic knowledge and the form of their knowledge interaction characterized by interactive learning processes:

1. *External stimulus.* Medium-tech sectors are characterized by close user–producer relationships. SMEs aim to respond to customer needs or are driven by the requirements of the client in highly integrated supply chains. Innovation is the result of the adaptation to local demand and aims to solve specific problems. In fact, the experiences of mismatch between plans and actual results push the generation of new knowledge. Firms receive incentives for innovation by the aim to exploit new opportunities or by fearing closure as the result of a selection mechanism prevailing in highly competitive markets. Policies for these sectors and these types of firms should promote competitiveness based on product innovation rather than only on costs advantages.

2. *Accessibility*. SMEs in medium-tech sectors are strongly embedded in their territory, which integrates cognitive, economic and social relationships among themselves. They participate in innovation networks, which have in most cases only a local dimension with weak international linkages. Policies should enhance the still low international accessibility of SMEs and their integration into international knowledge and innovation networks, while maintaining the high local accessibility. So far, however, the international openness in most European medium-tech networks is limited to commercial and production perspectives, while international linkages are missing for technology cooperation.

3. *Receptivity*. The high specialization of firms in medium-tech sectors leads to a high share of tacit knowledge within the knowledge base. Thus, the openness to external relationships is enhanced by the existence of rare internal specific capabilities suitable to be combined with external knowledge and by relational competencies in the development of cooperation with other actors. Firms are characterized by a high flexibility in their internal organization and in their relationships with external actors. The high specialization of internal human capabilities determine a high absorptive capacity of SMEs in their specific field of specialization, but limit the capability of cooperation with other sectors using different codes of knowledge. SMEs should invest more in 'exploration' into new fields and aim to extend their common specialized know-how for further diversification of the knowledge base.

4. *Identity*. SMEs in a sectoral cluster share common aims and mental models as well as trust and loyalty. Interactive learning processes lead to the development of individual and also collective knowledge. The sense of local identity and collaborative attitudes are enhanced by the creation of various intermediate institutions such as industry associations or specialized services or just common agreed routines, which are part of the 'social capital' of the regional economy. The high common identity of the local community and regional embeddedness of firms are points of strength, but may favour conservative solutions and cause a lock-in effect if the individual actors are not allowed to have more autonomy as within the network model. The international extension of knowledge networks of SMEs calls for the identification of common objectives and projects with external partners, while maintaining a strong local identity.

5. *Creativity*. Medium-tech sectors are characterized by informal processes of interactive learning instead of formal R&D. Innovation in SMEs requires better capabilities to select and combine in an original

way internal competencies with external and scattered competencies through networking and interactive learning for solving new specific problems.

6. *Governance.* The increasing focus on knowledge creation instead of investments and public subsidies makes it necessary for innovation policy for medium-tech sectors to see the development and implementation of new instruments as a major priority. These should be designed to enhance the six drivers of TKM indicated above. The dimensions of accessibility, identity and creativity seem particularly crucial for clusters of SMEs in medium-tech sectors. SMEs need supporting infrastructures due to their scarce resources; for example intermediate institutions and linkages should be developed systemically in order to reduce the institutional distance. Policy-making should be based on multilevel governance rather than on traditional planning or the free market approach and aim for the creation and strengthening of bridging institutions like competence centres based on the agreement between various local actors on a joint long-term development strategy.

4.21   THE INNOVATION PROCESS IN HIGH-TECH SECTORS

Clusters specialized in high-tech sectors indicate different key problems, such as: (1) a low local embeddedness of large firms, (2) problems in combining R&D activities or analytical and synthetic knowledge, which are science and technology-driven, with symbolic knowledge and creativity, which are driven by the users' needs and the demand, and (3) the need to avoid a too high concentration in large firms and to promote spin-offs and the participation also by SMEs and other social partners in strategic decision-making. These clusters can mostly be found in central and metropolitan urban areas. Innovation policies in central urban areas should take into account the nature of their knowledge base consisting of analytical and synthetic knowledge, and the form of the knowledge interaction characterized by knowledge flows coordinated by knowledge management and joint R&D projects. Knowledge networks in these areas are characterized by links between large firms and research institutions and by professional networks within knowledge-intensive business services:

1. *External stimulus.* The stimulus to innovation derives from new opportunities created by recent advances in science and technology at the world level, increasing international competition and the need

for firms to identify very specific fields of application for these technologies. In fact, the international enlargement of the market has created the need to look for a very narrow specialization in specific market niches, but spread at the world level. However, new markets may also emerge in large urban areas of most developed countries, as these areas serve as an incubator of innovation due to the fact that the 'knowledgeable citizens' expressing new needs and opportunities for new products and services are mostly located in these areas.

2. *Accessibility.* The international accessibility of urban areas specialized in high-tech sectors is rather favourable, as they are the nodes of international transport networks. The large dimension, increasing congestion and high diversity of citizens within these areas, however, lead to divides, exclusion and increases in social disparities and cognitive distances between the various very specialized social groups and production activities. Thus, policies should promote a greater accessibility between these groups and activities by creating soft infrastructures, performing as bridges between the different segments of the local economy and society.

3. *Receptivity.* On the contrary, the receptivity to innovation in urban areas specialized in high-tech sectors is relatively high, not only due to the high education level of the local labour force, related to the fact that knowledge workers concentrate in the urban areas, but also because of the high internal diversity and specialization of the various local activities, facilitating the access to the most diversified external sources of knowledge.

4. *Identity.* Urban areas specialized in high-tech sectors are characterized by the existence of well-developed associations, communities and organized groups in completely different economic and professional fields. Hence, sectoral identities are strong. On the other hand, the high diversity of local actors and the high internal congestion increase the cognitive distance among them and lead to segmentation and a rather weak place identity, thus lowering the commitment by the local actors to the development of their local area. Local policies should therefore reinforce the local identity and strengthen common values and aims, for example through the organization of major international events or the building of symbolic architectures.

5. *Creativity.* Creativity in urban areas specialized in high-tech sectors is mainly based on high-developed formal R&D activities, both in large firms and in research institutions. However, the local market plays an increasing importance for the development of highly qualified and complex new products and services, which may later become a part

of the local export base. That indicates the need to better connect symbolic (creativity based) knowledge with analytical and synthetic knowledge, which are the traditional strengths of urban areas in order to increase the brand value of new productions. Thus, policies should be capable of promoting new knowledge through interactive learning processes both within very specialized professional communities of interest and between fields that are highly diversified but may be complementary to solving these new emerging problems.

6. *Governance.* The international openness and role of urban areas specialized in high-tech sectors leads to the need for closer integration of local initiatives with national and European programmes. Usually, governance of knowledge networks in urban areas and high-tech sectors is characterized by the design of well-coordinated projects in rather specific fields. The various sectors and professional groups are characterized by high levels of self-government and close internal connectivity. On the other hand, the high internal diversity of urban areas and their congestion level indicate the need to improve the connectivity between the different economic activities and professional communities through the development of bridging institutions. Universities, large research institutions and competence centres may have an increasing role in promoting these links. Moreover, the development of new productions and the fast transformation of the local economy and society within cities also leads to the importance of accompanying these changes with new projects in physical planning aiming at the renewal of specific areas.

4.22   THE INNOVATION PROCESS IN LOW-TECH SECTORS

Clusters specialized in low-tech sectors are characterized by various weaknesses, such as: (1) too low international accessibility, (2) the lack of receptivity and qualified skills, and (3) the lack of identity, and fragmentation in decision-making. These clusters are typically located in less developed and peripheral areas, being dependent on public subsidization and so far exclusively on cost advantages. Innovation policies in the less developed peripheral areas specialized in low-tech sectors should take into account the nature of their knowledge base, mainly consisting of symbolic or creativity-based knowledge and sometimes synthetic or engineering-based knowledge, and the form of knowledge interaction in these regions, characterized by automatic knowledge spillover based on geographical proximity.

1. *External stimulus.* The pressure of international competition on costs is a factor that pushes the adoption of process innovation. However, the competitiveness of local productions should be less based on lower labour costs and more on product innovation and products of higher quality. This requires the improvement of the quality of human resources and productivity levels and focus on innovation. The low potential of the local market should create incentives to look for the development of productions addressed to the international markets according to the export-led strategy, which has been followed traditionally by all successful industrial clusters. That requires more specialization of local productions and integration into interregional and international supply chains.

2. *Accessibility.* The development or improvement of international transport and communication infrastructures is clearly a prerequisite for an export-led growth strategy. However, less developed regions are also often internally characterized by fragmentation and isolation of individual economic activities and need to improve internal communications.

3. *Receptivity.* The level of general education in less developed peripheral areas is often rather high, while there is a lack of specialized workers with high professional experience. Traditional production know-how should be oriented towards more specialized fields. However, the receptivity to innovation is not only limited by the technical capabilities of the labour force, but also by a traditional organizational culture. Firms should aim explicitly for a long-term growth strategy requiring a wider vision and larger investments instead of insuring the comfort of a smaller dimension and the exploitation of rents in a local market, as often occurs in small family-owned SMEs.

4. *Identity.* Peripheral and less developed areas are often characterized by fragmentation, internal conflicts and low levels of consensus on common values and long-term development strategies. This weakens the potential to promote a clearer role in external relations and often leads to a situation of closure or external dependence.

5. *Creativity.* Innovation is often limited to product differentiation and incremental innovations, which are related to the use of symbolic knowledge. On the other hand, policies often focus on promoting technology transfers and the adoption of modern production technologies, which represent forms of synthetic knowledge, in the traditional low-tech sectors of activity. A complementary strategy could be to focus less on process and more on product innovation, to enhance creativity, to increase the effort by individual firms in the design of business plans aiming at the reconversion to new productions and

at new markets, and to increase cooperation between the local and external firms aimed at the development of new and more complex production fields.

6. *Governance.* Less developed regions are often characterized by the weakness of the public administrative structures and by the need for a wider adoption of innovation in the public sector. Regional development policies have focused on the building of infrastructures and the provision of financial incentives to the firms, rather than on promoting innovation. The aim to create artificial clusters has often led to failure, due to a too low effort in promoting the key factors indicated above, such as international accessibility, receptivity and local identity.

Public funds should only complement the mobilization of private investments. Successful clusters require the participation of large and often external firms and forms of interregional cooperation between the local public institutions. Intermediate institutions should promote a better connectivity and specialization of local firms, a stronger local identity and a change in local culture favouring specialization, outsourcing to other local firms and subcontracting from major external firms. In fact, the creation of local knowledge networks is highly complementary to a strengthening of other networks as subcontracting networks and labour mobility networks.

The focus by innovation policies on 'analytical knowledge', rather than on 'synthetic knowledge' has often led to the creation in less developed peripheral regions of large centres of R&D excellence supported by public funds and separated from the rest of the regional economy. Regional development agencies and other public centres could have a more strategic role than aiming at the provision of technological services to individual firms in traditional production, if they supported the design of major projects striving for the reconversion of the local economy rather than aiming to provide technological services to the individual firms in traditional production cooperation between various local firms.

4.23 THE DEVELOPMENT OF INTERNATIONAL KNOWLEDGE AND INNOVATION NETWORKS

Firms in medium-tech sectors have organized complex production systems characterized by an increasing content of know-how and made by many different complementary partners. That has led to the internationalization of markets and industrial value chains. In fact, clusters specialized in medium-tech sectors have often been characterized by an intense network of international export flows for a long time. More recently, the internation-alization of production capacities through investment in foreign countries and through international subcontracting has become widely diffused.

However, many small firms have only few international contacts and little experience in international cooperation. While the internationaliza-tion of product markets and the industrial supply chain are well developed, the internationalization of knowledge links is still lagging behind. The geographical span of the various forms of technological cooperation by SMEs is mainly regional and the lack of trust and reciprocal knowledge as well as the high cognitive distance are hindering significant developments of international cooperation in innovation based on interactive learning with foreign or distant firms. The international extension of knowledge networks of SMEs calls for the identification of common objectives and collaboration in projects that go beyond their own territory, while main-taining a strong local identity. In fact, innovation and new knowledge are key factors of the international competitiveness of European firms and regions.

In the case of medium-technology sectors, the international competi-tiveness of European regions with respect to the less developed emerging countries is explained and may be further strengthened by their capability to:

- respond to the new emerging needs in more sophisticated markets;
- introduce new products characterized by high complexity and quality;
- organize complex production systems with a higher content of know-how and made by different complementary partners.

Within medium-technology clusters, some traditional intermediaries in international knowledge networks are:

- MNEs – multinational enterprises;
- investment banks and private equity funds;
- knowledge-intensive business services.

However, new intermediaries are emerging in international knowledge networks, such as:

- medium-sized ('leader') firms;
- universities and research centres;
- regional administrations and interregional cooperation programmes;
- European Union programmes.

Small firms are efficient from a production perspective, as they can focus on a precise product specialization and exploit the advantages of subcontracting relationships. However, small firms may prove ineffective when the innovation and internationalization of the firms become the most important competitive factors. On the contrary, medium-sized firms (100–500 employees) have been capable of combining an explicit effort in R&D with the process of internationalization of product markets and the supply chain. Moreover, medium-sized firms are strongly embedded in their regional territory, have easy access to tacit knowledge existing within other local actors and are capable of combining this regional knowledge with external knowledge available in other regions. Therefore, intermediate firms in medium-tech sectors may become important nodes of international knowledge networks linking clusters specialized in medium-technology sectors.

However, an international perspective indicates a series of challenges for medium-sized firms. A mental change is needed, as even some medium-size-firms are reluctant to internationalize from a knowledge perspective or to promote new forms of international interactive learning with foreign partners due to the fear losing their proprietary know-how, which they believe represents their most important tacit competitive asset. Moreover, medium-sized firms often rely only on forms of economic or commercial internationalization, which prove to be risky and short-sighted if they are not accompanied by the development of international linkages in the cultural and social field also by the other local partners, research centres and regional institutions. In fact, the internationalization process of individual firms is easier when it is supported by the respective economic, social and institutional system.

From a methodological perspective, the creation of international cooperation between SMEs implies first the decision on which field and with which partners it should be realized and then the choice of its specific form. Thus, international cooperation between SMEs depends on the aims of the firms, the fields to be considered and the characteristics of the partners. These factors affect the benefits that may accrue to the considered firms in a long-term perspective, as cooperation may be instrumental in order to get an easier or faster access to key specific technologies, to expand into new markets, to diversify the scope of products and to improve the image or the relational advantages with respect to specific clients or suppliers. In fact, SMEs often prefer alliances focused on commercial aims rather than on technological cooperation and prefer national or regional partners to foreign partners.

The advantages of an alliance with partners having complementary knowledge may be positively related to the specific characteristics of technology and it increases with increasing complexity, tacit nature, speed of change, specificity and strategic relevance. In particular, transaction costs are affected by the characteristics of technology and are higher if the technology is characterized by high complexity, tacit components, speed of change, specificity and strategic relevance.

On the other hand, next to the evaluation of the benefits, international cooperation in technology between SMEs may be unfeasible in the short term if the transaction costs are too high, as in the case of too high geographical distance, lack of trust or high social disparities and too distant technological level or cognitive distance. In fact, a lower distance may induce forms of closer integration between the firms, not only from a commercial or productive perspective but also from a financial or technological perspective. Moreover, a too high distance may lead to no relations and to autarchy, which hinders the development of interactive learning and knowledge creation. On the other hand, a too high proximity may not lead to cooperation, but rather to negative effects, such as a lock-in effect or local conflicts. Thus, an intermediate level of proximity seems more adequate.

The role of distance underlines the role of institutions. In fact, SMEs are often myopic and overestimate short-term costs of an international cooperation and underestimate the long-term opportunities. Thus, bridging institutions and international coordination of national innovation policies can promote a stronger awareness by the SMEs of the strategic benefits of cooperation, by helping them to identify realistic aims, key fields and complementary partners. In particular, bridging institutions may stimulate the firms to change their corporate strategy to a forward-looking and leadership model, which is more externally focused or more open to external knowledge and may promote strategic convergence between the various possible partners. Moreover, specific bridging institutions may be required to decrease the transaction costs of the international cooperation and to choose its most appropriate form. In fact, policies may promote a shorter cognitive distance and should be capable of improving the reciprocal trust, the sharing of common values, culture and institutions, sense of belonging, reciprocal knowledge and reputation. Finally, policies may also address those organizational factors that may lead to the failure of alliances, such as asymmetric incentives, lack of commitment, communication, project planning and flexibility.

The process of internationalization of firms from a technology perspective should be interpreted as a learning process where the single phases and forms of international alliances may lead to new and more complex phases and forms according to specific paths of evolution. Alliances with some firms may be terminated in order to develop alliances with other partners in the same or in different fields. The factors leading to the failure of alliances are similar to those determining its creation. Strategic divergence is the most important factor, accompanied by the failure in arranging the appropriate form of the alliance and to solve organizational differences.

We may conclude that the factors leading to an international alliance between SMEs are similar to those considered in the territorial knowledge management approach and that promote processes of interactive learning within knowledge and innovation networks. In particular, factors such as external stimulus, accessibility, receptivity, common identity, creativity and governance stimulate the creation and facilitate the success of an international alliance. Policies may promote a greater accessibility by reducing cultural and language barriers, promoting greater openness, making compatible different technologies and reducing their complexity, favouring frequent communication and transparency and the interaction within specific interregional working groups. Policies may also promote a greater receptivity, by building internal competencies, transferring skills and capabilities by exposure of workers to the culture of partnering organizations, changing corporate culture and promoting a learning culture. Policies may promote a greater common identity or sense of belonging, reciprocal trust, a cooperative rather than competitive posture, the identification of common strategic aims rather than short-term individual objectives and the design of common institutions with a relative power balance.

Finally, the governance of international cooperations between SMEs requires regional, national and European institutions. In fact, the development of international relations requires a more stable framework compared with what the market mechanisms, multinational companies or private forms of bottom-up international cooperation may be capable of providing. The process of internationalization has a selective character and a key role is played by 'gateways' or 'bridging' institutions. The economic strengths of medium-sized firms should be combined with the greater experience in international relations of other local actors, which may be much weaker in terms of economic strength than the industrial firms, as in the case of universities, research centres and the regional governments, but can perform a key role as intermediate nodes in international networks.

Institutions play a key role in promoting international economic integration and complement the role of market relations. Thus, from a market perspective, European integration allows the free flows of products and services and it is determined by the abolishment of custom tariffs, adoption of a common currency, improvement in transport and ICT infrastructure and decrease of other barriers, which imply monetary costs to the firms. However, European integration also has an institutional and

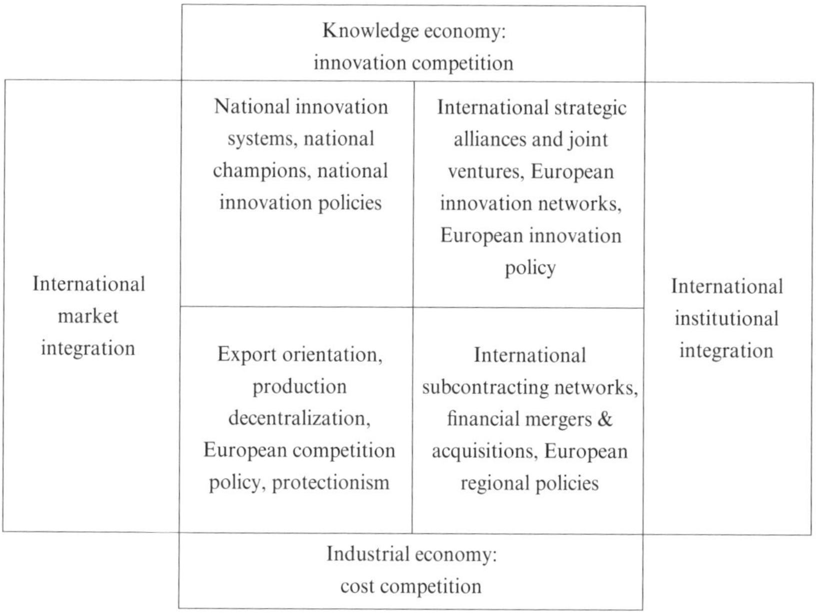

	Knowledge economy: innovation competition		
International market integration	National innovation systems, national champions, national innovation policies	International strategic alliances and joint ventures, European innovation networks, European innovation policy	International institutional integration
	Export orientation, production decentralization, European competition policy, protectionism	International subcontracting networks, financial mergers & acquisitions, European regional policies	
	Industrial economy: cost competition		

Figure 4.19　The process of international integration and the knowledge economy

organizational dimension, as the harmonization of the institutional and organizational framework is required to promote the flows of investments, labour and technological knowledge and social, cultural and institutional links.

As institutions play an important role in promoting the international integration of the economies, Figure 4.19 compares the role of institutions in a traditional industrial economy, where competition is determined by production costs, and in a modern knowledge economy, where competition is determined by the speed of innovation. The governance of international relations may be insured by individual private firms or by public institutions. In an industrial economy, firms have to create complex organizations to manage international subcontracting networks, mergers and acquisitions of foreign firms, while European regional policies play a key role in integrating the economic lagging regions in the European economy and in reducing the economic disparities that hinder European economic and political integration. On the other hand, in a modern knowledge economy, there is the need to overcome the negative effects of closure of the various national innovation systems. Thus, international strategic alliances and joint ventures between the firms and international knowledge and innovation networks and bridging institutions, to be created by the European innovation policy, may be appropriate instruments to promote a greater cognitive proximity between the various actors, to facilitate creativity through diversity and to accelerate the time of innovation.

Therefore, the process of internationalization is different from the growth of exports or also from the trade of patents and codified knowledge. It is based on a close integration not only of the markets of products, but also of the internal organization and production processes of the firms, as these latter become capable of closely working together with firms of other countries. Moreover, the internationalization process is affecting not only the industrial productions, but also the service sectors and the public administrations. The increased flows of intermediate products, services and production factors and the increased international sharing of codified and tacit knowledge require appropriate forms of governance through common private organizations and public, hard and soft, institutions. In fact, a first key difference of interregional relations with respect to international relations is the mobility not only of the final goods but also of the intermediate products and production factors. Thus, the international relations, once characterized by the mobility only of the final goods, are becoming increasingly similar to interregional relations, which are characterized by the mobility of production factors, due to the process of globalization and international integration. This process may be interpreted as a learning process extending the model of cooperation between many various private and also public actors existing within a cluster or a local production system to an international dimension.

However, a second difference is represented by the fact that institutional integration is the lowest in the international framework and it reaches its maximum within an individual country, as all regions within a country have in common the same institutional framework due to the existence of the state, laws, rules and institutions. In fact, in all countries, the process of economic integration at the interregional level, which implies the interregional mobility of intermediate products, material production factors and knowledge, would not be possible without a common institutional framework and the existence of trust relationships, common routines, norms, intermediate and also formal political institutions.

In particular, the European Union with its large share of international trade and of global GDP is a paradigmatic model of how a high and increasing market integration is closely linked with the process of building common political institutions and adopting common public policies (Cappellin, 2004b, 2004c, 2005). Economic growth increases as a result of increasing international openness and market integration, which promotes the mobility of final and intermediate products (Figure 4.20). However,

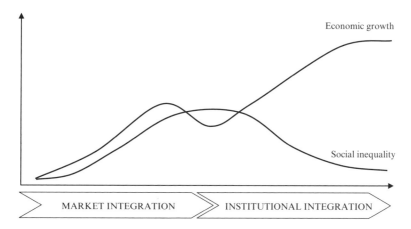

Figure 4.20   The trade-off between economic growth and social inequality

the integration of the markets of final products may be hindered or have a negative effects as it may determine an increase of regional growth disparities, disparities between the insiders and outsiders and various economic, social and environmental problems for specific firms, sectors or workers within the various regions. That determines a lower mobility of production factors and knowledge and it may also determine a declining speed of economic growth. Thus, the increasing European market integration should be accompanied by policies aiming at a greater institutional integration, reducing the 'organizational and institutional distance' between regions and sectors. A greater institutional integration may promote both the continuation of economic growth and the decrease of economic, social and environmental problems, by promoting knowledge creation, accessibility and receptivity to local and external knowledge and to other scarce resources and their use in innovative productions.

Thus, according to the model of interactive learning between firms illustrated in this book, a European economy that is moving towards the model of the knowledge society requires new tools in innovation policy for promoting and managing international knowledge and innovation networks between SMEs in medium-technology sectors. The next chapter will deal with these necessary policy changes at the European level.

5. The approach of knowledge networks in innovation policy

Riccardo Cappellin and Rüdiger Wink with Staszek Walukiewicz*

5.1 CLUSTER POLICY IN THE EUROPEAN UNION

The transition to the model of the knowledge economy implies a distinct change in the industrial development strategies and in the approach to innovation policies, focusing more on knowledge creation than on technology diffusion, more on networks with respect to individual firms and also more on a European perspective in innovation policies for medium-technology sectors.

The internationalization of markets and production processes indicates that innovation and new knowledge are the key factors of international competitiveness for European firms and regions. In fact, in the long term, the real factors of international competitiveness are neither taxes and corporate profits nor labour flexibility and labour costs, but rather productivity changes, innovation capabilities, knowledge and know-how.

Innovation is not only the key factor in competitiveness and success of the existing firms, but also the factor explaining the survival or crisis of firms or the factor leading to the creation of new firms. There are different factors of innovation, such as finance and entrepreneurship capabilities, but the role of knowledge, technological and organizational capabilities and know-how is becoming crucial. However, knowledge and innovation lead not only to economic and employment growth, but also to international division of labour, agglomeration and exclusion phenomena. In fact, the major factor of growth disparities between countries is the gap in technology and knowledge.

Thus, regional industrial and innovation policies should aim for a faster speed of innovation and a higher growth rate of labour productivity. Only the growth of productivity and increasing international competitiveness of regional industrial production will lead to increased or stable employment.

The processes of economic development in regions depend on their competitiveness in an increasingly integrated global economy. The aims of a European innovation policy are to increase the overall productivity, to promote a greater competitiveness of exports to non-European countries and to facilitate a fast transition toward a modern knowledge economy. Major factors of competitive advantage of the European economy with respect to the many and large emerging economies are related to:

- the high diversification of industrial productions within the various industrial clusters, allowing the creation of new productions as combination of traditional specializations;
- the emergence of new needs, which often have a collective nature, of consumers and citizens and the creation of new markets;
- a highly qualified labour force.

As already explained in the Chapter 2, medium-technology industry represents 57.9% of European manufacturing exports, 53.3% of manufacturing employment and 47.8% of manufacturing value-added, while the share of high-tech industry is only 17.1% of European manufacturing exports, 19.5% of manufacturing value-added and 5.8% of manufacturing employment (see Table 2.9 on p. 25). Medium-tech sectors are characterized by many specialized small firms. Large or medium-sized firms, however, are also important in these sectors, as for example in the case of the aeronautic, automobile and machinery productions.

The crucial role of medium-technology sectors is highlighted both by the focus on the evolution to the model of the knowledge economy and the increasing international interdependence determined by the globalization process. In fact, the knowledge economy requires a broader perspective to innovation and the consideration of many sectors different from the high-tech sectors, which represent a very minor share of total employment and value-added in a modern economy. The competitiveness and innovation of medium-technology sectors representing the largest share and the most dynamic component in European industry is becoming an issue that relates less to European R&D policy and scientific excellence and more to industrial policy and even to the macroeconomic performance of the aggregate European economy. This explains the importance of promoting strategic industrial projects in the medium-technology sectors. The actual slow growth rate of the European economy is much more due to the slow productivity increases in the medium-technology sectors than to the lags in the development of high-tech sectors, which could never represent a major component of the overall economy.

Moreover, the challenge by increasing export from emerging countries in Asia indicates that medium-technology sectors are going to play a key role in European international trade. The development of these sectors has been considered in the past as a secure element capable of creating the value-added and financial resources that could be devoted to long-term investment in R&D projects in high-tech sectors. However, there is now the need for a clearer focus on those factors that ensure the continuous innovation of these sectors facing increasing international competition. Thus, medium-technology sectors are going to play a strategic role and more private and public resources are needed in order to ensure the competitiveness of these sectors.

The increasing costs of energy, raw materials and food lead to inflation and to falling purchasing power or demand and production, which even imply falling real wages. A recovery would require a pronounced restructuring in the major sectors of the European economy such as the medium-technology sectors. A greater productivity increase would have a positive effect on costs and inflation, wages and demand and also international competition. In fact, the actual worsening of the terms of trade and of the purchasing power in Europe, which is related to the increase of oil, raw materials and agricultural products, can only be compensated by an increase of productivity in medium-technology sectors and the related increase of international competitiveness, as well as wages and incomes in these sectors.

The fast growth of emerging countries creates important opportunities for the exports and growth of medium-technology sectors. However, the success of these sectors depends on fast and continuous innovation as well as improvements in the quality of their products in order to ensure international competitiveness and avoid the delocation of productions from the European regions and countries. Thus, clusters specialized in these sectors should increasingly base their international competitiveness on innovation and the capability to create new knowledge especially in medium-tech industrial sectors. The international extension of knowledge networks of SMEs calls for the identification of common objectives and collaboration in projects that go beyond their own territory, while maintaining a strong local identity. In particular, the international competitiveness of developed European regions compared with less developed emerging countries can be explained and may be further strengthened by the capability of medium-technology sectors to:

- respond to the new emerging needs in more sophisticated markets;
- introduce new products characterized by high complexity and quality;

- organize complex production systems with a higher content of know-how and made by different complementary partners.

This changing economic and technological scenario calls for a new strategy in cluster policies, aiming to reorient existing clusters. Cluster policies should be based on the identification of the different evolution profiles of the individual clusters as well as their specific strengths and weaknesses and on the design of explicit strategies for the individual clusters.

The fourth chapter explained theoretically and generally the transition of clusters in medium-tech clusters towards the model of knowledge clusters and networks. In fact, the emerging 'knowledge clusters' are the result of the evolution from the traditional industrial or 'fordist' model, based on the exploitation of economies of scale external to the firms but internal to an industrial cluster, to the model of the 'knowledge economy' where regional innovation systems and innovation networks are characterized by intense knowledge interactions between the various local actors. This calls for changes in cluster policies, similar to changes that are widely adopted in the rest of the European economy and industry. The 'Cluster Memorandum' (Box 5.1) of the European Commission has emphasized that:

- clusters have positive effects on the competitiveness of firms;
- clusters most often emerge as the result of a bottom-up process and they cannot be completely planned exogenously from public institutions;
- cluster initiatives are nationally differentiated and European coordination should be highly flexible and focused on strategic initiatives.

5.2   CLUSTER POLICIES AT THE REGIONAL LEVEL

Within the second and third chapters, we explained the specificities of innovation in the medium-technology sector and the challenges SMEs face within the changing environment of these innovation processes. Our empirical investigation of SMEs in different European regions also serves to look for policy solutions at the regional level and for ways to connect and transfer them at the European level. One very important result of the empirical observation of networks referred to the greater importance of knowledge flows for the network linkages than material flows in almost all observed regions. This observation stresses the relevance of policies focusing on facilitation and competitiveness of knowledge interactions

BOX 5.1   THE EUROPEAN CLUSTER MEMORANDUM

The Commission's Directorate General Enterprise and Industry has recently launched an Open Consultation on the European Cluster Memorandum, a tool that could help to better target innovation policy toward increased competitiveness and growth. The Memorandum, supported by national and regional agencies for innovation and economic development, is addressed to policymakers at regional, national and European levels. It presents arguments why Europe needs stronger clusters and transnational cluster cooperation and provides 'an agenda for policy action' to promote European innovation through clusters.

The following selected statements of the Cluster Memorandum seem to share the same perspective as that illustrated in the IKINET project:

> Clusters – regional concentrations of specialized companies and institutions connected through multiple lineages and spillovers – provide an environment conducive to innovation.

> Clusters underline the importance of strong territorial policy in a world where both local and global networks are important for success.

> In modern competition, all clusters need to be innovation clusters.

> Furthermore it has become evident that innovation is heavily concentrated geographically.

> The more connections, relationships and interactions in a networked society, the higher the potential value-added, especially in the development of intellectual assets.

> Sometime industry-led networks will be the prime movers in clusters development and there can be a role for public authorities to support this process.

> The need to shift the innovation debate to a discussion on clusters and broader innovation has emerged at EU level.

> Cluster policies have already improved the efficiency of existing economic development efforts. But they have often been focused only on strengthening individual clusters, not on developing

mutually reinforcing portfolios of established and emerging clusters at the regional level.

Dynamic clusters become more visible and attractive if they have strong linkages with related clusters in other regions and countries. Europe needs stronger transnational cooperation between clusters with complementary strengths and between cluster initiatives learning from each other.

The success of government cluster policies depends on the actions of many different actors – multiple levels of government and public agencies, companies, investors, trade associations and chambers of commerce & industry, educational and research institutions, as well as other institutions affecting the business environment of clusters, for example the labour partners.

Strengthening the potential of clusters – moving them from co-located companies to dynamic clusters with high levels of competition, interaction and spillovers – is a central task that regional and national governments are best placed to address.

Effectiveness depends on defining and implementing action agendas that reflect the specific need of a particular cluster or region.

Source: www.proinno-europe.eu/NWEV/uploaded_documents/European_ Cluster_Memorandum.pdf, 23 November 2007.

on the regional level instead of more traditional instruments of regional development that concentrate on capital subsidies and infrastructures for material linkages within specialized clusters. The following subsections covering best practice cases in our investigation provide a summary of these political experiences and help to show how cluster policies support the emergence, growth and connection of knowledge networks in the medium-technology industries and the possibilities for the European level to build up interfaces between the regional initiatives.

5.2.1 Challenge: Incentives for Interaction Between SMEs and Actors with Diversified Knowledge as Prerequisites for Creativity

For many conventional SMEs in medium-technology industry, the internal knowledge base and contacts along the value chain still work as the main sources for new knowledge. These channels, however, are restricted.

Labour mobility of the workforce in conventional SMEs is lower than in big companies, enabling the long-term development of specified knowledge but limiting the acquisition of new insights, and most of the internal knowledge is driven by very specific internal routines with only few connections to knowledge production processes in other firms. This specificity of available knowledge interactions for SMEs limits the options for diversification and raises the dependence on just a few customers. Within the third chapter, the relevance of interaction and diversification for creativity has been stressed. Thus, regional policies have to look for ways to overcome the barriers of the medium-technology SMEs to creative environments.

The transition towards modular sourcing processes by OEMs causes further barriers to external knowledge for conventional SMEs, as traditional linkages to the OEMs to integrate new knowledge via orders are substituted by more formalized and organizational requirements of members of the value chain, which many conventional SMEs cannot meet. Therefore, SMEs are threatened with losing their most important connections to knowledge developments. These firms are restricted to positions as providers of simple components, which can easily be substituted by suppliers in low-cost countries. As a consequence, the incumbent SME structure in European medium-technology industries can no longer hold.

One traditional approach to help the conventional SMEs out of this difficulty refers to regional universities as partners in knowledge development. Close connections do not necessarily focus on formal R&D cooperation, which cannot be funded by the SMEs and is often too far away for practical application. Successful cooperation often includes joint development of topics for diploma theses, agreements on internships or even joint agreements on modules for under- and postgraduate programmes. Here, personal linkages between professors and firm leaders or employees often play the major role in cooperation. In some cases, the cooperation can even lead to spin-offs from the public institution and the professor or research assistants act as academic entrepreneurs.

Within all investigated areas, these linkages could be observed. In the case of Madrid, the engineering school does not only influence the regional knowledge interactions between firms and the university but also between the regional firms, as most of the engineers come from the same school and use their linkages for the development of joint technological standards. Similar experiences can be seen in the case of the mining industry in Silesia, where incumbent structures within the former state-owned firms and public research institutes dominate the interfirm linkages. Thus, cognitive and personal linkages are present in these cases.

Examples of instruments aiming at more systematic linkages can be found in Germany. One instrument focuses particularly on the cooperation between universities of applied sciences and SMEs. The 'industrial joint research' within the 'Working Group of Industrial Research Associations Otto von Guericke' (AiF) provides opportunities for SMEs to cooperate with public research institutes by partly funding the share of the public researchers. Besides the atmosphere of joint communication between firms and public researchers helping to overcome the gap between scientific research and practical application, firm managers stress the attractiveness of the possibility to test the contact within the bigger working group before taking the contact towards an exclusively private cooperation.

Another instrument to improve the exchange between public research and firm knowledge refers to the joint funding of research assistants. Both partner organizations share the contributions to the payment of the assistant, who at the beginning of the qualification programme works on theoretical issues in the research organization and then turns to the work in the private company to implement the more theoretical insights. These instruments, however, require capabilities in the firms to communicate directly with researchers, who are used to communicating in more science-driven terms.

An additional tool for more systematic interaction is offered by competence centres in Austria. These centres are based on cooperation between science, government and firms on issues of knowledge-specific technology fields and its strategic development, exchange and exploitation. The analysis of the knowledge flows within the regional networks of Styria clearly reveals the central role of these organizations to the networks, as they are accepted by the SMEs as partners due to their excellence in knowledge, while being simultaneously sufficiently independent from multinational firms and focused on support of SMEs to gain trust from the SMEs. In addition, the attractiveness of the competence centres for the multinational firms is driven by the access to a diversified set of SMEs with specialized tacit knowledge. This can be used as a starting point for the formation of more exclusive knowledge clubs. Without the knowledge centres, the OEMs would have to search for suitable partners themselves and would face problems due to a lack of trust by the SMEs, who fear being exploited. Within the context of competence centres, firms can first experience interaction within a protected, standardized and mutually acceptable environment and can then develop according to their specific needs. The approach of competence centres includes different features needed for the support of SMEs in regional knowledge networks:

- technology field orientation instead of a too specialized focus on one specific sector;
- cognitive capabilities within the centre to show necessary technological competences, while simultaneously interacting on practical applications, instead of focusing on one side of the interaction;
- strategic capabilities within the centre for initiating new projects on knowledge development instead of simply moderating the coordination between regional network members;
- acting as service organizations offering their products in competitive markets stressing the value of the knowledge provided instead of public subsidies;
- interregional focus on knowledge interaction enabling the integration of knowledge outside the region instead of being stuck in a lock-in constellation exclusively dependent on regional knowledge production.

Summing up, regional cluster policies to enhance regional knowledge networks support the diversification of the knowledge base within the region to generate stimuli and new challenges as necessary prerequisites for creative knowledge production processes. Table 5.1 shows the differences between the more incumbent approaches of regional development policies and the new regional knowledge policy strategies with regard to creativity.

For the European Union, this strategic change introduces important new functions. As for many regions the necessary diversity of knowledge can only be found beyond the regional borders, the EU can play a major role by supporting the coordination between regional competence centres. Here, the regional intermediaries can look for strategic partners in other regions and initiate joint activities to extend the existing knowledge base, develop new markets and new integrative combinations of knowledge in medium- and high-tech industries. This would not only require an information tool for regional competence centres but support for standardization of information and exchanges at intermediary level to understand exactly the specificities of knowledge bases in other regions.

5.2.2   Challenge: Strategic Exploitation and Development of the Knowledge Base as Prerequisites for Accelerated Innovation and Adjustment

SMEs face specific scarcities in resources for strategic planning. Traditionally, they cope with these restrictions by limiting their strategic planning processes to market niche strategies focused on a narrow set of regional markets. The changing international environment, however, makes it necessary to speed up innovation processes to accelerate the market exploitation of new products and processes and to adjust to

Table 5.1   Differences between incumbent and new regional policy strategies with regard to creativity

	Incumbent Regional Policies	Regional Knowledge Policy
Expected impact on the knowledge base	Strengthening the homogeneity of knowledge to achieve agglomeration effects	Supporting the diversity of knowledge to achieve stimuli for creativity
Focus on knowledge	Sector-specific knowledge with a high level of specificity	Technology platform knowledge with broad applications in different sectors
Focus on interaction	Concentration on formal R&D	Inclusion of tacit knowledge and joint qualification
Linkages	Driven by personal linkages without strategic direction	Institutional linkages supported by intermediaries between SMEs and other knowledge partners
Funding instruments	Subsidies for R&D	Subsidies for joint research, exchange and intermediaries
Coordinating institution	Weak coordination, parallel structures of chambers and university technology centres	Competence centres

structural changes in the international value chains. Furthermore, strategic processes are needed to integrate technological expertise from other sectors and disciplines to diversify existing markets. For most of the SMEs, however, resource scarcities still limit the strategic capabilities.

Traditional regional cluster policies focus simply on activities to extend agglomeration effects by active attraction of investors in already existing strong sectors, by offering additional infrastructures for the main sectors in the region or providing support for common events. Strategic development, however, is seen as a responsibility of the single firms without any political incentives. Consequently, SMEs are more or less forced to follow strategies of the OEMs within their value chain without having the resources for active reflections on alternative strategies.

In many European countries, regional contests have been established on a national level to create incentives for strategic projects within regional cluster networks. Within our investigation, Austria, France and Germany are examples of these contest approaches. In France, the contest on poles of competitiveness (*pôles de compétitivité*) offers a total of 1.5 billion euros to the successful regions within three years (2006–08). The region of Ile de France was the most successful within the contest to identify poles of competitiveness in France, as from a total of seven global competitiveness clusters three poles coming from this region are being supported by the French government within the next four years (finance innovation, medicine technologies and system technologies). Necessary prerequisites for success are the presentation of a strategic programme for the following years within a specific technology field with high global growth potential, the international competitiveness and visibility of the strategic programme and the firms involved and the development of suitable institutional infrastructures with several partnerships between the organizations involved for the implementation of the programme.

The optical industry in the Ile de France region, which was analysed within our empirical sample, is engaged within the SYSTEM@TIC PARIS-REGION pole, which focuses on embedded system technologies for sectors at the interface between electronics, IT and optics industries. All in all, 80 large firms, 100 SMEs and 134 research centres are involved in the pole. Within the optical sector, a strong deviation can be observed between young technology-driven start-ups with close connections to multinational firms and public research facilities and conventional firms facing problems in building up close knowledge cooperation with other firms. Geographical proximity cannot play a major role in cluster building within the region, as the distances between the firms are too big and the transport modes too poor to have frequent and spontaneous knowledge interactions via F2F contact. On the other hand, the regional government, multinational firms and associations look for intensive interactions based on common institutions. Relatively big lead projects help smaller firms to identify and follow mid- to long-term strategies. The basic problems for the conventional SMEs, however, are still the prerequisites for the institutional linkages. Formal knowledge and organizational standards can be met by the young specialized start-ups; the conventional firms, however, are only used to developing tacit knowledge and restricting their knowledge cooperation to their internal workforce, and few partners do not show the necessary knowledge capabilities required for the 'knowledge clubs'. Due to the good availability of knowledge capabilities for many different sectors, there are only few incentives for the policy in the region to improve the capabilities of conventional SMEs, as there are sufficient young firms to overcome the barrier towards the knowledge clubs.

Thus, the French approach of poles of competitiveness offers the possibility of extending strategic potentials to SMEs by creating incentives to open up the strategic projects of large multinational companies to SMEs with attractive knowledge resources. The institutional settings are dominated by the knowledge linkages between large companies, science-driven research institutes and small spin-off firms. Consequently, this programme strengthens regions with already existing formal knowledge resources and concentrates on metropolitan regions or industrial regions with high innovation focus and SMEs with suitable capabilities to fit in with the regional strategies.

Similarly, the German federal government uses contests for top clusters to create incentives for strategic projects in regional networks. Starting in 2007, a maximum of five clusters is supported for five years with up to 200 million euros. Again, the prerequisites for support are based on strategic projects of international competitiveness, the proof of economic and institutional capabilities, structural and sustainable changes towards international unique selling propositions of the clusters and the co-funding by private and public investors in the region. The aeronautical cluster of Hamburg is one of the five winners within the contest. As in the French case, the basis of this policy is the extension of lead technological projects of big firms to knowledge-intensive SMEs. The strategic planning process for the project is moderated by the regional government in Hamburg, but the main ideas come from the big OEMs in the region (Airbus, Lufthansa Technik), business-related service firms and research organizations. For the SMEs, the strategic discussion serves as a guiding rail for mid-term calculation of investments and organizational changes needed and goes beyond the already existing, more general communications from the OEMs on changes in the sourcing strategies and requirements for suppliers. In contrast to recent problems in adjusting to unforeseen challenges within the civil aeronautics markets – like the volatility in the foreign exchange rate markets, delays in delivering the new A380 and starting the new development process for the A350 – the joint strategic process will help to prepare for necessary adjustments and therefore speed up the assertion of innovation and adjustment processes.

The Austrian model of competence centres offers a slightly different focus. Here, the strategies are derived as a result of processes after establishing specific institutions. The establishment of the competence centres and their technological focus were the result of a contest at the end of the 1990s. First evaluations were made in 2003 and 2004 with slight adjustments of the approach. Again, strategic processes within the centres are mainly driven by the rationale in big multinational firms, as they are important customers and partners in the centre. The centres, however, can add ideas for further diversification to the existing projects of the multinational firms and initiate additional projects, in particular by extending the range of firms involved. They play a more active part than in the French case, where the institutions are only project-based, and include activities to raise the knowledge capabilities of SMEs.

Table 5.2 shows the main differences between incumbent regional policies and the knowledge policy approaches in the field of strategic

Table 5.2 Differences between incumbent and new regional policy strategies in the field of strategic development

	Incumbent Regional Policies	Regional Knowledge Policy
Objective of the activities	Support of single organizations to improve knowledge base	Strategic development of knowledge networks
Basis of policies	Allocation of national and EU funding according to needs	Contests on the national level
Concept of strategic development	Based on rationales of the OEMs	Based on strategic competitiveness of the cluster
Linkages	Driven by needs in supply chains based on social and organizational proximities	Institutional and cognitive linkages based on region-specific institutional settings
Funding instruments	Subsidies for organizations or subsidies for single projects	Subsidies for lead projects based on short- to mid-term evaluation
Coordinating institution	No external coordination, coordination restricted to private supply chains	Competence centres, poles of competitiveness

development. The main difference is the relevance of strategic development itself, as this focus was missing in many earlier concepts of incumbent regional policies. The provision of strategic consultancy by accepted intermediaries can help SMEs to overcome their structural weaknesses due to scarce management resources. The success of the regional initiatives depends on the active participation of the affected regional firms and strong incentives in the centres to play an active part in strategic development beyond the rationale of the big multinational firms in the region.

On the European level, an exploitation of the regional strategic processes is needed. This can first be achieved by organizing regional contests on the European level based on lead projects to achieve sustainable international competitiveness. Second, and even more important, the EU can support the global implementation of the strategic activities by using standardization policies or targeted support of demand, for example, in the context of renewable energies, environmental improvements in medium-technology industries or new service qualifications.

5.2.3 Challenge: Infrastructures for Regional Knowledge Networks

Traditionally, infrastructures play a major role in regional innovation policies. Typical examples are science parks, technology centres or technology transfer organizations. For SMEs, these organizations often seem to be too close to the scientific sector and high-technology markets and too far away from incremental innovation processes of medium-technology sectors. Thus, they might only be suitable in a context of analytical and formalized knowledge. Other shortcomings within traditional concepts of innovation policies refer to the role of IT infrastructures and the use of the internet. With broadband internet access and support from internet information tools, many policy-makers feel that the necessary prerequisites for knowledge interactions are provided. Actual communication between SMEs and other organizations, however, require ongoing incentives and capabilities for interactions, so that cognitive distances and mistrust can be overcome. Therefore, regional knowledge policies have to look for more inclusive infrastructures reducing the formal knowledge barriers for SMEs and improving prerequisites for qualification and creativity. On the other hand, R&D investments at the firm level are also needed within knowledge policies for medium-technology industries. These formal investments, however, have to be connected with interactions between the firms and activities to help SMEs in their development processes towards R&D. The following examples show those changes in the understanding of infrastructures for knowledge policies within the regions of observation.

Metropolitan areas have a specific position within the transition process towards knowledge economies. On the one hand, they have clear advantages due to their attractiveness for new business- and consumer-related services and high density of education suppliers. On the other hand, the high concentration of the population causes disparities between social groups not only in terms of economic strength but also knowledge and access to qualifications. Here, infrastructures are needed to offer attractive surroundings for creative service firms to exploit the benefits of geographical proximity and to attract other members of creative industries and to connect the service sectors with the regional industrial firms. Simultaneously, the regions need instruments to improve the inclusion of qualification schemes and the openness to foreign employees. Paris, Madrid and Hamburg are good examples of European metropolitan areas with a high attractiveness for international creative service firms and with a clear regional policy to exploit these strengths.

One traditional instrument, which gains additional importance in this context, is regional housing policy and spatial planning. Hamburg uses its restructuring of the traditional port area to develop attractive locations for media and design firms and attractive apartments for young employees in the creative sectors. Additionally, regional universities offer programmes in various creative service segments. Within aeronautics, a special focus is concentrated on the development of a centre for excellence in cabin interiors, including excellent facilities and capabilities in the design and advanced engineering service segment as well as joint projects between service companies and industrial producers. Similarly, Madrid supports the availability of areas for aeronautics engineering and related services. Around Paris, local concentration of areas for the optics and related electronics industries in several areas of the Ile de France region enables cooperation with urban service providers from design and IT and security engineering segments.

The connections between medium-technology SMEs and service firms as well as other suitable cooperation partners require more than simple material IT infrastructures. Joint events or projects, as in the context of poles of competitiveness or top clusters, offer possibilities for more intensive communication. The City of Hamburg offers a relatively huge programme to subsidize concrete R&D projects based on cooperation between regional partners and private co-funding with a strong demand by the firms. For SMEs, however, this programme is too focused on formal R&D and the rationale in multinational firms and public research institutes. Here, additional intermediaries will help.

Besides instruments to attract creative service companies and to connect them with medium-technology firms, instruments to overcome knowledge disparities in the regions become increasingly important for metropolitan regions. Here, qualification schemes with relatively low formal knowledge requirements and a high share of practical application are used to encourage the integration of less qualified persons. Due to the good performance in many medium-technology sectors, scarcities of qualified staff create additional incentives for the firms to participate in these programmes. Many SMEs fear, however, losing their best resources to bigger firms, which are able to pay higher salaries and offer international and more attractive career prospects. Thus, most of the programmes are dominated by qualifications in the bigger firms. Increasing scarcities, however, will put more pressure on the SMEs to attend these programmes.

Industrial regions face more problems in offering attractive conditions for creative service companies, as the restricted density of firm population causes difficulties in developing sales markets. In these cases, however, attractive education and qualification infrastructures and incentives for R&D investments can at least help to develop more specialized service capabilities. Styria is a good example of a region with severe structural challenges after the decline of traditional heavy metal industries in the 1980s. High public investments and incentives for private R&D made Styria one of the leading European regions according to formal innovation indicators. The strong role of these prerequisites in this specific case can be proved by analysing the regional network investigated in our sample. This region is almost exclusively based on knowledge flows instead of material flows and the centrality of actors within the network depends particularly on formal R&D investments. This clearly underlines the potential of an industrial region to catch up with innovation opportunities in metropolitan areas. Again, the role of competence centres has to be considered. These centres offer support to those SMEs with restricted R&D capacities and help them to overcome the knowledge barriers to the regional knowledge clubs. The success of this support, however, is restricted to those SMEs that already show specific – at least tacit – and synthetic knowledge capabilities and are willing and able to develop their capabilities along growing diversification and formalization lines.

Wales as the other industrial region within the investigation concentrates more on knowledge capabilities on the firm level. For a long time, this approach has worked within the aeronautical sector, as the Welsh firms concentrate on specific capabilities within metal wing production and maintenance, repair and overhaul. The structural change of materials for aeroplanes towards composites led to severe challenges for the Welsh firms, as no composite firm was available in the cluster and the public research capacities were not available in the region. Airbus tried to foster the capacities by cooperation with suppliers and by encouraging composite suppliers from other countries to locate in Wales. In the mid- to long term, however, the firms in the cluster see the lack of research capacities and qualification suppliers as a major threat to the competitiveness of the cluster. This again stresses the importance of regional knowledge policies for the European industries connecting traditional instruments to improve the formal knowledge base with structures for interaction between firms and inclusion of less qualified groups.

Campania and Silesia are the two lagging regions in our sample. Policy-making in these regions is heavily influenced by European cohesion policies. For a long time, policies in these regions have focused more on capital transfers and formal research capacities. During the last few years, Campania has developed new institutional structures to enhance the connections between the public research facilities, in particular in the regional universities, and the SMEs. So far, however, intermediaries acting as competence centres with the different functions already explained are missing. The need for infrastructures in regions like Campania mainly refers to the integration of conventional SMEs into knowledge interactions and the encouragement of spin-offs from the public research organizations to diversify the knowledge base. Similarly, Silesia is looking for institutional solutions to link the existing public research capacities and

Table 5.3   Differences between incumbent and new regional policy
strategies with regard to R&D infrastructures

	Incumbent Regional Policies	Regional Knowledge Policy
Target groups	Public research organizations, R&D-intensive firms	R&D-intensive firms, creative service firms, less qualified groups, conventional SMEs
Focus on knowledge	Formal analytical knowledge provided in scientific or high-technology research	Symbolic, analytical and synthetic knowledge considering tacit elements
Function of infrastructures	Delivery of R&D products	Platforms for interaction
Instruments	Public R&D investments and subsidies	Public research and education organizations, spatial planning, joint research projects
Coordinating institution	Science parks, technology transfer offices	Competence centres

existing linkages between former state firms towards knowledge cooperation including strategic development of skills and R&D capacities.

Table 5.3 provides a summary of the differences in the context of R&D
infrastructures. The main differences refer to the inclusion of creative services and less qualified groups. Besides classical R&D subsidies, instruments
are needed to enhance the connections between different organizations
and between groups with different knowledge capabilities. Furthermore,
spatial planning can help to integrate thus far separated groups and to
attract mobile highly qualified groups. Thus, knowledge infrastructures
have to be defined in a broader sense than before.

On the European level, a major role is the support of gateways to infrastructures in lagging regions. As explained above, the metropolitan areas
have sufficient locational advantages to attract highly qualified workforces and service segments and to develop new initiatives for social inclusion. In many lagging regions, the critical mass for interactions is often
missing, and these regions are threatened by massive emigration of better-
qualified citizens. In contrast to incumbent strategies of cohesion policies
that focus on capital transfers and formal organizations, programmes to
enhance linkages between the knowledge infrastructures in lagging and
more advanced regions are needed. These linkages, however, have to be
specified and adjusted to the needs and codes in the affected areas despite
existing programmes strengthening interregional cooperation in general.

5.2.4 Challenge: Funding Within Regional Knowledge Networks

Funding is always seen as a major hindrance towards competitiveness of innovative clusters. Consequently, the objectives of the Lisbon Process focus on the public and private expenditures for formal R&D. The importance of these investments has already been stressed within this section by showing the relevance of formal R&D capacities for the emergence of knowledge networks within our investigated regions. More important than the amount of money spent on formal R&D, however, is the way this money is used. In particular, medium technologies with their specificities in innovation processes are characterized by the need to synthesize the theoretical insights from formal knowledge with capabilities developed specifically for certain applications. Thus, funding for regional knowledge networks has to be oriented towards incentives for strategic knowledge interactions between regional firms and between firms and research organizations.

One important element of this incentive strategy is the allocation of responsibilities for funding and the control of its use. The case of the Austrian competence centres reveals the importance of co-funding structures: the share of the public funding is used to finance the resource basis of the intermediaries and the more long-term and specific aspects of their work, while private funding is used to pay for specific services and deliveries within projects. The participation of the private firms in the funding has two functions: first, it signals the value of the intermediary's services to the demanding firm and creates incentives to make as much as possible from this service, while a completely subsidized service would be used as a free good. Second, the competitive pressure to attract private funding creates incentives for the competence centre to focus on actual needs in the market and to utilize its resources efficiently. The public share in funding, however, is needed to finance the collective service of the competence centres: long-term strategies and initiatives for new projects are too uncertain and too weakly related to the exclusive benefits of specific firms to be sufficiently attractive for a private firm. This public share might change with maturity of the network and its capabilities: it might be higher in lagging regions with weaker companies, and it might be close to zero in very competitive areas with a high share of strong multinational firms and SMEs.

Another important element of the incentive strategy is the focus on funding to adjust to changes within the supply chain management of OEMs. Many SMEs in medium-technology industries are confronted with the requirements of the OEMs to take further financial risks with regard to the relocation of production sites, the development of new products or the market risks of the final product. These risks cannot be managed with traditional ways of finance by bank credits or loans within families. Therefore, some SMEs become the target of private equity funds or takeovers by bigger firms. Instruments to protect the sovereignty of the SMEs, while broadening the private equity sources, come particularly from mezzanine capital. These instruments are offered from private banks as well as from public development banks and consist in part of private equity – like, for example, profit participation certificates, silent partnerships or secondary loans – without changing the votes in the decision-making process of the management. These instruments are particularly available in Germany, but also in different forms in other European countries. So far, the supply exceeds the demand, as many SMEs fear the higher prices for capital and the uncertainties regarding the actual effects of this type of financing. Growing experience in management of SMEs and increasing pressure by takeovers, however, will lead to further demand in the near future.

Table 5.4 illustrates the main differences between incumbent regional policies and regional knowledge policies in the context of funding. Here, the priorities lie in the co-funding structure of the instruments and in the close relationships to private capital markets. In contrast to high-technology sectors where venture capital markets are used to finance high-risk investments with strong information asymmetries, firms in the

Table 5.4   Differences between incumbent and new regional policy strategies with regard to R&D funding

	Incumbent Regional Policies	Regional Knowledge Policy
Funding structure	Public funding to create incentives for R&D investments and exploitation	Public–private partnership to integrate private market elements and collective goods
Objective of the funding	Private R&D, formal knowledge	Strategic development, knowledge interactions and inclusion of different forms of knowledge
Evaluation of the instruments	Formal evaluation based on orders from public authorities	Private market evaluation based on the development of regional clusters and demand
Funding structure in the companies	Credit-based funding, increasing share of foreign equity	Mezzanine instruments strengthening private equity
Coordination of the funding	Coordination within public authority or experts commissions	Combination of contests and private (capital and R&D services) market assessment

medium-technology sectors can already offer a wide range of experiences and information. Thus, investments are less risky for the private market and the share of public subsidization within the mezzanine capital can usually be limited to small signals.

The experiences on the regional level offer important hints for the funding on the European level. Within the EU RTD Framework Programmes, many SMEs complain about the need for co-funding. Actually, the main source for complaint, however, is the dissatisfaction with the value of the subsidies compared with the costs to bear. By focusing on support for those regional intermediaries with a relatively high share of collective goods, for example in lagging regions or regions of transition, the EU would be able to show the specific worth of those supports, while the SMEs would have to pay for those services, where they find a clear benefit for themselves.

5.2.5   Challenge: Identity as a Regional Knowledge Network

In the third chapter, we argued that identity networks are typical for low-technology sectors. But even for other industrial firms in other technology segments, identity plays a major role in creating necessary trust for inter-actions, in overcoming fears of opportunistic behaviour by others and in inducing linkages between firms from high- and medium-technology indus-tries. Traditionally, identity is induced by long-term personal linkages of firm leaders in SMEs to the regions of origin, and networking is restricted to connections between SMEs. Structural challenges in medium-technol-ogy industries, however, hinder the identity of firms, as linkages between SMEs, system suppliers and big multinational firms are now needed. The increasing internationalization of production, however, restricts the connections between firms and regions, the disparities between big firms and SMEs cause fear in the SMEs of exploitation, and the higher labour mobility reduces the loyalty of employees and management to the regional firms. Consequently, regions need new programmes and instruments to overcome these difficulties.

The investigated regions in our samples follow different pathways towards identity. The firms in Campania have already been located for a relatively long time. Thus, the sense of belonging of the firm leaders to the region is rooted within personal experience. The main challenge in this context affects the linkage of these preconditions with institutional and cognitive linkages.

The situation in Hamburg is completely different, as the aeronautics cluster is relatively young with many firms entering the cluster only after the decision of Airbus in the 1990s to locate the final assembly in Hamburg. At the beginning of the decade, firms, research organizations, associations, universities and regional government developed a joint location initiative for aeronautics based on social events and joint activities in specific areas. The social events include presentations by firm leaders, exchanges of entrepreneurs from other areas (Midi-Pyrénées or Aquitaine) or joint seminars. Typical examples of joint activities are qualification programmes and finance and technological issue-related activities. For the SMEs within the sample, the connection between the issue-related activities and personal linkages play an important role, as it enables the firms to gain experience with the partners and to work on concrete solutions for structural challenges. The joint activities are supported by the regional association of SMEs in the aeronautical sector, which uses its reputation as a private association of entrepreneurs to encourage the participation of the firms. The initiative has its own website and communication on trade and industry fairs. Furthermore, it is integrated into the list of German competence networks and the nucleus for its application as a top cluster. Limits to these activities within the initiative, however, affect the linkages between the social links and the cooperation on formal R&D.

Similar initiatives can be observed in Wales. Here, a regional association (Aerospace Wales Forum) organizes conferences and other social events and tries to establish itself as a moderating intermediary between the regional firms. As in the case of Hamburg, Airbus plays a central role as a supporter of the initiative. Again, the impact on knowledge flows is limited due to the weak formal knowledge base of many firms and the lack of available research organizations in the region. These activities, however, are an important first step for a region with only weak linkages thus far.

Summing up, Table 5.5 shows the major differences between incumbent regional policies and knowledge policies in the context of regional identity. Within knowledge policies, these activities serve as prerequisites for further initiatives to intensify knowledge linkages and interactions, as they reduce the uncertainties about the reliability of partners. Although the internationalization of markets strengthens tendencies towards formal linkages between cooperation partners based on technological standards and requirements of formal knowledge, many SMEs in medium-technology industries are still used to personal linkages and joint social norms. Therefore, these social events help to integrate the SMEs into strategic regional processes and reduce transaction costs. The higher the share of international firms and workforce in the regions, the more important are these integrative measures to prevent segmentation. These activities focusing on identity are typical for the regional level. On the European level, the only need for action refers to coordination of different regional initiatives, for example to use social events as starting points for future knowledge interactions beyond regional boundaries.

Table 5.5   Differences between incumbent and new regional policy strategies in the context of identity

	Incumbent Regional Policies	Regional Knowledge Policy
Objective of activities	Exploitation of existing personal and social linkages	Identity as prerequisite for strategy processes
Activities	Social events within existing associations and clubs	Organized social events linked with topics of general interest within the cluster
Linkages	Personal and social proximities	Personal linkages as starting point for cognitive and organizational linkages
Funding	Private associations	Public–private partnerships
Coordination	Weak coordination based on private associations	Competence centres

5.2.6   Challenge: Openness Towards Knowledge from Other Regional Knowledge Networks

Cluster policies in many regions concentrate on the development of knowledge flows within the region. This concentration on intra-regional knowledge flows, however, causes risks of lock-in situations. Structural changes in medium-technology industries require even more transregional knowledge flows to diversify the knowledge base, accelerate the generation and exploitation of innovations and to attract human resources beyond the regional boundaries. The extension of regional networks beyond the spatial boundaries, however, causes additional challenges: social control mechanisms are limited, as well as possibilities to exploit F2F contacts and to use joint cultural and social norms. Therefore, regional knowledge policies need additional instruments and programmes to build up gatekeepers and gateways between regional networks.

A gatekeeper approach can be observed in Styria. Here, competence centres not only offer their services to regional firms, but also to multinational firms from other regions, and cooperate with firms and research organizations, in particular in German regions, where automotive clusters exist for a long time. Other gatekeepers in Styria are multinational firms acting as gatekeepers for knowledge flows both ways. On the one hand, they use experience in other regions, where the knowledge development might be more advanced in specific areas, to send new stimuli to the regional knowledge interactions. On the other hand, they attempt to export experience to less advanced, in particular Central and Eastern, regions to exploit cost advantages. In these cases, however, the firm managers face limits to successful transfers of experience: some Styrian firms even halted their relocation processes to low-cost regions.

In contrast to gatekeeper approaches, gateway models try to establish linkages between regions and to improve the absorptive capacities of regional firms. The firms in the aeronautical cluster in Hamburg have several of these instruments available. One of the most traditional instruments for transregional linkages in medium-technology industries is the establishment of trade and industry fairs: Hamburg applied successfully for the relocation of the leading global fair on aircraft interiors. The regional association of SMEs in the aeronautical sector organizes joint presentations not only on the fair in Hamburg but also for fairs in Asia and other European countries. Instruments developed by the regional government refer to joint qualification schemes with Midi-Pyrénées and Aquitaine: the most concrete initiative on qualification schemes affect vocational training courses based on general agreements on curricula with an exchange year for students. During this year, the students work in internships. Other activities within this context are the organization of cooperation between university staff from the different regional universities and exchange programmes of entrepreneurs visiting each other at least once a year. As a result, the first joint university courses are being offered with stays in Hamburg and Toulouse.

European approaches to strengthening transregional linkages, particularly in the aeronautical sector, focus on the provision of funding for information technologies. Within the sixth EU RTD Framework Programme, three different European organizations compete with each other in offering gateways towards European co-funding for joint research projects. The participation rates, however, are thus far limited, as the SMEs face only limited incentives for participation: the benefits for the firms are limited to cost savings within the application process (the firms receive the opportunity to register themselves on a search programme for cooperation, and the European organizations shoulder the burden of coordination with big firms and administrative costs). On the other hand, the firms have to organize the co-funding and administrative prerequisites and expect only limited benefits from R&D cooperation. Consequently, only few firms take the opportunity to register on the sites. Further developments of the existing approaches are directed towards the emergence of strategic partnerships with big multinational firms. The linkages to the regional SMEs will be intensified by the regional associations of the SMEs. These linkages, however, are limited due to the too indirect benefits of European linkages.

These experiences in one sector are similar to developments in other contexts of intermediaries, where European organizations serve as an umbrella for transregional cooperation, for example, technology transfer offices, business incubators, innovation relay centres or regional development agencies. Those services are particularly important for SMEs in medium-technology sectors, as they often lack contacts to firms in other regions or countries and need information to develop internationalization strategies. The members of these transboundary networks often achieve a high level of cooperation due to similar functions and experiences strengthening the cognitive proximity. The main challenge, however, remains in the context of diffusion. Here, the impact is limited to concrete cases, where firms in the region see the benefits of contacts with and information about other regions. Regional representatives can try to raise the awareness for more international contacts, but without a clear market perspective these attempts remain limited in their impact. Consequently, the organizational umbrella can help to manage the interface between representatives in the different regions; the actual diffusion of learning experiences, however, is limited to regions with emerging economic relationships.

Table 5.6 illustrates the main differences between incumbent regional development policies and new regional knowledge policies with regard to transregional cooperation. The strong focus on transregional interactions is already a major difference, as so far most of the regional policies have been restricted to the region. The examples of joint qualification schemes, exchange programmes and institutional support stress the importance of standardization in the European context to facilitate the cooperation and identify common objectives. The actual impact of these initiatives as

Table 5.6   Differences between incumbent and new regional policy strategies referring to transregional cooperation

	Incumbent Regional Policies	Regional Knowledge Policy
Objective of the activities	Exchange of experiences, general coordination	Transboundary knowledge flows extending the diversity of the knowledge base
Core activities	Mutual visits by politicians and regional representatives	Incentives for gatekeeper organizations and gateway products like joint qualification schemes
Funding	Based on EU programmes	Public–private partnerships based on strategic deliberation
Linkages	Personal linkages between representatives	Organizational and cognitive linkages
Coordinating institution	Regional development agency	Competence centres and their European umbrella

well as the services provided by the intermediaries organized in European umbrella associations, however, will be always dependent on the actual motivation and capabilities in the SMEs.

In this context, the European Union can play a major role by providing the coordinating infrastructures for the umbrella organizations and by intensifying standardization of qualification programmes and other issues of possible cooperation.

5.3   THE ROLE OF KNOWLEDGE CREATION IN INNOVATION POLICY

The innovation process in medium-tech sectors is different from the 'linear' approach focusing on R&D expenditure and the rational process of optimization of individual firms, and it can be interpreted according to a 'systemic' approach. This approach focuses on the related processes of knowledge creation and collective interactive learning (Lundvall and Johnson, 1994; Florida, 1995; Morgan, 1997; Keeble et al., 1999; Lawson and Lorenz, 1999; Steiner and Hartmann, 2006), on the iterative adaptation between the different partners and on an implicit automatic selection of the most competitive innovations. While a linear approach aims to promote transfers of information and modern technology or to provide customized expertise to individual firms, a systemic approach (Lundvall, 1992; Antonelli, 2005) focuses on promoting knowledge networks and cooperation between the various local and external actors in regional innovation systems and on the development of their internal capabilities.

The innovation process in SMEs and in medium-technology sectors is of a gradual nature and is driven by an intensive interaction between the suppliers and the customers and other actors. This process of interactive learning leads to the development of 'tacit' knowledge represented by a complex set of capabilities, which are localized or idiosyncratic and cannot easily be transferred (Nonaka and Konno, 1998; Rizzello, 1999; Cohendet and Steinmueller, 2000; Howells, 2002; Cappellin, 2003b, 2004a; Wink, 2003). The emerging 'knowledge clusters', characterized by intense knowledge interactions between the various local actors (Maillat and Kebir, 1999; Simmie, 2005; Cooke et al., 2006; van Geenhuizen and Nijkamp, 2006), are the result of the evolution from the traditional industrial 'fordist' model, based on the exploitation of economies of scale external to the firms but internal to the cluster, to the model of the 'knowledge economy' (Lundvall, 1992; Nelson, 1993; Braczyk et al., 1997; Cooke and Morgan, 1998; Asheim and Clark, 2001; Bougrain and Haudeville, 2002; Asheim, Coenen, et al., 2007).

From a policy perspective, the research in the IKINET project has clarified that:

- not only large firms but SMEs also compete through innovation;
- clusters of SMEs promote innovation and the most important innovations are not the result of a single entrepreneur, but of the interaction between various economic actors;
- while codified knowledge may diffuse in international networks, the process of knowledge creation works in a localized framework;
- medium-technology sectors are the largest positive component in the European trade balance;
- competitiveness in medium-technology sectors is determined by the speed of innovation and creativity rather than by lower production costs;
- R&D is not the main factor of innovation in medium-technology sectors, but rather tacit knowledge, human competencies, learning processes and networks;
- innovation policies in medium-technology sectors should shift from a focus on technology transfers to a focus on knowledge creation;
- human resources should not be considered as a factor of resistance to the adoption of innovation but rather as the source of core capabilities and the key actors in learning and knowledge creation;
- networks represent institutions that favour knowledge creation and innovation;
- the spontaneous clustering processes of innovative activities is not always sufficient for competitiveness and it needs to be complemented by the design of an explicit cluster strategy.

Thus, the transition to the model of the knowledge economy and the above indicated empirical analysis and theoretical framework imply a distinct change in the industrial development strategies and in the policy approach to technological change. According to the traditional industrial model, technologies are basically a product, similar to the case of new equipment. This implies that firms have to invest in R&D, since this allows the generatation of new technologies. However, they may also directly buy the required technology in the technology market. Technology would lead to an increase of productivity, a decrease of labour inputs and a decrease of costs. Thus, technology would directly solve the problem of the competitiveness of a firm. Resistance to the adoption of technologies by labour would require an effort to increase its receptivity. The ideal model, according to the traditional linear approach, would be a totally automated plant or a firm run by a single person, where production is completely outsourced or performed by machines. Thus, technologies are similar to a bitter medicine, which implies both a direct cost for its internal production or its external acquisition and also various indirect costs related to the need to downsize and re-skill the labour force.

On the other hand, in the model of knowledge economy, the aim of the firms is not the adoption of modern technologies but rather the fast adoption of product and process innovation, in order to respond to the changed needs of the users of the product or service. Innovation is not a product, but rather a dynamic process, and flexibility and speed of adoption are the key factors of competitiveness and not production costs. Innovation requires information, new knowledge and technical and organizational capabilities. These latter are the result of collective processes of interactive learning, where the key actors are the people, such as the entrepreneurs, skilled technicians and workers. Creativity is not the result of the individual inventors, but of the collective and continuous effort by a specific team or by a professional community. Therefore, the labour force is not the object on which technology has an impact, but rather the key actor that promotes innovation (Almeida and Kogut, 1999; Florida, 2002; Handly et al., 2006; Andersson, 2003; Van Oort, Weterings and Verlinde, 2003; Stambøl, 2005; Felix, 2006; Amin and Roberts, 2008; Duguid, 2008). Hence, investment in continuous education at all levels of the organization is needed as well as the promotion of interactions between various individuals by investing in the creation of networks, clusters, intermediate institutions and 'social capital' (Coleman, 1988; Putnam, 1993; Cappellin, 1997, 2004b, 2004c; Lagendijk and Cornford, 2000).

Table 5.7 highlights the crucial points that distinguish a systemic approach from a linear approach in promoting innovation in medium-technology sectors. According to a systemic approach, focus should shift from the aim to promote the adoption of modern technology to that of enhancing internal capabilities and knowledge. The stimulus to change and innovation within firms is not only determined by the pressure of competition, the need to increase productivity and reduce costs, or the opportunity created by the supply of modern technologies and to adopt modern equipment, but by the identification of new markets, the aim to adapt to changes in the demand and the opportunity to satisfy users, new needs.

While in the linear process of innovation the formal process of R&D investment plays a key role, the systemic approach of innovation pronounces that solutions are gradually discovered through a process of interactive learning involving many different actors also outside the R&D laboratories. The desired outcomes are not just the increase of productivity indicators, often interpreted as a disjoint result, but rather the speed of a continuous process of innovation, where each change is the evolution of previous changes. Entrepreneurship and governance, through

Table 5.7   Why the process of innovation in SMEs and in medium-technology sectors differs from that of large firms in high-tech sectors

	Linear Approach	Systemic Approach
Keyword	Technology	Knowledge
Stimulus	Cost competition, supply changes and new equipment	Market orientation, demand changes and user needs
Process	In-house R&D and technology transfers	Interactive learning
Role of human resources	Labour substitution and receptivity to new technologies	Competencies of the actors, creativity and entrepreneurship
Competitive-ness factor	Productivity increase and economies of scale	Continuous innovation, flexibility and fast change
Governance process	Rational optimization by individual firms and market competition	Connectivity, iterative adaptation and selection within innovation networks
Policies	Public finance to R&D and public market regulation	Multilevel governance, bridging institutions and public–private partnership

public–private partnership, are required to organize the joint effort of different actors and firms. The focus shifts from stimulating competition between the local actors to promoting connectivity and iterative processes of reciprocal adaptation and selection of the best productive combinations. Innovation policies should promote the process of knowledge creation, instead of solely the adoption of technologies, and creativity, which is based on diversity, close interaction between different and dispersed actors and on the capability to establish new connections between different pieces of information and knowledge. In fact, networks organize diversity and facilitate the combination of information and knowledge.

Medium-tech industries should not only integrate knowledge from new high-technology and scientific segments but also develop internal competencies through interactive learning processes to obtain competitive knowledge advantages on the global markets and in new production fields. Thus, cluster policies should promote investment in intangible assets in the regions, such as investments in the continuous professional training of the labour force. Moreover, cluster policies should invest in a better organization of the cognitive relationships between the local actors, as indicated by the approach of territorial knowledge management (Cappellin, 2003b, 2007; Wink, 2003; Benzler and Wink, 2005; Harmaakorpi and Melkas,

2005). The existing technological know-how or 'synthetic' knowledge in production activities should be connected with greater creativity, improved quality of products and modern services and with the capability to respond to new needs of users.

This requires a change in the corporate culture to promote knowledge sharing and the willingness to collaborate within and between the firms. Human resources should not be considered only for their absorptive capacity and the resistance to the adoption of modern technologies, but rather as the actors who are endowed with specific capabilities and promote innovation. Formal education and life-long learning are instruments that enable the building of competencies of various partners in a local knowledge network and their ability to use external tacit and codified knowledge in the process of innovation. As creativity may be hindered by the lack of required competencies in the local economy, there is the need for cooperation with international universities and major international companies. In particular, clusters should be better capable of combining synthetic or engineering knowledge with analytic or scientific knowledge. That requires an improvement of the relationships between firms, universities and research institutions in cooperative research projects.

As indicated in the previous chapter, different types of clusters are characterized by different types of knowledge flows and different levels of institutional integration. In particular, ecological networks are characterized by a low level of connectivity, identity networks by an intermediate level and strategic networks by a high level of connectivity. Moreover, science-based sectors are characterized by analytical or science-based knowledge, medium-technology sectors are characterized by the importance of synthetic or engineering knowledge and low-tech sectors are often characterized only by knowledge based on symbolic creativity. Therefore, the policy tools needed to promote the flows of various types of knowledge (that is, symbolic, synthetic and analytic knowledge) vary according to the specific network type to be considered (that is, ecological, identity and strategic networks), as indicated in Table 5.8.

First, from a pure free market perspective, as in 'ecological networks', the firms are individual independent units causing a focus on the provision of general non-material infrastructures, which may enable the contacts between the firms and the circulation of information, such as cultural expositions, industrial fairs, university education and scientific publications. Instead, the concept of 'identity networks' leads to the consideration of not only the individual firms but also collective structures, such as an industrial cluster. This leads to the adoption of a multilevel governance approach and the development of policy tools aiming to promote and strengthen the cultural, technical, entrepreneurial and scientific

Table 5.8   The policy instruments in innovation policy

Types of Knowledge	Forms of Governance		
	In ecological networks	In identity networks	In strategic networks
Symbolic knowledge	Expositions	Cultural and professional associations	Specialized schools and joint projects for international contests or tenders (call for proposals)
Synthetic knowledge	Fairs	Industry and professional associations	Territorial knowledge management, joint projects, networks of competence centres
Analytic knowledge	University education and publications	Scientific associations and networks	Joint R&D projects and networks of centres of excellence

associations that may link the individual actors, firms or workers within various professional communities and networks. Finally, the concept of 'strategic networks' indicates the need for a coordinated action towards common aims and using dedicated resources. This leads to the identification of a complex set of policy instruments that represent 'intermediate' institutions or 'bridging' institutions, capable of designing and organizing strategic joint actions, such as for example:

- specialized schools;
- international contests or tenders (call for proposals);
- joint industrial projects;
- strategic planning contracts with large firms;
- cooperative research projects between SMEs;
- regional innovative start-up funds;
- joint R&D projects;
- autonomous non-governmental research institutions or foundations;
- regional technological parks and centres;
- local stakeholders coordination tables;
- territorial pacts with local actors;
- RIS – regional innovation systems;
- national programmes for R&D and innovation networks;
- territorial knowledge management;
- networks of research centres of excellence;
- networks of competence centres.

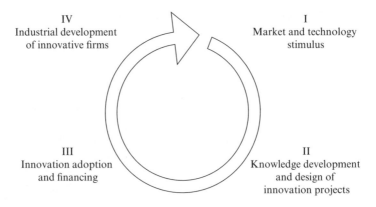

IV
Industrial development
of innovative firms

I
Market and technology
stimulus

III
Innovation adoption
and financing

II
Knowledge development
and design of
innovation projects

Figure 5.1   The fields of innovation policies

In conclusion, a systemic approach leads to the identification of a more complex set of policy actions for innovation policies, rather than the single financing of R&D, as indicated in Figure 5.1. In fact, policies should first promote openness and receptivity of the firms to the stimulus coming from international competition, from the creation of new market needs and from the availability of new technologies. Second, policies should also promote the creation of new knowledge suitable for solving the problems and stimulate the design of innovative projects proposed by large firms and by groups of SMEs. Then, policies should promote the receptivity of the local actors in the adoption of innovation and facilitate a proper evaluation and financing of the innovation projects by banking institutions. Finally, policies should promote the coordination between the various large and small firms, their reciprocal adaptation and the integration of innovative firms in international and local technology and production networks.

5.4   THE GOVERNANCE OF NETWORKS IN MEDIUM-TECHNOLOGY SECTORS

The approach of learning networks underlines the fact that time is the key dimension of innovation. The competitiveness of firms in regional innovation systems requires a faster speed of the process of change than in competing firms and regions. Well-structured production and innovation networks reduce transaction costs and adjustment costs and that allows a faster speed of the process of change to accelerate the policy-making process and to decrease the decision and implementation times. Innovation requires flexible forms of cooperation between many different private and public, regional and international actors, such as large firms, SMEs' suppliers, knowledge-intensive services, higher education and research institutions, financial intermediaries, public administration and many other partners such as professional associations and media. Innovation requires the combination of different competencies within a process of collective learning, as firms must cooperate to increase and diversify their knowledge base.

The speed of information flows and decision-making processes and a faster adoption of innovation are closely related to the stability of the organizational forms and depend on the existence of a well-developed institutional system. A diversified typology of institutions plays a leading role in defining a long-term strategy of innovation of medium-technology sectors within different regions. These institutions represent the 'social capital' of these regions and play the role of non-material infrastructures that organize the knowledge flows between various firms. Moreover, institutional solutions to overcome lack of resources by SMEs are regionally specific and influenced by long-term historical and cultural heritage within the region.

However, the problem seems not to be the creation of new geographical clusters, but rather the promotion of new strategic projects in existing clusters and regions. In particular, the challenge of increasing international competition in medium-technology sectors calls for large projects realized within national thematic networks and building on the existing strengths and innovative capacities of various regions.

Cluster policies require new forms of governance of the relationships between various local actors and also the identification and selection of new actors. Thus, while medium-sized firms have developed vertical flows of tacit knowledge within their respective supply chain, they need to be supported to develop horizontal linkages between different technologies.

Moreover, industrial clusters specialized in medium-technology sectors require a better connection between industrial firms and modern knowledge-intensive business services (KIBS) and also an improvement of the relationship between industrial firms and financial institutions, such as private equity, to improve the evaluation procedures of risk for investment in innovation. Clearly, universities may play a key role in modern 'knowledge-based' clusters. They can develop new fields of activity ('third sectors'), for example, organize life-long training programmes together with professional associations and the promotion of creativity and entrepreneurship of their researchers by joining firms in the design of large complex innovation projects and in the creation of new specialized firms.

A policy for the knowledge economy based on the approach of 'governance' or 'dynamic coordination' implies the use of different policy instruments compared with those usually adopted in traditional innovation policies, such as:

- public R&D;
- public subsidies to private R&D;
- public demand for innovative products and services;
- IPR (intellectual property rights) in order to ensure a monopoly power to innovators.

The multiplication of players and layers of negotiation – international, national and local – demands a different model of government, called 'multilevel governance', based on organizational structures of interaction and partnership. The adoption of a governance approach in innovation policies for medium-technology sectors highlights different types of priorities. In particular, the adoption of a network approach in regional innovation policies highlights the importance of two major policy issues: the problem of adapting the structure of innovation networks and the problem of changing the behaviours of actors and nodes, as indicated in Box 5.2.

BOX 5.2   THE ADOPTION OF A NETWORK APPROACH IN INNOVATION POLICY

The development of knowledge and innovation networks in medium-technology sectors requires a modern governance approach, rather than relying on the traditional free market approach or the hierarchical planning approach. Innovation policies should promote the interaction between the various actors and the combination of their various capabilities.

I. *From the focus on individual firms to the governance of the network of firms*

Innovation policies according to a governance approach should adapt the structure of innovation and knowledge networks to external and internal changes. This requires measures addressed to the following elements and characteristics of a network:

1. Focus on key nodes rather than adopt general measures. Networks mostly have a quasi-hierarchical character and gateways in the knowledge and innovation networks may be made by firms, research institutions, public administration, customers, associations of people, geographical areas.

2. Create new nodes and promote diversity. Enhance innovative spin-offs from firms, recognize competence and technological centres as new actors in innovation networks and attract new actors, in order to avoid lock-in effects.

3. Create missing links and promote integration between weakly connected nodes. Enhance the direct relationships between various selected actors in order to avoid closure and the incompatibility between two nodes.

4. Promote international links and avoid regional closure. Promote the interconnectivity between regional networks and international networks and identify nodes performing the role of international gateways. Innovation policies should promote international networking of knowledge flows rather than only stimulate exports or production decentralization. International technological cooperation with non-local research centres and also multinational firms should complement local knowledge and capabilities.

5. Create intermediate institutions and reduce transaction costs. The creation and development of bridging institutions requires ad hoc investment. They represent non-material and material infrastructures facilitating the flows of knowledge and information between the nodes of a network.

6. Reorient the form of the networks. Governance of knowledge networks requires the adjustment of the paths of relationships between two nodes and the transformation of indirect links into direct links, and the cancellation of previous links in knowledge networks, in subcontracting and in financial networks.

7. Promote the speed of innovation and flexibility. Accelerate the time of changes by reducing the adjustment costs or switching costs in the change of the various links of the knowledge and innovation networks and increase their flexibility. Governance aims to decrease the adjustment costs in the change of the links between the nodes of innovation networks and to promote iterative and interactive adjustments, rather than general and static optimization, as systematic incremental innovation may bring about systemic radical innovation in the long term.

8. Adopt more hierarchical forms of organization and identify leaders and a strategy. Innovation policies should promote the evolution from informal to formal routines, from communities or

'ecological' networks and 'identity' networks to 'strategic' networks. The design and organization of strategic projects in existing clusters and regional innovation systems is preferable to the creation of new organizations and new clusters.

II. *From the distribution of R&D public funds to the connection of innovative capabilities*

Innovation policies should orient the working of knowledge and innovation networks in medium-technology sectors by enhancing and connecting the capabilities and the behaviours of the various actors, as indicated in the territorial knowledge management approach. That implies facilitating the following functions and capabilities:

1. Respond to the demand of markets and sectors. Innovation stimulus in medium-technology sectors is driven by the demand of clients and markets rather than being supplier dominated. Innovation should be more oriented to solving localized problems than being pushed by the application of scientific discoveries.
2. Promote receptivity and attractivity. Promote 'cognitive proximity', rather than just geographical accessibility and transfer of codified knowledge, and promote interactive learning between the workers, experts and entrepreneurs in the firms, aimed at the creation of collective tacit knowledge.
3. Promote the building of a common identity, trust, the consensus on common values. Governance aims to promote cooperation and innovation differently from a free market approach focusing on competition and price flexibility. Trust and networks are required for ensuring lower transaction costs, lower information asymmetries and the sharing of tacit knowledge and allow interactive learning in local innovation networks. Innovation policies should promote joint investments and the commitment to long-term investment in innovative projects, based on the alignment to common goals and ex ante coordination rather than just commercial short-term exchange and subcontracting.
4. Enhance the creative capabilities and the diversity of the actors in innovation networks. Innovation policies should focus on the capability to combine complementary knowl-

edge components in an original way and allow the creative destruction of old technologies, and not just promote technology transfers, imitation and adoption, incremental increase of fixed capital and financing of R&D.

5. Promote the capabilities of collective governance. Innovation policy should adopt a multilevel governance approach, which is based on negotiations and represents an alternative to the free market model and the planning policy-making model, based on competition and hierarchical control. The key questions in multilevel governance are 'how' and 'who' rather than 'what' to do.

6. Design and adopt new regulations and defend weak and dispersed interests. Governance should link the various nodes and anticipate the latent demand and use them to determine the creation of new markets for innovative products and services. Governance should not only focus on the regulation of the relationships between the major stakeholders, but it should also adopt new regulations and defend weak and dispersed interests, such as in security and environmental protection.

In fact, all recent regional innovation theories, such as industrial districts and clusters (Becattini, 1990; Pyke et al., 1990; Cappellin, 1998; Brenner, 2004), 'innovative milieux' (Capello, 1999; Crevoisier and Camagni, 2000; Capello and Faggian, 2005), regional innovation systems (Cooke, 1998; Cooke and Morgan 1998), the dynamics of proximity (Bellet et al., 1993; Rallet and Torre, 1998; Torre, 2003; Torre and Gallaud, 2004; Boschma, 2005; Torre and Rallet, 2005; Torre, 2008) and the learning regions (Florida, 1995; Morgan, 1997; Maillat and Kebir, 1999; van Geenhuizen and P. Nijkamp, 2006) stress the increasing importance of a network approach and closely related elements, such as territorial embeddedness, interactive learning and institutional thickness.

Therefore, the empirical and theoretical research on innovation within medium-technology sectors highlights the need for an evolution of regional innovation policies:

*   from the traditional free market approach or the hierarchical planning approach to a modern governance approach;
*   from the focus on individual firms to the governance of the network of firms;
*   from the distribution of R&D public funds to the connection of innovative capabilities;

- from a focus on exploitation of specific technologies to the exploration of diverse technologies;
- from sectoral specialization to intersectoral integration and sectoral diversification;
- from a focus on process innovation and cost competition to product innovation and time competition;
- from a focus on accessibility to technological sources to receptivity by the local actors;
- from the supply of R&D infrastructures to the identification of the new demand by the final and intermediate users;
- from the distribution of public funds to the stimulation of private investments;
- from informal cooperation based on trust to formal commitment on strategic projects.

Innovation policies should devise different instruments for specific target groups. Moreover, the subject matter of innovation and technology policy is highly heterogeneous in scope, and is made by a variety of policy fields, diverse institutions and numerous agents. Thus, any potential solution will require highly complex strategies of intervention.

Innovation policy is a field of competing legislation between various levels of government (Karl and Wink, 2006), and a closer vertical cooperation should be complemented by an increasing specialization of the policy field of individual institutions according to the subsidiarity principle. Thus, innovation policies increasingly require a European dimension. In fact, not only high-technology sectors, but also medium-technology sectors need to be integrated in a 'European knowledge economy', as they represent a major component of European international competitiveness. Moreover, regional innovation systems specialized in medium-technology sectors require that the effects of market mechanism are integrated by European policy and institutions to ensure a continuous growth and a long-term sustainability by managing the economic, political, social, environmental imbalances related to economic and technological change.

5.5 THE CHARACTERISTICS OF THE COMPETENCE CENTRES POLICY

National and regional competence centres (see Box 5.3) are designed to stimulate cooperation in research and technological development in strategic important production fields between companies, academia, the public sector and other organizations involved in promoting innovation,

---

BOX 5.3   THE IKINET POLICY FORUM ON COMPETENCE CENTRES

The Policy Forum on 'Regional Competence Centres and European Knowledge and Innovation Networks: An International Comparison of Innovation Cluster Policies'[a] organized by the IKINET project has aimed to discuss the role of competence centres in innovation and industrial policies at the European, national and regional level. The Policy Forum of the IKINET project was held on 19–20 September, 2007 in Rome at the Department for Public Administration of the Presidency of the Council of Ministers, Palazzo Vidoni. It was promoted by the Italian Ministry for Innovation in Public Administration, Ministry of Economic Development, Ministry of Research and the Italian National Economic and Social Council. Almost 50 experts from many competence centres, regional administrations, Italian and foreign national agencies and public institutions, and of the European Commission participated in three sessions devoted to the discussion of:

Theme 1: How to promote international accessibility and cooperation between competence centres.
Theme 2: How to promote creativity and new innovative projects and companies.
Theme 3: How to promote an effective governance of networks of competence centres.

The Policy Forum advocated the need for international learning and benchmarking and the launch of programmes for the creation of networks of competence centres in countries and regions that do not have them. In particular, it aimed to investigate how competence centres can promote the international competitiveness of SMEs and how these latter can be linked in international networks of knowledge and innovation.

These programmes are highly similar in the various countries, while having different names, such as national networks of clusters, 'pôles de compétitivité', competence centres, centres of expertise or technological districts. Examples of national programmes include the following:

France: www.compétitivité.gouv.fr/;
Finland: www.oske.net/en/what_is_oske/objectives and
www.tekes.fi/eng/;
Austria: www.ffg.at and www.ffg.at/content.php.

The results of the IKINET research may help to illustrate the different dimensions of the process of knowledge creation at the local level and to provide guidelines for defining the strategy of competence centres.

[a] The contributions to this Forum can be downloaded at http://www.ikinet. uniroma2.it/Policy_Forum.htm.

overcoming the gap between precompetitive technological research and practical industrial application.

The idea of cluster policies and competence centres in various European countries is based on the following characteristics of competence centres:

- part of a national or regional network created by a national or regional public programme, which has defined a competitive mechanism for the selection of various proposals of competence centres and a national or regional agency for the steering of the overall network of competence centres;
- a regional focus but actions on an international scale;
- concentration on a specific thematic production field;
- capabilities to generate innovations with a particularly high value-added potential;
- coverage of many links in the value chain and connection between multiple sectors of industry and scientific disciplines;
- an outstanding communication and cooperation platform by promoting public–private partnership and existing networks between large and small firms and other regional actors in close cooperation with universities and research, educational and vocational centres;
- a common strategy of innovation and economic development for a specific territorial cluster or regional innovation system;
- an innovative and operational mode of 'governance' or a 'soft infrastructure' aiming at the development of synergies around specific collective innovation projects oriented toward one or more well-focused markets;

- a critical mass to develop international visibility in an industrial and/ or technological perspective and to increase the attractiveness of a cluster with respect to international competitors.

The experience of some countries where competence centres have been created in the last few years should be extended to many other European countries that still lack an explicit national programme for the creation and management of a national network of competence centres. Competence centres are new instruments of innovation policy that are suitable for the SMEs in medium-tech sectors.

5.6 THE AIMS OF A COMPETENCE CENTRE

The creation of competence centres (see, for example, Figure 5.2) and a focus on knowledge links indicate the need for a new framework for innovation policies at the regional, national and European level. Competence centres contribute to developing a new vision and long-term strategy and increase the awareness of needed changes in the clusters and the stimulus to firms and other actors in the clusters to innovate. Regional competence centres focused on new fields of production, related to traditional specializations in the various regions, may promote the collaboration between firms of different sectors having complementary competencies.

According to a systemic or network-oriented approach to innovation, competence centres should not only focus on financing precompetitive and competitive R&D and promoting technology transfers to individual firms: they should also aim to promote knowledge creation, network building, knowledge exchange, interactive learning, the development of labour competencies and the creativity capabilities of the clusters in the design of new projects. Competence centres should work as knowledge intermediaries and not only act as intermediaries that foster social and institutional proximity.

While in the case of 'analytical' knowledge national financing may be adequate, the cases of 'synthetic' knowledge and of 'symbolic' knowledge call more for the promotion of relations at the regional level. In particular, innovation in medium-tech sectors is facilitated by horizontal relations within territorial clusters, which may be accelerated by the creation of competence centres.

Competence centres are different from research 'centres of excellence', which mostly belong to larger research institutions and focus on well-defined fields of advanced precompetitive research, often in close

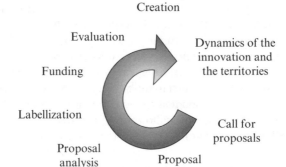

The 'Pôles de Compétitivité'
Creation

Evaluation

Dynamics of the
innovation and
Funding   the territories

Labellization

Call for
proposals
Proposal
analysis   Proposal

Source: Nicoulaud, B., 'The Pôles de Compétitivité', Ministry of Industry, Paris.

Figure 5.2   The stages in the creation of a competence centre

cooperation with specific industries aiming to raise the quality of research and to improve their international visibility and reputation. Competence centres should aim to promote the accumulation of knowledge between different firms and sectors through processes of interactive learning, rather than to focus only on the investment in R&D, as exchanges of tacit knowledge and building of specialized competencies should play a key role. However, competence centres may clearly contribute to the enlargement of the technological and general information base required for cultural and social development by focusing on innovative industrial projects and specifically on the competitiveness of national and regional industrial and innovation systems.

Competence centres are also different from the traditional 'technological centres' that have been created by local and regional institutions and aim to provide new technological and business services to individual SMEs within territorial clusters. Indeed, competence centres aim for the design and management of large joint projects with several firms and other partners for the development of innovative productions for the industrial diversification of a cluster.

Competence centres should not only focus on the needs of individual companies or vertical supply chains. They should also adopt a territorial perspective, that is, dealing with horizontal relations between different sectors, and an institutional perspective, that is, promoting new forms of multilevel governance.

Competence centres should carry out an exploration activity leading to the design of many large and small projects and not just represent ad hoc organizations created to manage one single specific large project. They should identify emerging needs in existing and new markets and create coalitions of regional and also international partners needed to solve the problems.

5.7   THE PARTNERS AND GOVERNANCE IN COMPETENCE CENTRES

Competence centres may be organized as a public–private partnership (see Figure 5.3.), where the regional government acts as a coordinator together with a consortium of private actors or the regional business promotion agency acting as supporting and managing institution. Cluster policies require new forms of governance of the relationships between the various local actors and they should also enhance the identification and selection of new actors. They should promote flexible forms of multilevel govern-ance through horizontal cooperation between firms belonging to different sectors and an improved cooperation between local, regional, national and European organizations and institutions instead of hierarchical forms of coordination by large firms within their respective specific supply chain to exploit economies of scale and cost decreases.

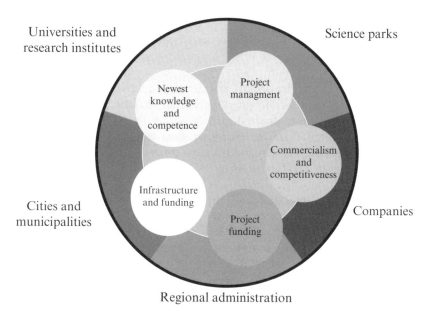

Figure 5.3   Main partners within a competence centre at the regional level

Competence centres may stimulate the firms to change their corporate strategy to a forward-looking model and represent a stimulus to the international openness of regional clusters by promoting forms of collaboration with external partners such as international research institutions and large international firms. Competence centres aim to free the innovation and entrepreneurial potential of a cluster or regional innovation system, since innovation depends on the contribution of many partners and small and medium-sized firms may take innovative choices to be followed later by large firms. Openness to new actors within the various clusters is a decisive prerequisite for sustainability to avoid path dependencies and lock-in effects or the emergence of an elitist club formed by few firms isolated from the rest of the cluster.

5.8   THE SELECTION OF STRATEGIC FIELDS IN A COMPETENCE CENTRE

Competence centres should adopt a selective approach and aim to identify and develop new strategic projects by exploiting intersectoral cognitive interdependencies at the local and international level rather than to sustain the existing fields of specialization in a given cluster (Figure 5.4).

As indicated above, the selection of these sectors can be guided by the acknowledgement that the factors of competitiveness of the European economy with respect to the many and large emerging economies are related to:

- the high diversification of industrial productions within various industrial clusters allowing the creation of new productions as a combination of traditional specializations;
- the emergence of new needs, which often have a collective nature, by consumers and citizens and the creation of new markets;
- a highly qualified labour force.

Regional policy should identify regional fields of competence and relevant target areas of new technology (Figure 5.5). The following three fields of competence can be identified as candidates for cluster policies according to their respective stage of development: (1) developed fields of competence well connected with the current specializations of the regional economy, (2) developing fields, where strength in the supply by research institutions does not correspond to the actual demand by the regional firms, (3) emerging fields in an early stage of research undertaken, which are in need of policy support for future development.

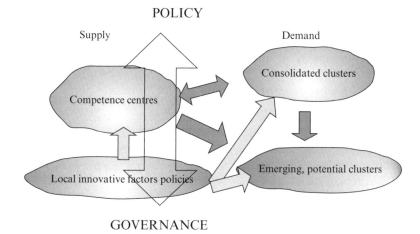

POLICY

Supply

Demand

Competence centres

Consolidated clusters

Local innovative factors policies

Emerging, potential clusters

GOVERNANCE

Source: Silvano Bertini, Economic Development Unit – Emilia-Romagna region.

Figure 5.4 The choice of the fields in a competence centre

	Mechanical and engineering clusters	Multimedia	Construction	Food	Traditional clusters	Energy environment	Health	Management, labour, organization
Microelectronics	X						X	
Sensoristics, Optoelectronics	X						X	
Nanotechnnologies	X		X	X			X	
Advanced materials	X		X				X	
Advanced engineering	X						X	
Software	X	X		X				
Industrial chemistry	X		X		X	X		
Chemistry			X		X	X	X	
Biotechnologies			X			X	X	
Food technologies			X					
Humanistic and Social Sciences		X	X	X	X			X

Source: Silvano Bertini, Economic Development Unit – Emilia-Romagna region.

Figure 5.5 Matching clusters and knowledge resources

Competence centres can promote various activities such as animation of the innovation network, create working groups, trainings, thematic events, elaborate prospective studies, provide support to find qualified human resources, promote research contracts with universities and research centres, technology surveys carried out on a regular basis, specific alliances with universities and research centres, provide support to international development and create strategic partnerships for international development.

5.9   THE FINANCIAL SUPPORT TO COMPETENCE CENTRES

Organizations operating in clusters are providers of new services that over the short-term are to be developed with the help of initial start-up funding, but that over the longer term should not be supported by government financing. This in-built need for self-financing makes it necessary for clusters to focus on developing services that generate clear operational benefits for companies in a short space of time. While clusters therefore support the development of new, company-related service structures, the prevailing financial considerations mean that short-term operational benefits are pushed to the fore, and long-term, strategic concerns tend to recede into the background.

The development of knowledge clusters requires time to build up internal codes and reputation. Public support via projects sometimes only leads to short-term structures, which run the risk of losing the engagement of partners after the end of external funding. However, pure long-term public funding would destroy incentives of the private partners to look for efficiency. Thus, a suitable way out for funding cluster structures could be public–private partnerships and collaboration with private financial intermediaries together with public funding for more long-term strategic projects of public interest. Thus, it seems appropriate to define more precisely the tasks to be accomplished by clusters and to identify three distinct fields of activity:

- support core cluster themes with public funding by devising long-term programmes lasting several years, as clusters can take on functions related more closely to the public sphere;
- integrate policies for clusters with a variety of policy fields, due to the multidimensional nature of innovation policies;
- understand clusters as providers of specific company-relevant services at normal market rates.

5.10 IKINET GUIDELINES FOR COMPETENCE CENTRES

Competence centres should combine a strategic approach focusing on the central decision on selected R&D projects with a decentralized approach aiming for the creation of wide and flexible networks for interactive learning and knowledge sharing. Competence centres should be characterized by an:

- intersectoral integrative approach;
- transparent governance structure;
- openness and mid-term perspective.

Competence centres are crucial in order to reduce the 'switching costs' to innovation and to accelerate the speed of the process of adoption of innovation, thus avoiding the risk of a lock-in effect in territorial clusters and promoting a horizontal and vertical diversification of the traditional productions in these clusters. Knowledge clusters are no longer organized along the boundaries of sectors, as the knowledge and technology can be used in different product segments. The diversity of final products even raise incentives for cooperation, as direct rivalry between the partners can be excluded. Consequently, any support of knowledge clusters should not be concentrated on single sectors but on broad platforms.

Therefore, research in the IKINET project highlights that regional and national policies for competence centres should:

- respond to the emerging needs of the users, identify and aggregate new demand, explore new markets with high growth potential or new 'lead markets' for the regional productions;
- promote the use of the knowledge accumulated within the cluster, the circulation of tacit knowledge and the development of new competencies through the process of interactive learning between the local actors;
- create new activities or 'strategic spin-offs', which can lead to a production diversification of the regional economy into new sectors of application, by investing in projects close to the phase of market exploitation, since it is not precompetitive research, to avoid path dependencies and lock-in effects;
- promote the design and adoption of new large strategic projects of innovation, requiring the coordination and cooperation of many partners in the existing clusters and regions rather than the creation of new geographical clusters;

- raise new funding through public–private partnership, involve modern financial intermediaries in strategic industrial projects and provide key competence in the selection of innovative projects submitted for financial support, as the problem is the abundance of funding and the lack of profitable projects;
- build new formal and informal institutions, infrastructures, norms, rules and routines, adopt new forms of 'governance' of the knowledge and innovation networks and design an explicit long-term strategy of the competence centre;
- promote the participation of new partners in innovation networks, such as KIBS and universities, thus promoting a greater effort in innovation and a mid-term development strategy;
- represent a bridging institution and promote local contacts between SMEs and large firms on the one hand, and between them and the research institutions on the other;
- promote international links between competence centres of different countries, the participation to European projects and enhance a greater international integration and competitiveness in an increasingly complex and connected world.

5.11   THE EUROPEAN DIMENSION AND THE INTERNATIONALIZATION OF COMPETENCE CENTRES

The international extension of knowledge networks of SMEs calls for the identification of common objectives and projects with external partners, while maintaining a strong local identity. It is necessary to find ways of combining regional public assistance with firm collaboration in projects that go beyond their own territory. Competence centres may represent a stimulus to the international openness and competitiveness of the regional clusters.

Clusters may contribute to the evolution of European industry towards a knowledge economy. In particular, the transition to the knowledge economy of the European economy is not only demanding large international investments in new strategic industrial sectors or 'structural reforms', but also the creation of new 'knowledge clusters' due to the localized nature of the processes of knowledge creation. Thus, a cluster approach is also needed in European policy for the knowledge economy.

While the internationalization of product markets and industrial supply chains is well developed, the internationalization of knowledge links is still lagging behind. Barriers to international clusters for SMEs can be rooted in different problems. For more conventional SMEs, general deficits of contacts and experience are particularly relevant, while for more advanced SMEs, commercialization strategies and institutional security are more relevant. Accordingly, different organizations can act as gatekeepers to secure necessary openness of cluster structures in these cases. For any public support, the type or structure of gatekeepers should be less decisive than the actual impact on integrating SMEs.

Even medium-sized firms are reluctant to internationalize from a knowledge perspective or to promote new forms of international interactive learning with foreign partners due to the fear of losing their proprietary know-how, as they believe that it represents their most important tacit competitive asset. Regional, national and European institutions are required to promote international forms of cooperation between SMEs, both at the regional and national levels. In fact, the development of international relations requires a more stable framework and specific bridging institutions than market mechanisms and private forms of bottom-up international cooperation may be capable of providing.

The process of internationalization is a gradual learning process and requires a new mental model by the firms. Moreover, the internationalization process has a selective character and a key role is played by 'gateways' or 'bridging' institutions. Thus, competence centres may create that institutional framework made by trust, reciprocal commitment and well-designed governance, which allow the firms from distant regions to exchange tacit knowledge and to participate in joint projects. In particular, gatekeepers are important for lagging regions, as in these regions the necessary density of partners might not be enough to form clusters, but single partners might use contacts to regional gatekeepers to find access to clusters in other regions.

The spatial dimension of innovation is increasingly clear, enabling the adoption of policy schemes that focus on the creation of regional clusters. The choice of new specific production fields of specialization and the creation of specific 'competence centres' in many European countries may be the result of previous local initiatives or may be left to the regional governments that know the production specializations of their region and the potentials of the various sectoral clusters. However, a complex interaction is needed between regional policies and national or European innovation policies. Several sectors (such as aerospace, environment, energy, finance, major international infrastructures, and so on) seem to require a higher national or European coordination and the initiatives to be taken at the regional level should be stimulated and orientated within the framework of national and also European networks.

The national governments may take various important initiatives in order to promote the competence centres, such as to:

- launch programmes for the creation of networks of competence centres in regions that do not have them;
- focus on the problems in the implementation phase of the competence centres, and not only on the creation of new competence centres, and identify success factors and evaluation criteria;
- generate new organizational and institutional solutions and create a consensus on a new common model of action;
- develop systemic linkages between the various competence centres at the national and European level, organize working groups and periodic events, allow an easier exchange of knowledge, promote international learning and benchmarking, create a platform for exchanging experiences and best practices and compare the management models;
- define a concrete set of proposals and possibly interregional strategic projects based on the cooperation of various competence centres and promote the creation of new competence centres in fields of national and international relevance;
- promote studies dealing with innovation, human resources, internationalization, and so on in clusters and organize training sessions dealing with cluster management;
- design new public–private funding solutions.

As firms are increasingly integrated in international production networks, competence centres also have to build international networks. The creation of European networks of competence centres would increase their specialization with respect to those of other regions at the international level and widen the knowledge base of existing clusters.

There is a close relation between clusters and the European economy and policies. Increasing international competition and the globalization process require that European institutions make a distinct contribution to the cluster policies of the various regions, as the transition of industrial clusters to the knowledge economy can be facilitated by European policies. The role of the European Union changes in this context. In reality, direct R&D and capital subsidies rarely reach SMEs in medium-technology sectors, as the SMEs miss necessary formal R&D and strategic resources to cope with EU preconditions in order to participate in large R&D European projects. Instead, EU policy should focus on:

- support of competence centres as intermediaries for SMEs;
- subsidization of public–private funding of competence centres in lagging regions aiming to extend the cooperation between these regions and leading agglomerations;
- initiating contests on strategic lead projects on a regional and inter-regional level, enhancing the participation of new companies;
- promoting projects integrating medium-technology industries with universities and high-technology services, aiming to extend industrial value chains and to diversify in new qualified productions;
- promoting European linkages between regional competence centres by standardization of information, qualification courses for the managers of competence centres, technological norms and support to bridging organizations;
- adopting strategic regulations to strengthen European technical safety and environmental standards in the global market and promoting the development of new productions.

NOTE

* Staszek Walukiewicz is Full Professor of Systems Science at the Systems Research Institute of the Polish Academy of Sciences in Warsaw. He was a main partner in several EU research projects and he has coordinated the PHARE project on Universities–Academy–Industry collaboration. He has published a book on mathematical programming as well as many papers on operations research and recently on social capital and clustering.

The authors would like to thank Professor Walukiewicz for his active participation in the IKINET Policy Forum and the continuous discussions on the implications of the research results for European innovation policies.

Bibliography

Abernathy, W.J. and Clarke, K. (1985), Innovation: mapping the winds of creative destruction, *Research Policy*, **14**(1), 3–22.

Abramowitz, M. and David, P. (1996), Technological change and the rise of intangible investments: the US economy's growth path in the twentieth century, *Employment and Growth in the Knowledge-based Economy*, OECD.

Acs, Z.J. (2002), *Innovation and the Growth of Cities*, Cheltenham, UK and Northampton, MA, USA: Edward Elgar.

Aerts, K. and Schmidt, T. (2008), Two for the price of one? Additionality effects of R&D subsidies: a comparison between Flanders and Germany, Research Policy, **38**(10), 806–22.

Agarwal, R., Echambadi, R., Franco, A.M. and Sarkar, M.B. (2004), Knowledge transfer through inheritance: spin-out generation, development, and survival, *Academy of Management Journal*, **47**(4), 501–22.

Akbar, H. (2003), Knowledge levels and their transformation: towards the integration of knowledge creation and individual learning, *Journal of Management Studies*, **40**(8), 1997–2021.

Akkermans, D., Castaldi, C. and Los, B. (2007), Do 'Liberal Market Economies' Really Innovate More Radically than 'Coordinated Market Economies'? Hall & Soskice Reconsidered, GGDC Research Memorandum GD-91, Groningen Growth and Development Centre, University of Groningen.

Alazmi, M. and Zairi, M. (2003), Knowledge management critical success factors, *Total Quality Management*, **14**(2), 199–204.

Alfonso-Gil, J. and Talbot, D. (2007), The aeronautical sector: recent tendencies, in: Alfonso-Gil, J. (ed.) *European Aeronautics. The Southwestern Axis*, Berlin and Heidelburg: Springer, pp. 23–73.

Alfonso-Gil, J. and Vazquez-Baquero, A. (2009), Networking and innovation. Lessons from the aeronautical cluster of Madrid, *International Journal of Technology Management*, forthcoming.

Almeida P. and Kogut B. (1999), Localization of knowledge and the mobility of engineers in regional networks, *Management Science*, **45**(7), 905–17.

Al-Waqfi, M.A. and Agarwal, N.C. (2006), Determinants of role orientation and organisational commitment under skill-based pay: a path model, *International Journal of Human Resources Development and Management*, **6**(1), 4–21.

Amin, A. and Cohendet, P. (2003), *Architecture of Knowledge*, Oxford: Oxford University Press.

Amin, A. and Roberts, J. (2008), Beyond communities-of-practice: knowledge in action, *Research Policy*, **37**(2), 353–69.

Amo, B.W. (2006), What motivates knowledge workers to involve themselves in employee innovation behaviour? *International Journal of Knowledge Management Studies*, **1**(1–2), 160–77.

Andersson, U. (2003), Managing the transfer of capabilities in multinational corporations: the dual role of the subsidiary, *Scandinavian Journal of Management*, **19**(4), 425–42.

Andersson, U. and Forsgren, M. (2000), In search of centre of excellence: network embeddedness and subsidiary roles in multinational corporations, *Management International Review*, **40**(4), 329–50.

Andersson, M. and Hellerstedt, K. (2008), Location Attributes and Start-ups in Knowledge-intensive Business Services, Centre of Excellence for Science and Innovation Studies, Working Paper Series in Economics and Institutions of Innovation No. 116.

Antonelli, C. (2005), Models of Knowledge and Systems of Governance, Department of Economics 'Cognetti de Martiis', Università di Torino, Working paper No. 01/2005.

Antonelli, C. (2007), Localized Technological Knowledge: Pecuniary Knowledge Externalities and Appropriability, Max Planck Institute for Economics, WP No. 0709, Jena.

Argyris, C. (1993), *Knowledge for Action: A Guide to Overcoming Barriers to Organizational Change*, San Francisco: Jossey Bass.

Argyris, C. and Schön, D. (1996), Organizational Learning II. Theory, Method, and Practice, Reading, MA: Addison Wesley.

Asheim, B. (1996), Industrial districts as 'learning regions': a condition for prosperity, *European Planning Studies*, **4**(4), 379–400.

Asheim, B.T. (2002), Temporary organisations and spatial embeddedness of learning and knowledge creation, *Geografiska Annaler, Series B: Human Geography*, **84**(2), 111–24.

Asheim, B. and Clark, E. (2001), Creativity and cost in urban and regional development of the new economy, *European Planning Studies*, **9**(7), 805–11.

Asheim B.T. and Coenen L. (2005), Knowledge bases and regional innovation systems: comparing Nordic clusters, *Research Policy*, **34**(8), 1173–90.

Asheim, B., Boschma, R. and Cooke, P. (2007), Constructing Regional Advantage: Platform Policies Based on Related Variety and Differentiated Knowledge Bases, Utrecht University, Urban and Regional Research Centre, Utrecht, Papers in Evolutionary Economic Geography, No. 07.09.

Asheim, B., Coenen L., Moodysson J. and Vang, J. (2007), Constructing knowledge-based regional advantage: implications for regional innovation policy, *International Journal of Entrepreneurship and Innovation*, **7**(2), p. 140.

Audretsch, D. and Feldman, M. (1996), R&D spillovers and the geography of innovation and production, *American Economic Review*, **86**(3), 630–40.

Bathelt, H. and Schuldt, N. (2005), Between Luminaries and Meat Grinders: International Trade Fairs as Temporary Clusters, Marburg: Spaces Discussion Paper No. 05-06.

Bathelt, H., Malmberg, A. and Maskell, P. (2004), Clusters and knowledge: local buzz, global pipelines and the process of knowledge creation, *Progress in Human Geography*, **28**(1), 31–56.

Becattini, G. (1990), The Marshallian industrial district as a socio-economic notion, in: Pyke P., Becattini G. and Sengenberger W. (eds), *Industrial Districts & Inter-firm Co-operation in Italy*, pp. 37–51, Geneva: International Institute for Labour Studies.

Bellet, M. Colletis, G. and Lung, Y. (1993), Economie de proximites, *Numero Spécial, Revue d'Economie Régionale et Urbaine*, **3**.

Benzler, G. and Wink, R. (2005), Managing changes to integrative technologies – the case of biophotonics, *International Journal of Learning and Change*, **1**(1), 11–27.

Bergek, A., Jacobsson, S., Carisson, B., Lindmask, S. and Rickne, A. (2008), Analyzing the functional dynamics of technological innovation systems: a scheme of analysis, *Research Policy*, **37**(3), 407–29.

Bhatt, G.D. (2000), Information dynamics, learning and knowledge creation in organizations, *The Learning Organization*, **7**(2), 89–98.

Bianchi, P. (1995), *Le Politiche Industriali dell'Unione Europea*, Bologna: Il Mulino.

Bleeke, J. and Ernst, D. (1995), Is your strategic alliance really a sale? *Harvard Business Review*, **73**(1) January–February, 13–23.

Blum, U. and Müller, S. (2004), The role of intellectual property rights regimes for R&D cooperation between industry and academia, in: Wink, R. (ed.), *Academia Business Links: European Strategies and Lessons Learnt*, Houndmills: Palgrave Macmillan, pp. 90–105.

Boisot, M.H. (1998), *Knowledge Assets. Securing Competitive Advantage in the Information Economy*, Oxford: Oxford University Press.

Boschma, R.A. (2005), Proximity and innovation: a critical assessment, *Regional Studies*, **39**(1), 61–73.

Bottazzi; G., Dosi. G. and Fagiolo, G. (2002), On the ubiquitous nature of agglomeration economies and their diverse determinants: some notes, in: Quadrio Curzo, A. and Fortis, M. (eds) *Complexity and Industrial Clusters. Dynamics and Models in Theory and Practice*, Heidelberg: Physica-Verlag.

Bougrain, F. and Haudeville, B. (2002), Innovation, collaboration and SMEs' internal research capacities, *Research Policy*, **31**(5), 735–47.

Boyer, W. (1990), Political science in the 21st century: from government to governance, *Political Science and Politics*, **23**, 50–54.

Brandes, H., Lilliecreutz, J. and Brege, S. (1997), Outsourcing – success or failure, *European Journal of Purchasing and Supply Chain Management*, **3**(1), 63–75.

Bredin, K. and Söderlund, J. (2006), Perspectives on human resource management: an explorative study of the consequences of projectification in four firms, *International Journal of Human Resource Development and Management*, **6**(1), 92–113.

Brenner, T. (2004), *Industrial Clusters: Existence, Emergence and Evolution*, London: Routledge.

Brenner, T. and Mühlig, A. (2007), Factors and Mechanisms Causing the Emergence of Local Industrial Clusters. A Meta-study of 159 Cases, Max Planck Institute of Economics, Working Paper No. 0723, Jena.

Breschi, S. and Lissoni, F. (2001), Knowledge spillovers and local innovation systems: a critical survey, *Industrial and Corporate Change*, **10**(4), 975–1005.

Broström, A. (2008), Firms' Rationales for Interaction with Research Universities, Centre of Excellence for Science and Innovation Studies, Working Paper Series in Economics and Institutions of Innovation No. 115.

Brown, J.S. and Duguid, P. (1991), Organizational learning and communities-of-practice. Toward a unified view of working, learning, and innovation, *Organization Science*, **2**(1), 40–57.

Callan, B. (2001), Generating spin-offs: evidence from across the OECD, *STI Review*, **26**(14), 13–55.

Cantner, U. and Graf, H. (2006), The network of innovators in Jena: an application of social network analysis, *Research Policy*, **35**(4), 463–80.

Cantwell, J.A. and Piscitello, L. (2005), Recent location of foreign-owned research and development activities by large multinational corporations in the European regions: the role of spillovers and externalities, *Regional Studies*, **39**(1), 1–16.

Capello, R. (1999), Spatial transfer of knowledge in high-technology milieux: learning versus collective learning processes, *Regional Studies*, **33**(4), 353–65.

Capello, R. and Faggian, A. (2005), Collective learning and relational capital in local innovation processes, *Regional Studies*, **39**(1), 75–87.

Cappellin, R. (1983), Productivity growth and technological change in a regional perspective, *Giornale degli Economisti e Annali di Economia*, March, 459–82.

Cappellin, R. (1988), Transaction costs and urban agglomeration, *Revue d'Economie Régionale et Urbaine*, No. 2.

Cappellin, R. (1997), Federalism and the network paradigm: guidelines for a new approach in national regional policy, in M. Danson (ed.), *Regional Governance and Economic Development*. London: Pion.

Cappellin, R. (1998), The transformation of local production systems: international networking and territorial competitiveness, in: Steiner, M. (ed.), *From Agglomeration Economies to Innovative Clusters*, London: Pion.

Cappellin, R. (2002), Regional industrial policy and the new economy, in: Atalik, G. and Fischer, M.M. (eds.), *Regional Development Reconsidered*, Berlin: Springer Verlag.

Cappellin, R. (2003a), Networks and technological change in regional clusters, in: Bröcker, J., Dohse, D. and Soltwedel, R. (eds), *Innovation Clusters and Interregional Competition*, Heidelberg: Springer Verlag, pp. 52–78.

Cappellin, R. (2003b), Territorial knowledge management: towards a metrics of the cognitive dimension of agglomeration economies, *International Journal of Technology Management*, **26**(2–4), 303–25.

Cappellin, R. (2004a), International knowledge and innovation networks for European integration, cohesion and enlargement, *International Social Science Journal*, UNESCO, **56**(180), 207–25.

Cappellin, R. (2004c), The role of institutional distance in the process of international integration, *Transition Studies Review*, **37**, 65–78.

Cappellin, R. (2005), The governance of regional networks and the process of globalization, in: Gangopadhyay, P. and Chatterji, M. (eds), *Economics of Globalization*, Burlington, VT: Ashgate, pp. 145–61.

Cappellin, R. (2007), Learning, spatial changes, and regional and urban policies: the territorial dimension of the knowledge economy, *American Behavioral Scientist*, **50**(7), 897–921.

Cappellin, R. and Orsenigo, L. (2000), The territorial dimension of modern industry and the scope of regional industrial and labour market policies, in: Klemmer, P. and Wink, R. (eds), *Preventing Unemployment in Europe. A New Framework for Labour Market Policy*, Cheltenham, UK and Northampton, MA, USA: Edward Elgar, pp. 166–87.

Cappellin, R. (2004b), Il ruolo della distanza istituzionale nel processo di integrazione internazionale: l'approccio dei network, in: Quadrio

Curzio, A. (ed.), *La Globalizzazione e i Rapporti Nord-Est-Sud*, Bologna, Il Mulino, pp. 155–87.

Carabelli, A., Hirsch, G. and Rabellotti, R. (2006), Italian SMEs and Industrial Districts on the Move: Where are They Going? Working Paper No. 3/2006, University of Bologna.

Carayannis, E.G., Rogers, E.M., Kurhara, K. and Allbritton, M.M. (1998), High-technology spin-offs from government R&D laboratories and research universities, *Technovation*, **18**(1), 1–11.

Carbonara, N., Giannoccaro, I. and Pontrandolfo, P. (2002), Supply chains within industrial districts: a theoretical framework, *International Journal of Production Economics*, **76**(2), 159–76.

Chetty, S. and Agndal, H. (2008), Role of inter-organizational networks and interpersonal networks in an industrial district, *Regional Studies*, **42**(2), 175–88.

Chiarvesio, M., di Maria, E. and Micelli, S. (2004), From local networks of SMEs to virtual districts? Evidence from recent trends in Italy, *Research Policy*, **33**(10), 1509–28.

Christensen, C. (1997), *The Innovator's Dilemma*, Cambridge, MA: Harvard Business School Press.

Christensen, J.L. and Drejer, I. (2005), The strategic importance of location: location decisions and the effects of firm location on innovation and knowledge acquisition, *European Planning Studies*, **13**, 807–14.

Coase, R.H. (1992), The institutional structure of production, *American Economic Review*, **82**(4), 713–19.

Cohen, W. and Levinthal, D. (1989), Innovation and learning: the two faces of R&D, *The Economic Journal*, **99**(397), 569–96.

Cohendet, P. and Steinmueller, W.E. (2000), The codification of knowledge: a conceptual and empirical exploration, *Industrial and Corporate Change*, **9**(2), 195–209.

Coleman, J.S. (1988), Social capital in the creation of human capital, *American Journal of Sociology, Supplement*, **94**, 95–120.

Cooke, P. (1998), Introduction: origins of the concept, in Braczyk, H.J., Cooke, P. and Heidenreich, M. (eds), *Regional Innovation Systems. The Role of Governances in a Globalized World*, London: UCL Press, pp. 2–27.

Cooke, P. and Morgan, K. (1998), *The Associational Economy: Firms, Regions and Innovation*, Oxford: Oxford University Press.

Cooke, P., De Laurentis, C., Tödtling, F. and Trippl, M. (2006), *Regional Knowledge Economies*, Cheltenham, UK and Northampton, MA, USA: Edward Elgar.

Cooke, P., Heidenreich, M. and Braczyk, M. (2004), *Regional Innovation Systems*, 2nd ed., London: Routledge.

Coviello, N.E. and Martin, K.A. (1999), Internationalisation of service SMEs: an integrated perspective from the engineering consulting sector, *Journal of International Marketing*, **7**(4), 42–66.

Crevoisier O. and Camagni R. (eds) (2000), *Les Milieux Urbains: Innovation, Systèmes de Production et Ancrage*, EDES, Neuchâtel

D'Aveni, D. (1994), *Hypercompetition: Managing the Dynamics of Strategic Maneuvering*, New York.

Dahl, M.S. and Pedersen, C.O.R. (2003), Knowledge Flows through Informal Contacts in Industrial Clusters: Myths or Realities?, DRUID Working Paper No. 03-01, Copenhagen.

Damijan, J.P., Kostovec, C. and Polanec, S. (2008), From Innovation to Export or Vice Versa? Causal Link Between Innovation Activity and Exporting in Slovenian Microdata, LICOS Centre for Institutions and Economic Performance Discussion Paper, Ljublijana.

Danilovic, M. and Winroth, M. (2006), Corporate manufacturing network: from hierarchy to self-organising system, *International Journal of Integrated Supply Chain Management*, **2**(1–2), 106–31.

Danov, M.A., Smith, Brock J. and Mitchell, R. (2003), Relationship prioritization for technology commercialization, *Journal of Marketing Theory and Practice*, **11**(3), 59–70.

Davenport, S. (2005), Exploring the role of proximity in SME knowledge-acquisition, *Research Policy*, **34**(5), 683–702.

Davenport, T.H. and Prusak, L. (1998), *Working Knowledge: How Organizations Manage What They Know*, Boston, MA: Harvard Business School Press.

De Vries, M.J. (2003), The nature of technological knowledge: extending empirically informed studies on what engineers know, *Techné*, **6**(3), 1–21.

Dobson, W. and Safarian, A.E. (2008), The Transition from Imitation to Innovation: an Enquiry in China's Evolving Institutions and Firm Capabilities, IIB Discussion Paper No. 8, Rotman School of Management, Toronto.

Drejer, A. (2000), Organizational learning and competence development, *The Learning Organization*, **7**(3–4), 206–20.

Drejer, A., Christensen, K.S. and Ulhoi, J.P. (2004), Understanding intra-preneurship by means of state-of-the-art knowledge management and organizational learning theory, *International Journal of Management and Enterprise Development*, **1**(2), 102–19.

Duguid, P. (2008), Communities of practice then and now, in: Amin, A. and Roberts, J. (eds), *Community, Economic Creativity, and Organizations*, New York: Oxford University Press.

Duhovnik, J., Starbek, M., Dwivedi, S.M. and Prasad, B. (2003), Development of innovative products in a small and medium-sized enterprise, *International Journal of Computer Applications in Technology*, **17**(4), 187–201.

Dumais, D., Ellison, G. and Glaeser, E. (2002), Geographical concentration as a dynamic process, *Review of Economics and Statistics*, **84**, 193–204.

Dunning, J.H. (1988), The eclectic paradigm of international production: a restatement, *Journal of International Business Studies*, **19**(1), 1–31.

Dupuy C. and Torre A. (2006), Local clusters, trust, confidence and proximity, in: Christos, P., Sugden, R. and Wilson, J. (eds), *Clusters and Globalisation: The Development of Urban and Regional Economies*, Cheltenham, UK and Northampton, MA, USA: Edward Elgar.

Egeln, J., Gottschalk, S., Rammer, C. and Spielkamp, A. (2004), Are research spin-offs a local phenomenon? Empirical findings from Germany, in: Wink, R. (ed.), *Academia Business Links. European Policy Strategies and Lessons Learnt*, Houndmills: Palgrave Macmillan, pp. 28–47.

Egidi, M. and Rizzello, S. (2003), Cognitive Economics: Foundations and Historical Evolution, Working Paper Series Cognitive Economics: Foundations and Historical Evolution, CESMEP, Università di Torino, No. 04.

Eickelpasch, A. and Fritsch, M. (2005), Contests for cooperation – a new approach in German innovation policy, *Research Policy*, **34**(8), 1269–89.

Ekeledo, I. and Sivakumar, K. (1998), Foreign market entry mode by service firms: a contingency approach, *Academy of Marketing Science Journal*, **26**(4), 274–92.

El Hajj Chehade, H. and Vigneron, L. (2007), SME's Main Bank Choice and Organizational Structure: Evidence from France, Working Papers of Labouratoire de Recherche en Gestion et Economie, No. 2007-06.

European Commission (2001), Multi-level Governance: Linking and Networking the Various Regional and Local Levels, Report by Working Group 4c, Brussels, May 2001.

European Commission (2002), Cooperation Between the Research System and Industry to Promote Innovative Firms, Brussels; Innovation Paper No. 26.

European Commission (2005), European Innovation Scoreboard. Comparative Analysis of Innovation Performance, Brussels: European Commission.

European Commission (2007), Growing Regions, Growing Europe, 4th Report on Economic and Social Cohesion, European Commission, Brussels.

European Union (2000), Lisbon European Council 23 and 24 March 2001 Presidency Conclusions, Brussels: European Union.

Fawcett, S.E. and McCarter, M.W. (2008), Behavioural issues in supply chain collaboration: communicating the literature via interactive learning, *International Journal of Integrated Supply Management*, **4**(2), 159–80.

Federico, S. (2005), The internationalization of production and industrial districts: an analysis of Italy's foreign direct investments, in: Signorini, L.F. (ed.), *Local Economies and Internationalization in Italy*, Rome: Banca d'Italia, pp. 313–42.

Felix, B. (2006), Employment in high technology, science and technology, *Eurostat, Statistics in Focus*, 2006/1.

Feller, I., Ailes, C.P. and Roessner, J.D. (2002), Impact of research universities on technological innovation in industry: evidence from engineering research centres, *Research Policy*, **31**(3), 457–74.

Ferlie, E., Fitzgerald, L., Wood, M. and Hawkins, C. (2005), The non-spread of innovations: the mediating role of professionals, *Academy of Management Journal*, **48**(1), 117–34.

Field J. (2003), *Social Capital*, London-New York: Routledge.

Fisher, M. (1997), What is the right value chain for your product? *Harvard Business Review*, **75**(2), 105–16.

Fisher, M.L., Hammond, J., Obermeyer, W. and Raman, A. (1997), Configuring a supply chain to reduce the costs of demand uncertainty, *Production and Operations Management*, **6**(3), 211–25.

Florida, R. (1995), Towards the learning region, *Futures*, **27**(5), 527–36.

Florida, R. (2002), *The Rise of the Creative Class*, New York: Basic Books.

Florida, R., Mellander, C. and Stollarick, K. (2007), Inside the Black Box of Regional Development: Human Capital, the Creative Class, and Tolerance, CESIS Working Paper No. 88, Toronto.

Foray, D. and Lundvall, B.-A. (1996), The Knowledge-based economy: from the economics of knowledge to the learning economy, in: Foray, D. and Lundvall, B.-A. (eds), *Employment and Growth in the Knowledge-based Economy*, OECD.

Frank, O. (1979), The estimation of population totals by snowball samples, in: Holland, P. and Leinhardt, S. (eds) *Perspectives on Social Network Research*, New York, Academic Press, pp. 319–47.

Friedkin, N.E. (1981), The development of structure in random networks, *Social Networks*, **3**, 41–52.

Frormann, D. (2006), Medium-sized business in Germany, *International Journal for Entrepreneurship and Innovation Management*, **6**(1/2), 18–23.

Fujita, M. and Thisse, J.-F. (2002), *Economics of Agglomeration. Cities, Industrial Location and Regional Growth*, Cambridge: Cambridge University Press.

Gallouj, F. and Weinstein, O. (1997), Innovation in services, *Research Policy*, **26**(4–5), 537–56.

Gann, D.M. and Salter, A.J. (2000), Innovation in project-based, service-enhanced firms: the construction of complex products and systems, *Research Policy*, **29**(7–8), 955–72.

Garcia-Vega, M. (2006), Does technological diversification promote innovation? An empirical analysis for European firms, *Research Policy*, **35**(2), 230–46.

Gay, B. and Dousset, B. (2005), Innovation and network structural dynamics: study of the alliance network of a major sector of the biotechnology sector, *Research Policy*, **34**(10), 1457–75.

van Geenhuizen, M. (2007), Modeling dynamics of knowledge networks and local connectedness: a case study of urban high-tech companies in the Netherlands, *Annals of Regional Science*, **41**(4), 813–33.

van Geenhuizen, M. and Nijkamp, P. (2006), Learning regions in an evolutionary context: policymaking for high technology firms, *International Journal of Entrepreneurship and Innovation Management*, **6**(3), 265–82.

Gertler, M., Wolfe, D. and Garkut, D. (2000), No place like home? The embeddedness of innovation in a regional economy, *Review of International Political Economy*, **7**(4), 688–718.

Gherardi, S. (2006), *Organizational Knowledge: The Texture of Workplace Learning*, Oxford: Blackwell.

Gold, A.H., Malhotra, A. and Segars, A.H. (2001), Knowledge management: an organizational capabilities perspective, *Journal of Management Information Systems*, **18**, 185–214.

Gonzalez, X. and Pazo, C. (2008), Do public subsidies stimulate private R&D spending? *Research Policy*, **37**(3), 371–89.

Gordon, I.R. and McCann, P. (2000), Industrial clusters: complexes, agglomeration and/or social networks, *Urban Studies*, **37**(3), 513–32.

Gore, C. and Gore, E. (1999), Knowledge management: the way forward, *Total Quality Management*, **10**(1), 554–60.

Grabher, G. (2004), Learning in projects, remembering in networks? Communality, sociality, connectivity in project ecologies, *European Urban and Regional Studies*, **11**(2), 103–23.

Grabher, G. and Ibert, O. (2006), Bad company? The ambiguity of personal knowledge networks, *Journal of Economic Geography*, **6**(3), 251–71.

Grant, R.M. (1996), Towards a knowledge-based theory of the firm, *Academy of Management Executive*, **17**(1), 109–22.

Grieves, J., McMillan, J. and Wilding, P. (2006), Barriers to learning: conflicts that occur between and within organizational systems, *International Journal of Learning and Intellectual Capital*, **3**(1), 86–103.

Gronroos, C. (1998), Marketing services: the case of a missing product, *Journal of Business and Industrial Marketing*, **13**(45), 322–38.

Gustafson, L. and Reger, R. (1995), Using organizational identity to achieve stability and change in high velocity environments, in: Moore, D. (ed.), *Academy of Management Best Papers, Proceedings*, pp. 464–8.

Gutierrez, A. and Serrano, A. (2008), Assessing strategic, tactical and operational alignment factors for SMEs: alignment across the organisation's value chain, *International Journal of Supply Chain Management*, **2**(1), 33–56.

Hall, A.R. (1974), What did the industrial revolution in Britain owe to science? in: McKendrick, N. (ed.), *Historical Perspectives: Studies in English Thought and Society*, London: Europa, pp. 129–51.

Hall, P.A. and Soskice, D. (eds) (2001), *Varieties of Capitalism. The Institutional Foundation of Comparative Advantage*, Oxford: Oxford University Press.

Hall, P.A. and Soskice, D. (2003), Varieties of capitalism and institutional change: a response to three critics, *Comparative European Politics*, **1**(2), 241–50.

Handly, K., Sturdy, A., Fincham, R. and Clark, T. (2006), Within and beyond communities of practice: making sense of learning through participation, identity and practice, *Journal of Management Studies*, **43**(3), 641–53.

Harada, T. (2003), Three steps in knowledge communication: the emergence of knowledge transformers, *Research Policy*, **32**(10), 1737–51.

Harmaakorpi, V. and Melkas, H. (2005), Knowledge management in regional innovation systems: the case of Lahti, Finland, *European Planning Studies*, **13**(5), 641–59.

Hashai, N. and Almor, T. (2008), R&D intensity, value appropriation, and integration patterns within organizational boundaries, *Research Policy*, **37**, 1022–34.

Hassink, R. (2005), How to unlock regional economies from path dependencies? From learning region to learning cluster, *European Planning Studies*, **13**(4), 521–35.

Hayek F.A. (1952), *The Sensory Order*, Chicago: University of Chicago Press.

Hayton, J.C. (2005), Promoting corporate entrepreneurship through human resource management practices: a review of empirical research, *Human Resource Management Review*, **15**(1), 21–41.

Hayward, K. (2005), UK Aerospace: Position & Prospects, lecture organized by Royal Aeronautical Society, Rhoose, Wales 13 October.

Heneman, H.G., Ledford, G.E. and Gresham, M.T. (2000), The changing nature of work and its effects on compensation design and delivery, in: Rynes, S.L. and Gerhart, B. (eds), *Compensation in Organizations: Current Research and Practice*, San Francisco: Jossey-Bass, pp. 195–240.

Héritier, A. (2002), Introduction, in: Héritier, Adrienne (ed.), *Common Goods. Reinventing European and International Governance*, Lanham: Rowman & Littlefield Publishers, pp. 1–12.

Héritier, A. and Eckert S. (2007), New Modes of Governance in the Shadow of Hierarchy: Self-Regulation by Industry in Europe, EUI Working Papers, RCAS 2007/20.

Hoffman, K., Parejo, M., Bessent, J. and Perren, L. (1998), Small firms, R&D, technology and innovation in the UK: a literature review, *Technovation*, **18**(1), 39–55.

Holland, J.H (2002), Complex adaptive systems and spontaneous emergence, in: Quadrio Curzio, A. and Fortis, M. (eds), *Complexity and Industrial Clusters: Dynamics and Models in Theory and Practice*, Heidelberg: Physica-Verlag, pp. 25–34.

Hooghe, L. and Marks, G. (2003), Unravelling the central state, but how? Types of multi-level governance, *American Political Science Review*, **97**(2), 233–43.

Howells, J.R.L. (2002), Tacit knowledge, innovation and economic geography, *Urban Studies*, **39**(5–6), 871–84.

Hung, S.Y., Dai, C.I. and Chang, C.M. (2007), A longitudinal study of virtual teamwork with and without group support systems, *International Journal of Management and Enterprise Development*, **4**(6), 703–19.

Iakovou, E., Vlachos, D. and Xanthopoulos, A. (2007), An analytical methodological framework for the optimal design of resilient supply chains, *International Journal of Logistics Economics and Globalisation*, **1**(1), 1–20.

Iammarino, S. and McCann, P. (2006), The structure and evolution of industrial clusters: transactions, technology and knowledge spillovers, *Research Policy*, **35**(7), 1018–36.

IKINET Project, Policy conclusions of the Policy Forum presented at the Policy Forum of the IKINET project on: 'Regional Competence Centres and European Knowledge and Innovation Networks', Rome, 19–20 September 2007 (www.ikinet.uniroma2.it/contributions.htm).

Ilyas, R.M., Banwet, D.K. and Shankar, R. (2008), Value chain outsourcing? A solution for flex-lean-agile manufacturing, *International Journal of Supply Chain Management*, **2**(2), 227–68.

Jack, R., As-Saber, S. and Edwards, R. (2006), Service embeddedness and its impact on the value chain and firm internationalisation: in search of a framework, *International Journal on Value Chain Management*, **1**(1), 33–43.

Jacobs, J. (1969), *The Economy of Cities*, New York: Random House.

Jalabert, G., Zuliani, J.-M., Gilly, J.-P., Kechidi, M., Wink, R. et al. (2008), Dynamique et Compétitivité du Pôle Aéronautique Espace et Systèmes Embarqués. Un mise en perspective avec le cluster de Hamburg, Toulouse.

Jeng, L.A. and Wells, P.C. (2000), The determinants of venture capital funding. Evidence across countries, *Journal of Corporate Finance*, **6**(3), 241–89.

Johanson, J. and Vahlne, J.E. (1990), The mechanism of internationalisation, *International Marketing Review*, **7**(4), 11–24.

Junold, R. and Wink, R. (2006), Nurturing stem cell business – lessons from recombinant drugs markets?, *International Journal of Biotechnology*, **8**(3–4), 187–205.

Kaiser, R. (2008), Governance and the Knowledge Economy: Relevance and Potentialities of the 'Analytical Governance Concept' Within the EURODITE Context, Eurodite Project, Sixth Framework Programme, Institute of Political Science, University of Hamburg,

Kaiser, R. and Prange, H. (2004), Managing diversity in a system of multilevel governance: the open method of coordination in innovation policy, *Journal of European Public Policy*, **11**(2), 249–66.

Karl, H. and Wink, R. (2006), Innovation policy and federalism. The German experience, *International Journal of Foresight and Innovation Policy*, **2**, 265–84.

Karl, H., Janson, B., Möller, A. and Wink, R. (2004), Innovation Policies in Germany, CERIS-Working Paper, Torino.

Karlsson, C. (1997), Product development, innovation networks, and agglomeration economies, *The Annals of Regional Science*, **31**(3), 235–58.

Karlsson, C. and Andersson, M. (2007), Knowledge in regional economic growth – the role of knowledge accessibility, *Industry and Innovation*, **14**, 129–49.

Karlsson, C. and Ejermo, O. (2006), Spatial inventor networks as studied by patent coinventorships, *Research Policy*, **35**(3), 412–30.

Karlsson, C. and Johansson, B. (2006), Towards a dynamic theory for the spatial knowledge economy, in: Johansson, B., Karlsson, C. and Stough, R.R. (eds), *Entrepreneurship and Dynamics in the Knowledge Economy*, London & New York: Routledge, pp. 12–46.

Kechidi, M. et al. (2007), Dynamiques et Compétitivité du Pole

Aéronautique Espaces et Systemes Embarques. Une Mise en Perspective avec le Cluster de Hamburg, LEREPS, CIEU, RUFIS, Toulouse.

Keeble, D., Lawson, C., Moore, B. and Wilkinson, F. (1999), Collective learning processes, networking and 'institutional thickness' in the Cambridge region, *Regional Studies*, **33**(4), 319–32.

Keogh, W. and Steward, V. (2001), Identifying the skill requirements of the workforce in SMEs: findings from a European Social Fund project, *Journal of Small Business and Enterprise Development*, **8**(2), 140–49.

Keuschnigg, C. (2008), Tax Policy for Venture Capital-backed Entrepreneurship, University of St. Gallen Discussion Paper No. 2008-07.

Kilger, C. and Reuter, B. (2002), Collaborative planning, in: Stadtler, H., Kilger, C. (eds), *Supply Chain Management and Advanced Planning: Concepts, Models, Software and Case Studies*, Berlin: Springer, pp. 223–37.

Kim, J.Y. and Zhang, L.Y. (2008), Formation of foreign direct investment clustering – a new path to local economic development? The case of Quingdao, *Regional Studies*, **42**(2), 265–80.

Klepper, S. (2001), Employee start-ups in high-tech industries, *Industrial and Corporate Change*, **10**, 639–72.

Kohtamaki, M. and Kautonen, T. (2008), Conceptualising the dimensions of sourcing strategy: a governance-based approach, *International Journal of Supply Chain Management*, **2**(2), 206–26.

König, W. (1993), Technical education and industrial performance in Germany: a triumph of heterogeneity? in: Fox, R. and Guagnini, A. (eds), *Education, Technology and Industrial Performance in Europe, 1850–1939*, Cambridge: Cambridge University Press, pp. 65–87.

Krätke, S. (2002), Network analysis of production clusters: the Potsdam/Babelsberg film industry as an example, *European Planning Studies*, **10**(1), 27–54.

Krugman, P.R. (1991), *Geography and Trade*, Cambridge, MA: MIT Press.

Lagendijk, A. and Cornford, J. (2000), Regional institutions and knowledge – tracking new forms of regional development policy, *Geoforum*, **31**(2), 209–18.

Lawson, C. and Lorenz, E. (1999), Collective learning, tacit knowledge and regional innovative capacity, *Regional Studies*, **33**, 305–17.

Lehmbruch, G. (1977), Liberal Corporatism and Party Government, *Comparative Political Studies*, **10**(1), 91–126.

Lindkvist, L. (2004), Governing project-based firms: promoting market-like processes within hierarchies, *Journal of Management and Governance*, **8**(1), 3–25.

Liyanage, S., Nordberg, M. and Wink, R. (2007), *Managing Path-breaking Innovations*, New York: Praeger.

Loasby, B.J. (2001), Time, knowledge and evolutionary dynamics: why connections matter, *Journal of Evolutionary Economics*, **11**(4), 393–412.

Loasby, B.J. (2002), The evolution of knowledge: beyond the biological model, *Research Policy*, **31**(8–9), 1227–39.

Loasby, B.J. (2003), Organisation and the Human Mind, paper presented at the Università Commerciale Luigi Bocconi, 14 October 2003.

Lockett, A., Wright, M. and Franklin, S. (2003), Technology transfer and universities' spin-out strategies, *Small Business Economics*, **20**(2), 185–200.

López Iturriaga, F. and Martin Cruz, N. (2008), Antecedents of corporate spin-offs in Spain: a resource-based approach, *Research Policy*, **37**(6–7), 1047–56.

Lubatkin, M., Florin, J. and Lane, P. (2001), Learning together and apart: a model of reciprocal interfirm learning, *Human Resources*, **54**(10), 1353–82.

Lublinski, A.E. (2003), Does geographic proximity matter? Evidence from clustered and non-clustered firms in Germany, *Regional Studies*, **37**(5), 453–67.

Lundvall, B.A. (ed.) (1992), *National Systems of Innovations: Towards a Theory of Innovation and Interactive Learning*, London: Pinter Publishers.

Lundvall, B.A. and Johnson, B. (1994), The learning economy, *Journal of Industrial Studies*, **1**(2), 23–42.

MacPherson, A. (2002), The contribution of academy–industry interactions to product innovation: the case of New York's state medical devices sector, *Papers in Regional Science*, **81**, 121–59.

Maillat, D. (1995), Territorial dynamic, innovative milieus and regional policy, *Entrepreneurship & Regional Development*, **7**(1), 157–65.

Maillat, D. and Kebir. L. (1999), 'Learning region' et systèmes territoriaux de production, *Révue d'Economie Régionale et Urbaine*, **3**, 430–48.

Mariotti, S., Mutinelli, M. and Piscitello, L. (2008), The internationalization of production by Italian industrial districts' firms: structural and behavioural determinants, *Regional Studies*, **42**(5), 719–35.

Markman, G.D., Gianiodis, P.T., Phan, P.H. and Balkin, D.B. (2005), Innovation speed: transferring university technology to market, *Research Policy*, **34**, 1058–75.

Marsh, D. and Smith, M. (2000), Understanding policy networks: towards a dialectical approach, *Political Studies*, **48**(4), 4–21.

Marshall, A. (1919), *Industry and Trade*, London: Macmillan.

Marshall, A. (1920), *Principles of Economics*, London: Macmillan.

Marshall, A. (1994), Ye machine, *Research in the History of Economic Thought and Methodology, Archival Supplement*, **4**, JAI Press, Greenwich CT, 116–32.

Martinez, V. and Bititci, U.S. (2006), Aligning value propositions in supply chains, *International Journal of Value Chain Management*, **1**(1), 6–18.

Maskell, P. (1999), Social capital, innovation, and competitiveness, in: Baron, S. and Schuller, T. (eds), *Social Capital. Critical Perspectives*, Oxford: Oxford University Press, 111–23.

Mazaud, F. and Lagasse, M. (2007), Vertical Sub-contracting Relationships Strategy: The Airbus First-tier Suppliers' Coordination, Toulouse, GRES Working Paper No. 02-2007.

McCracken, M. and Wallace, M. (2000), Towards a redefinition of strategic HRD, *Journal of European Industrial Training*, **24**(5), 281–90.

Mehran, H. (1995), Executive compensation structure, ownership, and firm performance, *Journal of Financial Economics*, **38**(2), 163–84.

Metcalfe, J.S. and Ramlogan, R. (2005), Limits to the economy of knowledge and knowledge of the economy, *Futures*, **37**(7), 655–74.

Meyer, K.E. (2006), Globalfocusing. From domestic conglomerate to global specialist, *Journal of Management Studies*, **43**(5), 1109–44.

Michna, J. and Kalka, M. (2006), Small and medium-sized enterprises development in Central and Eastern Europe, *International Journal for Entrepreneurship and Innovation Management*, **6**(1/2), 59–73.

Miotti, L. and Sachwald, F. (2003), Co-operative R&D: why and with whom? An integrated framework of analysis, *Research Policy*, **32**(8), 1481–99.

Mol, M.J. (2005), Does being R&D intensive still discourage outsourcing? Evidence from Dutch manufacturing, *Research Policy*, **34**(4), 571–82.

Morgan, K. (1997), The learning region: institutions, innovation and regional renewal, *Regional Studies*, **31**(5), 491–504.

Muller, E. and Zenker, A. (2001), Business services as actors of knowledge transformation: the role of KIBS in regional and national innovation systems, *Research Policy*, **30**(9), 1501–16.

Nelson, R. (ed.) (1993) *National Systems of Innovation: A Comparative Analysis*, Oxford: Oxford University Press.

Nonaka, I. (1994), A dynamic theory of organization knowledge creation, *Organization Science*, **5**(1), 14–37.

Nonaka, I. and Konno, N. (1998), The concept of 'Ba': building a foundation for knowledge creation, *California Management Review*, **40**(3), 40–54.

Nooteboom, B. (2002), *Trust: Forms, Foundations, Functions, Failures and Figures*, Cheltenham, UK and Northampton, MA, USA: Edward Elgar.

North, D.C. (1990), *Institutions, Institutional Change and Economic Performance*, Cambridge, MA: Cambridge University Press.

O'Dell, C. and Grayson, C. (1998), If only we knew what we know: identification and transfer of internal best practices, *California Management Review*, **40**(3), 154–74.

OECD (1996), *The Knowledge-based Economy*, Paris: OECD.

OECD – Organisation for Economic Co-operation and Development (2001), *STI Review No: 26: Special Issue on Fostering High Tech Spin-offs: A Public Strategy for Innovation*, Paris: OECD.

OECD – Organisation for Economic Co-operation and Development (2007), *OECD Science, Technology and Industry Scoreboard 2007. Innovation and Performance in the Global Economy*, Paris: OECD.

Olhager, J., Selldin, E. and Wikner, J. (2006), Decoupling the value chain, *International Journal of Value Chain Management*, **1**(1), 19–32.

Olk, P. and Young, C. (1997), Why members stay or leave an R&D consortium: performance and conditions of membership as determinants of continuity, *Strategic Management Journal*, **18**, 855–77.

Orlikowski, W.J. (2002), Knowing in practice: enacting a collective capability in distributing organizing, *Organization Science*, **13**, 249–73.

Paniccia, I. (2002), *Industrial Districts: Evolution and Competitiveness in Italian Firms*, Cheltenham, UK and Northampton, MA, USA: Edward Elgar.

Parhankangas, A. and Arenius, P. (2003), From a corporate venture to an independent company: a base for a taxonomy for corporate spin-off firms, *Research Policy*, **32**(9), 463–81.

Pavlovich, K. and Corner, P.D. (2006), Knowledge creation through co-entrepreneurship, *International Journal of Knowledge Management Studies*, **1**(1–2), 178–97.

Pibernik, R. and Sucky, E. (2006), Centralised and decentralised supply chain planning, *International Journal of Integrated Supply Chain Management*, **2**(1–2), 6–27.

Pierre, J. (2000), Introduction: understanding governance, in: Pierre, J. (ed.) *Debating Governance*, Oxford: Oxford University Press, pp.1–10.

Piore, M.J. and Sabel, C.F. (1984), *The Second Industrial Divide*, New York: Basic Books.

Piscitello, L. and Rabbiosi, R. (2006), How does Knowledge Transfer from Foreign Subsidiaries Affect Parent Companies' Innovative Capacity?, Copenhagen, DRUID Working Paper No. 06-22.

Pistor, K. (2005), Legal Ground Rules in Coordinated and Liberal Market Economies, Columbia University School of Law, ECGI – Law Working Paper No. 30 Political Studies, Vol. 48, pp. 4–21.

Poon, J.P.H., Hsu, J.Y. and Jeongwook, S. (2006), The geography of learning and knowledge acquisition among Asian latecomers, *Journal of Economic Geography*, **6**(4), 541–59.

Porter M. (1990), *The Competitive Advantage of Nations*, London: Macmillan.

Porter, M. (1998), Clusters and the new economics of competition, *Harvard Business Review*, **76**(6), 77–90.

Porter, M. (2000), Locations, clusters and company strategy, in: Clark, G.L., Feldman, M.P. and Gertler, M.S. (eds), *The Oxford Handbook of Economic Geography*, Oxford: Oxford University Press, pp. 253–74.

Poutsma, E., de Nijs, W. and Poole, W. (2003), The global phenomenon of employee financial participation, *International Journal of Human Resource Management*, **14**(6), 855–62.

Powell, W. (1990), Neither market nor hierarchy: network forms of organization, *Research in Organizational Behaviour*, **12**, 74–96.

Power, D. (2006), Adoption of supply-chain management enabling technologies in SMEs: the view from the top vs. the view from the middle, *International Journal of Supply Chain Management*, **1**(1), 64–93.

PRSA, Knowledge spillovers and space, Papers in Regional Science, *Special Issue*, **86**(3).

Putnam, R. (1993), *Making Democracy Work: Civic Traditions in Modern Italy*, Princeton, NJ: Princeton University Press.

Pyke, F., Becattini, G. and Sengenberger, W. (eds) (1990), *Industrial Districts and Inter-Firm Co-operation in Italy*, Geneva: International Institute for Labour Studies, ILO.

Qi, X., Bard, J.F. and Yu, G. (2004), Supply chain coordination with demand disruptions, *Omega: The International Journal of Management Science*, **32**(4), 301–12.

Quinn, J.B (2000), Outsourcing innovation: the new wheel engine of growth, *Sloane Management Review*, **41**(4), 13–28.

Quintana-Garcia, C. and Benavides-Velasco, C.A. (2008), Innovative competence, exploration and exploitation: the influence of technological diversification, *Research Policy*, **37**(3), 492–507.

Raffaelli, T. (2003), *Marshall's Evolutionary Economics*, London: Routledge.

Rallet, A. and Torre, A. (1998), On geography and technology: proximity relations in localised innovation networks, in: M. Steiner (eds), *From agglomeration economies to innovative clusters*, London: Pion, European Research in Regional Science.

Reger, R., Mullane, J., Gustafson, L. and DeMarie, S. (1994), Creating earthquakes to change organisational mindsets, *Academy of Management Executive*, **8**(4), 31–46.

Rhodes, R.A.W. (2008), Peripheral vision. Understanding governance: ten years on, *Organization Studies*, **28**, 1243–64.

Rizzello, S. (1999), *The Economics of the Mind*, Cheltenham, UK and Northampton, MA, USA: Edward Elgar.

Rizzello, S. (2003), Towards a Cognitive Evolutionary Economics, Università di Torino, CESMEP, Working Paper No. 03/2003.

Roper, S., Du, J. and Love, J.H. (2008), Modelling the innovation value chain, *Research Policy*, **37**(6–7), 961–77.

Rosenthal, S.S. and Strange, W.C. (2001), The determinants of agglomeration, *Journal of Urban Economics*, **50**(2), 191–229.

Ruiz-Torres, A.J. and Mahmoodi, F. (2008), Outsourcing decision in manufacturing supply chains considering production failure and operation costs, *International Journal of Integrated Supply Management*, **4**(2), 141–58.

Rullani, E. (1998), Riforma delle istituzioni e sviluppo locale, *Sviluppo Locale*, **V**(8), 5–46.

Salamon, L.M. (2002), *The Tools of Government. A Guide to New Governance*, Oxford: Oxford University Press.

Santalainen, T. (2006), *Strategic Thinking*, Helsinki: Talentum.

Schein, E.H. (1996), Three cultures of management: the key to organizational learning, *Sloan Management Review*, **38**(1), 40–51.

Schertler, A. (2003), *Dynamic Efficiency and Path Dependencies in Venture Capital Markets*, Berlin and Heidelberg: Springer.

Schmitter, P.C. and Lehmbruch, G. (eds) (1982), *Patterns of Corporatist Policy-making*, London/Beverly Hills: Sage Publications.

Schumpeter, J.A. ([1942]1975), *Capitalism, Socialism and Democracy*, New York: Harper.

Scott, J. (2000), *Social Network Analysis. A Handbook*, London: Sage.

Selldin, E. (2004), Supply chain frontier: achieving excellence in efficiency and responsiveness, in: van Wassenhove, L.N., De Meyer, A., Yücesan, E., Didem Günes, E. and Muyyldermans, L. (eds), *Operations Management as a Change Agent*, INSEAD, **1**, pp. 537–46.

Siegel, D.S., Westhead, P. and Wright, M. (2003), Science parks and the performance of new technology-based firms: a review of recent UK evidence and an agenda for future research, *Small Business Economics*, **20**(2), 177–84.

Simmie, J. (ed.) (2001), *Innovative Cities*, London: Spon Press.

Simmie, J. (2005), Innovation and space: a critical review of the literature, *Regional Studies*, **39**(6), 789–804.

Simon, H. (1996), *Hidden Champions. Lessons from 500 of the World's Best Unknown Companies*, Boston, MA: Harvard Business School Press.

Smith, A. (1976 [1776]), *An Inquiry into the Nature and Causes of the Wealth of Nations*, Campbell, R.H., Skinner, A.S. and Todd, W.B. (eds), Oxford: Oxford University Press.

Smith, A. ([1795] 1980), The principles which lead and direct philosophical inquiries: illustrated by the history of astronomy, in: Wightman, W.P.D. (ed.), *Essays on Philosophical Subjects*, Oxford: Oxford University Press, pp. 33–105.

Sorensen, O. (2003), Social networks and industrial geography, *Journal of Evolutionary Economics*, **13**(5), 513–27.

Sorge, A. and Streeck, W. (1988), Industrial relations and technical change: the case for an extended perspective, in: Hyman, R. and Streeck, W. (eds), *New Technology and Industrial Relations*, Oxford/New York: Blackwell, pp. 19–47.

Sparrow, J., Mooney, M. and Lancaster, N. (2006), Perceptions of a UK university as a knowledge-intensive business service enhancing organisational and regional service innovation, *International Journal of Business Innovation and Research*, **1**(1–2), 191–203.

Stambøl L.S. (2005), The Function of Labour Market Mobility to Regional Economic Growth Generally and by New Service Economy and Labour Force Nationality Especially, ERSA Conference Papers from European Regional Science Association.

Steels, N.O. (2000), Success factors for virtual libraries, *Wilton*, **23**(5), 68–71.

Stein, E.W. and Zwass, V. (1995), Actualizing organizational memory with information systems, *Information System Research*, **6**(2), 85–117.

Steiner, M. (1998), The discrete charm of clusters: an introduction, in: Steiner, M. (ed.), *From Agglomeration Economies to Innovative Clusters*, London: Pion, European Research in Regional Science.

Steiner, M. and Hartmann, C. (2006), Organizational learning in clusters: a case study on material and immaterial dimensions of cooperation, *Regional Studies*, **40**(5), 493–506.

Steiner, M. and Ploder, M. (2008), Structure and strategy within heterogeneity: Multiple dimensions of regional networking, *Regional Studies*, **42**(6), 793–815.

Sterlacchini, A. (2008), R&D, higher education and regional growth: uneven linkages among European regions, *Research Policy*, **37**(6–7), 1096–107.

Streeck, W. and Kenworthy, L. (2005), Theories and practices of neo-corporatism, in: Janowski, T., Alford, R., Hicks, A. and Schwartz, M. (eds), *The Handbook of Political Sociology*, Cambridge, MA: Cambridge University Press, pp. 441–60.

Streeck, W. and Schmitter, P.C. (eds) (1985), *Private Interest Government: Beyond Market and State*, Beverly Hills: Sage.

Swanson, R. (2001), Human resource development and its underlying theory, *Human Resource Development International*, **4**(3), 299–312.

Szulanski, G. (1996), Exploring internal stickiness: impediments to the transfer of best practice within the firm, *Strategic Management Journal*, **17**(4), 27–43.

Tan, B. and Hung, H.C. (2006), A knowledge management system introduction model for small and medium-sized enterprises, *International Journal of Management and Enterprise Development*, **3**, 53–69.

Teichert, T. and Harder-Nowka, A. (2007), *Erfolgsfaktoren im Technologiemarketing für Hamburger Luftfahrtzulieferer*, Universität Hamburg, Studie.

Teirlinck, P. and Spithoven, A. (2008), The spatial organization of innovation: open innovation, external relations and urban structure, *Regional Studies*, **42**, 705–18.

Tether, B.S. (2002), Knowledge and investment: the sources of innovation in industry, *Research Policy*, **31**, 183–4.

Tether, B.S. and Tajar, A. (2008), The organisational-cooperation mode of innovation and its prominence amongst European service firms, *Research Policy*, **37**(4), 720–39.

Thompson, J.R. and LeHew, C.W. (2000), Skill-based pay as an organizational innovation, *Review of Public Personnel Administration*, **20**(1), 20–40.

Tiwana, A. (2001), *The Knowledge Management Toolkit: Practical Techniques for Building Knowledge Management Systems*, Upper Saddle River, NJ: Prentice Hall.

Torre, A. (2003), Local organisations and institutions. How can geographical proximity be activated by collective projects?, *International Journal of Technology Management*, **26**(2–4), 386–400.

Torre, A. (2008), On the role played by temporary geographical proximity in knowledge transmission, *Regional Studies*, **42**(6), 869–89.

Torre, A. and Gallaud, D. (2004), Geographical proximity and circulation of knowledge through inter-firm cooperation, in: Wink, R. (ed.), *Academia-Business Links*, London: Palgrave, Macmillan.

Torre, A. and Rallet, A. (2005), Proximity and localization, *Regional Studies*, **39**(1), 47–60.

UNCTAD – United Nations Conference on Trade and Development (2005), *World Investment Report: Transnational Corporations and the Internationalizatin of R&D*, Geneva: UNCTAD.

UNCTAD – United Nations Conference on Trade and Development (2007), *World Investment Report: Transnational Corporations, Extractive Industries and Development*, Geneva, UNCTAD.

Utterback, J. (1996), *Mastering the Dynamics of Innovation*, Boston, MA: Harvard Business School Press.

Van der Bent, J., Paauwe, J. and Williams, R. (1999), Organizational learning: an exploration of organizational memory and its role in organizational change processes, *Journal of Organizational Change Management*, **12**(5), 377–404.

Van Kersbergen, K. and Van Waarden, F. (2004), Governance as a bridge between disciplines: cross-disciplinary inspiration regarding shifts in governance and problems of governability, accountability and legitimacy, *European Journal of Political Research*, **43**(2), 143–71.

Van Oort, F.G., Weterings, A. and Verlinde, H. (2003), Residential amenities of knowledge workers and the location of ICT-firms in the Netherlands, *Journal of Economic and Social Geography* (TESG), **94**(4), 516–23.

Vázquez Barquero, A. (1990), Endogenous development: analytical and policy issues, in: Scott, A. and Garofoli, G. (eds), *Development on the Ground*, London and New York: Routledge

Venohr, B. and Meyer, K.E. (2007), The German Miracle Keeps Running: How Germany's Hidden Champions Stay Ahead in the Global Economy, Berlin: Berlin School of Economics, Working Paper No. 30.

Vincenti, W.G. (1990), *What Engineers Know and How They Know It*, Baltimore, MD: Johns Hopkins University Press.

von Tunzelmann, G.N. (1998), Localized technological search and multitechnology companies, *Economics of Innovation and New Technology*, **6**(2–3), 231–55.

Warnecke, H.J. (1993), *The Fractal Company: A Revolution in Corporate Culture*, Berlin: Springer.

Wickramasinghe, N. and Sharma, S.K. (2005), Key factors that hinder SMEs in succeeding in today's knowledge-based economy, *International Journal of Management and Enterprise Development*, **2**(2), 141–58.

Williamson, O.E. (1981), The modern corporation: origins, evolution, attributes, *Journal of Economic Literature*, **19**(4), 1537–68.

Wink, R. (2003), Transregional effects of knowledge management: implications for policy and evaluation design, *International Journal of Technology and Management*, **26**(2–4), 421–38;

Wink, R. (2004a), Commercialisation of bio-pharmaceutical therapies and risk management: the impact on the sustainability of markets for recombinant drugs, *International Journal of Biotechnology*, **6**(2/3), 186–201.

Wink, R. (2004b), Universities as hubs to global knowledge pipelines? A strategy-focused perspective on regional university policies, in: Wink, R. (ed.) *Academia Business Links. European Policy Strategies and Lessons Learnt*, Houndmills: Palgrave Macmillan, pp. 246–62.

Wink, R. (2007), Creativity and openness: the interrelationships between outsourcing knowledge business services and metropolitan regions, in: Cooke, P. and Schwartz, D. (eds), *Creative Regions. Entrepreneurship and Creativity*, London: Routledge.

Wink, R. (2008), Gatekeepers and proximity in science-driven sectors in Europe and Asia: The case of human embryonic stem cell research, *Regional Studies*, **42**(6), 777–92.

Wink, R. (2009a), Transregional institutional learning in Europe: prereq-uisites, actors, and limitations, *Regional Studies*, forthcoming.

Wink, R. (2009b), Examination knowledge and its role in medium-technology innovation: the case of European aeronautics clusters, *International Journal of Technology Management*, forthcoming.

Witt, U. (2000), Changing cognitive frames – changing organizational forms. An entrepreneurial theory of organizational development, *Industrial and Corporate Change*, **9**(4), 733–55.

Womack, J.P. and Jones, D.T. (1994), From lean production to lean enter-prise, *Harvard Business Review*, **72**(2), March-April, 93–103.

World Trade Organization (2008), Statistics database 2008, http://stat. wto.org/Home/WSDBHome.aspx? Language=E, accessed 14 January, 2009.

Zingheim, P.K. and Schuster, J.R. (2002), Reassessing the value of skill based pay, *World at Work Journal*, **11**(3), 72–7.

Zook, M.A. (2004), The knowledge brokers: venture capitalists, tacit knowledge and regional development, *International Journal of Urban and Regional Research*, **28**(3), 621–41.

Zucker L., Darby M. and Armstrong J. (1998), Geographically localized knowledge: spillovers or markets?, *Economic Inquiry*, **36**(1), 65–86.

Index